AFRICAN MEDIA, AFRICAN CHILDREN

Yearbook 2008

AFRICAN MEDIA, AFRICAN CHILDREN

Editors:
Norma Pecora, Enyonam Osei-Hwere & Ulla Carlsson

WITH AN INTRODUCTION BY FIRDOZE BULBULIA

The International Clearinghouse on Children, Youth and Media

NORDICOM
University of Gothenburg

Yearbook 2008

African Media, African Children

Editors:
Norma Pecora, Enyonam Osei-Hwere & Ulla Carlsson

ISSN 1651-6028
ISBN 978-91-89471-68-9

Published by:
The International Clearinghouse on Children, Youth and Media

Nordicom
University of Gothenburg
Box 713
SE 405 30 GÖTEBORG
Sweden

Cover by:
Karin Persson
Printed by:
Livréna AB, Göteborg, Sweden, 2008
Environmental certification according to ISO 14001

Contents

Acknowledgement

A number of people have been involved in this project and we would first like to thank all those who have contributed to this discussion. The authors of these chapters have been a joy to work with and it is exciting to see their work in print. We would also like to thank Ulla Carlsson and Cecilia von Felitzen for their commitment to this project and to the International Clearinghouse on Children, Youth and Media for making this collection of work available. We would also like to acknowledge Firdoze Bulbulia's outstanding and valuable work, both personal and professional, in bringing African children into the discussion. In addition, we wish to thank and acknowledge the Institute for the African Child at Ohio University for beginning this dialogue in the summer of June 2006 at their conference on African Children in African Media on the Ohio University Campus.

Foreword

Ulla Carlsson

African Media, African Children is the title of this tenth Yearbook of the International Clearinghouse on Children, Youth and Media. Over the years, we have focused attention on a wide range of topics, from issues relating to media violence, new media technologies, soap operas and globalization of media to issues of regulation, media education and media literacy. This is the first Yearbook with a geographical focus, and a vast continent at that. That the choice fell on Africa is hardly by chance. The 5th World Summit on Children, Youth and Media, held in Johannesburg, South Africa, a year or so ago, sent echoes ringing around the world.

Although media, digital and information divides certainly do exist in the world, more and more people have access to a steadily swelling flow of material through many new channels. An interactive and mobile media society has grown up alongside the traditional mass media society. Once passive media consumers are becoming active media producers. The medialized symbolic environment we live in today largely shapes the choices, values and knowledge that determine our everyday lives. In the midst of these developments are children and youth. Helping to develop fruitful insights and a better understanding of children, youth and the media in a perspective that includes all parts of the world is a top priority for the International Clearinghouse on Children Youth and Media – in the light of the UN Convention on the Rights of the Child.

Contemporary global and multicultural societies raise more complex issues than ever before. To be able to respond effectively to this situation, the research community needs to revive its curiosity and explore new phenomena. What do we need in order to be able to formulate the real and really difficult questions? This question occupies many researchers today, and one often-heard answer is a call for greater internationalization and regionalization of media studies. Equally important, we need to regain our sense of context and to broaden our perspectives in a holistic direction.

This implies a learning process. Quite definitely, we need more collaboration – within our field, with other disciplines, with society around us and collaboration across national frontiers. We need to learn more from one another, to share knowledge and context. Internationalization is both enriching and necessary with regard to our common interest in broader, more all-inclusive paradigms. But, we also have to maintain and further develop national and regional collaboration, not least as a means to ensure that internationalization does not take place at the expense of knowledge about, and reflection on, scholars' own societies and cultures. Fruitful national and regional dialogues are a great boon in international exchanges and vice versa.

We have to build on past work but break new ground. We need fresh, unexpected insights and new comparative research questions. And, not least, there is a need for a de-Westernizing of the research agenda – it has to embrace non-Western thoughts and cross-cultural approaches to a much higher degree than it does today. This is an absolute prerequisite for a robust development of our understanding of young people and media.

These needs have guided every Yearbook from the International Clearinghouse on Children Youth and Media to date. But the rapid pace of development in the media sector at all levels – national, regional, global – has, year by year, made it increasingly urgent that the needs be addressed and problems resolved. The gap between the rich and poor countries of the world still prevails. It is a product of disparities in access to resources, knowledge and technology, especially in rural areas. What is more, the divide is reproduced within virtually every country of the world and often reflects other gaps – those between income groups, the sexes and ethnic groups.

Against this background a focus on Africa seems both timely and important. The reasons cannot be set out any better than Francis B. Nyamnjoh does in his article in this volume:

> *The time has come to pay greater attention to changing not only what is produced as knowledge on Africa but, even more importantly, the institutional cultures within which that knowledge is produced, in view of encouraging greater and more genuine collaboration between African, non-African and African-plus scholars. We need to redress the inequalities, prejudices and tensions that continue to stand in the way of meaningful research on children's agency in Africa. The contributions in this volume offer useful building blocks in this connection.*

I am deeply indebted to the main editors, Norma Pecora and Enyonam Osei-Hwere, and all the contributors in many African nations who have made this publication possible. I also wish to express my great appreciation of the support provided by Firdoze Bulbulia, Director, Moments Entertainment and President of the International Center of Films for Children and Young People (CIFEJ). It is my hope that this volume will be useful to a wide range of readers, that it will provide new insights and knowledge, inform policy and stimulate further research.

Göteborg in November 2008

Ulla Carlsson
Director
The International Clearinghouse on Children, Youth and Media

Introduction

Firdoze Bulbulia

The 5th World Summit on Media for Children (5WSMC) was premised on the African philosophy of "Umuntu ngumuntu ngabantu" – simply put *ubuntu*, meaning 'I am because you are' – or one owes one's humanity to other people.

During the 3-year preparatory phase we worked with many partners in the Children's Media environment who greatly assisted with ideas, logistics and support with regards to the agenda. This was an unprecedented phase that allowed us to travel from Africa to The Middle East, Europe, North and South America, the Caribbean and Asia. During this period we developed important bonds and profound partnerships that aided a process that we hoped would be democratic and peaceful and would indeed encompass the spirit of ubuntu. One of our Swedish partners called the process the 'building-blocks of Peace and Democracy'.

This publication is one of those building blocks – it resulted from our partnership with Ohio University's (OH) African Studies Department under the leadership of Prof. Steve Howard who is also the Director of the Institute of The African Child (IAC). In 2003 as a graduate of the Master's degree in the African Studies programme I taught a Summer course on Media and The African Child. It was during this period that Faith Isiakpere – CBFA and 5WSMC Board Member informed us that the Children and Broadcasting Foundation for Africa (CBFA) would bid to host the 5WSMC. Our initial response was one of ambivalence. However, Faith's enthusiasm soon excited the rest of the CBFA Board. I recall mentioning this to the OH post-graduate students who were taking my class at the time and their excitement at the possibility of Africa hosting a world summit! Most of the students were from Africa or African American so there was an immediate comradeship. How would Africa host such a summit – could we? This was 2003 and already we started planning the African agenda for the 5WSMC!

As an African producer, content creator and advocate of children's media for more than 15 years I am aware of the grave disparities between African children's media and global media for children. My philosophy however, is that Africans must take charge of their destiny and it is our responsibility to improve the media environment of the African child. It is important for us as Africans to ensure that we de-colonize Africa including its children's media. As Africans we have a responsibility to tell our own stories and to allow our children to become involved in their storytelling. We must take control of our media and we must be the researches and producers of our media. We must ensure that the texts written about us are written by us! My impetus was thus to encourage African students to focus on research in Media with a spotlight on the African Child. This lead to a greater interest and support for further teaching and workshops that would result in a proposal to ensure that at the Ohio pre-summit in June 2006 we would include on the agenda a comparative African country report on the state of Children's Media for which Prof. Norma Pecora and her PhD Student Enyonam Osei-Hwere were responsible. The concluding session of this pre-summit prompted the first discussions of the possibility of a publication on Media and the African Child. It was discussed that we should try to have a publication ready for the 5WSMC. However, when it proved impossible to prepare an African Publication at such a short notice – the idea of the proposed publication was presented by Prof. Norma Pecora and Enyonam Osei-Hwere at the 5WSMC. It is therefore, astounding to see that this "idea" has so quickly become a reality and we thank the generous support of The Clearinghouse under the leadership of Prof. Ulla Carlsson and Prof. Cecilia von Feilitzen.

This publication is therefore, an extremely important one – firstly because we have an entire international publication dedicated to children's media in Africa! Secondly and most importantly it will offer a window into the world of children's media in Africa and thus encourage further research and greater interest in media and the African child. Many of the contributors to this publication are friends and partners of the Children and Broadcasting Foundation for Africa (CBFA) – the hosts of the 5WSMC and assisted us tremendously with the African agenda of the 5WSMC.

The 5WSMC was conceived to offer opportunities for global partnerships with local emphasis. The spirit of ubuntu created spaces wherein our global partners could experience African media, cultures and traditions without feeling that a dominant globalised culture was present. From the Gala Opening speeches and entertainment we wove a tapestry of western and African presentations but we kept the balance in Africa's favour. We wanted the delegates to always acknowledge that they were in Africa and that the fusion of all our worlds would lead to an enriching experience that would continue to generate quality media for all our children.

The need to succeed with an African or south-south agenda is a challenging one, but this publication is proof that it is possible to focus on the south – in this case Africa – thus ensuring that our friends in the north have a glimpse into our world, our challenges, and our achievements. We are sure that you will benefit greatly from this publication and that the many contributors will also be available as resources for future collaborations, advise and support.

The 5WSMC Post- Summit Publication of 2007 however, is a global reference on Children's Media and highlights all the remarkable children's media initiatives globally – it is a resource that all media practitioners and development communications activists will find extremely useful. We sought in that publication to offer the diversity of children's media so as to give prominence of formal, non-formal and informal media projects which are being created in commercial, public and non-governmental sectors.

Conclusion

As we pondered the concept of ubuntu we thought we should share the following from Prof Musa Xulu an ethnomusicologist and cultural researcher from South Africa, who wrote:

> *After putting an emphasis of one's dependence on others for the completion of one's identity, it is possible to think that in African thought there is no concept of individuality. To the contrary, there is a lot of individuality, but its acceptable existence exists within the self same context of umuntu ngumuntu ngabantu.*
>
> *Its meaning is that one needs the communal whole to advance one's individuality. In traditional Zulu society the biggest marker of one's individuality was one's set of praises – izibongo. But one seldom composed their own izibongo; this being left to the discretion of others, who compose their praises based on their known and accepted achievements. But such achievements must meet with the criteria for generally accepted public behavior. To have no praises or to have short praises would be indicative of one's ineptness.*

The izibongo for this publication is left to your discretion.
Peace!

Firdoze Bulbulia
Chairperson: CBFA, 5WSMC
Sec-General: CIFEJ

Children's Media in Sub-Saharan Africa

Enyonam Osei-Hwere & Norma Pecora

> *The child shall have the right to freedom of expression; this right shall include freedom to seek, receive and impart information and ideas of all kinds, regardless of frontiers, either orally, in writing or in print, in the form of art, or through any other media of the child's choice.*
>
> Convention on the Rights of the Child: Article 13 (1989)

In 1989 when the Convention rights on the child were being drawn up by the Office of the High Commissioner for Human Rights at the United Nations, among the rights granted children were access to information (Convention on the Rights 1989). While it is unlikely that those drawing up the rights had *SpongeBob SquarePants* in mind, certainly they did have the right to learn about their own and other cultures and to participate "through any ... media of the child's choice." As we know children's media, as addressed in the Convention on the Rights of the Child (UNCHR), can take many forms and children can be producers and creators as well as an audience; indeed increasingly we have recognized the importance of children as media makers. According to Hamlink:

> The crucial challenge that the Convention on the Rights of the Child poses to adults is to listen to children, to consult them, work with them and to make them active partners in shaping humanity's common communication future. (2008: 517)

Yet what has come to define children's media is hardly what the writers had in mind but rather the commercial broadcasting industry dominated by the West. Much has been written on the subject from a Western perspective but we know little about the experiences of African children either as audiences or creators. For example, in twenty years of analyzing the research on children and television there has never been a discussion on African children published in U.S. academic journals (Pecora, Murray, Wartella 2007) and a recent 'global study' by MTV included 16 countries – none on the African continent (Biz-Community 2007). In addition, attempts to document the global distribution of U.S. children's programming or the programming available to children in Africa[1] have been difficult because of the one-way flow of information (Lustyik and Pecora 2005). This is not to argue for the continued expansion of U.S or British entertainment such as Nickelodeon, Disney, and CBBC but rather to examine the conditions that allow such programming to become a part of the global world creating a culture of youth defined by the Western world and to consider some of the challenges that face African broadcasters in programming indigenous or local children's program. For, according to a UN Report on youth:

> While some boundaries are becoming blurred, others are becoming more strongly defined. With young people's increased access to media technology, they no longer have to watch or read what their parents choose. As the youth niche market grows in importance, young people are increasingly able to confine themselves to media that are produced specifically for them. The new post, postmodern cultural forms that characterize contemporary youth culture are in many respects highly exclusive of adults; they require particular cultural competencies and a prior knowledge of specific media texts (or in other words, a form of media literacy only available to the young. While youth around the world are increasingly sharing a global media culture with one another, they appear to be sharing less and less with their own parents. (World Youth Report 2005: 95).

This is a youth culture all too often driven by the characters, stories, and values of the global network of imported children's programming. So what does it mean that the Nickelodeon television channel is available in at least 171 world markets (Nickelodeon 2001; Hendershort 2004; Pecora 2004) and the popular Nickelodeon character, *SpongeBob*, is available to children in countries such as Kenya, Nigeria, Ghana, and South Africa?

Although mandated to offer children indigenous programming and programming that reflects their heritage and culture, African broadcasters face a number of challenges to abide by such mandates, and as broadcasting systems are increasingly privatized Western programming becomes the programming of choice because of its ready availability and commercialized structure. This becomes problematic, not in the sense of a theory of media imperialism where "ideology drips into people's veins in the manner of a hypodermic needle" (Chalaby quoted in Moran and Chung 2008) but rather identity among youth and children where "local identities are constructed out of material and symbolic resources that may not be local in their origins" (Strelitz 2004: 2; see also Strelitz and Boshoff 2008).

Mandates for children's mass media

At the first World Summit on Media and Children held in March 1995, The Children's Television Charter was signed by 38 countries (Children's Television Charter

2008) and later ratified at Prix Jeuness in 1997. Building on The Convention on the Rights of the Child, this charter advocated for consideration of the best interest of children by the broadcast media when programming and providing information and entertainment targeted to and produced by child and youth audiences. Additionally, the Charter stated that the interests, opinions, and participation of children should be included in the broadcast media production process aimed at children (von Feilitzen and Bucht 2001). Its significance becomes apparent when, according to *The World Youth Report* published by the United Nations (2005): "The emergence of the global media-driven youth culture signifies the building of a new landscape of socialization. With the structures and traditional roles of families undergoing major changes, youth cultures and youth media have emerged as entirely new agents of socialization, given rise to new forms of socialization" (p. 85) – a socialization that is too often based on a Western image. Building on the World Summit charter, in 1995, the Africa Charter on Children's Broadcasting was affirmed and ratified.

Broadcasters in sub-Saharan Africa, particular when addressing children, face serious and sometimes overwhelming challenges, such as geography, politics, language, and resources. Too often marginal access; lack of interest by government, industry, and academics; as well as economic constraints all contribute to a complex arrangement when trying to understand African children's media. It is estimated that 42 percent of the sub-Saharan African population is under age 15, while Asia and Latin America and the Caribbean have about 30 percent of their population under 15 and in Europe (16 percent) and in North America (20 percent) the numbers are far below those of sub-Saharan Africa (Ashford, 2007; Prospectus, 2007). These figures are significant when addressing the critical role television and radio play in shaping children's lives (UNICEF 2006; McConnell 2001), the importance of children's access to information (Convention on the Rights of the Child 1989), and the global nature of communication and information (Straubhaar 1997; Curran and Park 2000; McMillan 2007).

In a world where technology, not nation states, defines boundaries and frontiers the right to information and access to media is an essential ingredient and resource necessary for including individual nations within the global village; otherwise, they are left out of the debate. It is therefore imperative that the media in Africa equip its children and youth to become citizens in this global world. In less developed countries mass media for children is often a luxury and often receive little or no attention from governments, media practitioners, or researchers. To explore the state of children's broadcasting in Africa, we will examine some of the challenges faced by the broadcasting industry and the regulatory systems in place that either promote or discourage the introduction of Western programming such as *Sesame Street* and *SpongeBob* or indigenous programming as called for by the Convention and Charters. There is, in this essay, no attempt to offer answers – after all, children's broadcasting in the West meets few of the criteria set out by the Convention or the Charters – but it is an attempt to put forward some of the particular concerns of African children's media.

The United Nations adopted the Rights of the Child to affirm that children have the right to "be fully prepared to live an individual life in society, to do so, children were also assured the right "to preserve his or her identity, including nationality, name and family relations" (Article 7) and their views were to be "given due weight in accordance with the age and maturity of the child" (Article 12). In addition, children are to be granted the right to freedom of expression (Article 13). The Convention on the Rights of the Child also acknowledged the importance of the mass media and outlined the responsibilities of States Parties (Article 17), these included:

- the recognition of the educational benefits to the child;
- the dissemination of information from a diversity of sources;
- the regard for linguistic needs of minority and indigenous groups;
- and, guidelines for the protection of the child from injurious information and material.[2]

These rights were further affirmed in the 1995 Children's Television Charter presented at the first World Summit on Television and Children and adopted later that year at Prix Jeunesse.[3] In 1997 at the Africa Summit on Children and Broadcasting held in Accra Ghana, the Africa Charter on Children's television was adopted. This Charter addressed the particular needs and wants of the children of Africa. The Africa Charter on Children's Broadcasting also held that children should have quality, well-funded programming addressing the developmental needs of children. However, in addition the Africa Charter offered three amendments:

- children should be protected from commercial exploitation;
- children must be ensured equitable access to programmes and where possible be involved in the production process;
- children's programmes must empower children and there should be ongoing research into the child audience, including the child's needs and wants.[4]

Over the almost twenty years of the Rights of the Child, we have called for age-appropriate, programming with guidelines that both protect the child from commercial exploitation while offering him or her a place for the exchange of a diverse range of ideas. Recognizing the need for international co-operation and a range of genre and content and the significance of diverse voices, these Charters and the Convention also address the importance of a space for indigenous programming:

> Governments, production, distribution and funding organizations should recognize both the importance and vulnerability of indigenous children's television, and take steps to support and protect it. (Children's Television Charter 1995)

Unfortunately, all too often children's programming on every continent has come to be defined by the United States. In a recent survey of children's television in 24 countries it was found that except for the United States, Great Britain, Australia, Canada, and China – on average – 80 percent of the programming was imported and most of that from the United States (Götz 2008; Osei-Hwere 2008). In African states like South Africa, Kenya, and Ghana much of what the children have available is from the Disney Channel, Nickelodeon, or the Cartoon Network. Very little, if any, is indigenous programming. Clearly governments, program creators, and funding organizations are failing the children. While there are some very exciting projects funded by NGOs, these rarely have the broad reach of commercial broadcasting.

Challenges to Sub-Saharan African children's television

It is important to note that Africa is a large and diverse continent and to speak of one solution for all would be unacceptable.[5] However there are within the continent social, political, and economic problems that come from a history of colonization that are not inherent in other world regions. While every nation-state has its history of invasion, Africa has been plundered as no other. In addition, issues like geography, colonialism, economics, political unrests, foreign imports, religion, cultural beliefs, linguistic differences, and lack of interest in the media industries by investors have all presented problems to media in general and children's broadcasting in particular. Its reputation as a much less developed continent also creates a barrier, on the one hand, to local, foreign, public and private investors but allows for cheap imports on the other. Historical issues like colonialism and its impact on the development of the continent and its resources have caused serious setbacks and impact on media advancements and development. Most African media systems were inherited from countries that colonized them like the British and French. Consequently, the British BBC has been a foundational institution upon which many African media systems were established; thus encouraging a model not open to indigenous or local programming.

In addition to historical and political circumstances that impede the development of a national broadcasting system, African states must address challenges to the system such as access, often created by language and geography; limited research directed towards children and youth; and economic constraints that restrict technological growth and program development.

Language and literacy. The wide range of languages and dialects that are a part of African culture constitute challenges for children's media in Africa. Challenges such as low rates of literacy and multiple languages in many African communities create a problem for media content and programming. The continent of Africa is blessed with hundreds of indigenous languages that differ from country to country along with colonial languages like French, English, German and Portuguese.

The challenge however, is in which of these many languages do you program in when it comes to broadcasting? On a continent with limited resources, challenges with language when it comes to media content become increasingly complex particularly when attempting to address mandates for indigenous programming. Literacy which is closely connected to language is another stumbling block for media programming. Media personnel are faced with challenges of being able to reach an audience made of adults, youth and children often with exceptional to limited literacy skills.

Access. As traditional forms of media are joined by 'new' technologies, these challenges of access and language appear to remain. In a global economy dependent on information and communication technologies (ICTs) and the ability to access information which is important in a knowledge economy, Africa remains behind. Figures for youth are difficult to come by but, according to the United Nations, overall figures indicate there were over 580 million Internet users: 200 million in the US and Canada; 185 million in Europe; 170 million for East Asia and the Pacific combined; 33 million for Latin America; and 6 million in Africa, half of who reside in South Africa. (World Youth Report 2004; p. 318). This disparity whether adult or youth oriented (and there are arguments for it being both) has consequences as increasingly broadcasting moves to the web and children's television is driven by websites.

Compared to children in advanced countries, children in Africa constitute a larger percentage of the population yet what we do know is that they have less access to both information and the skills and equipment to create their own work. It is no secret that children in advanced and developed countries have greater access and fewer obstacles to participation in the media compared to children in developing countries. In developing and third world countries mass media for children is a luxury and therefore receives little to no attention from governments, media practitioners and organizations.

Economics. One of the major challenges for broadcasting in Africa is setup, licensing fees, and equipment cost. Television is a very expensive system. Often, governments demand large amounts of money from private investors interested in acquiring licenses for new television stations. In addition equipment, signal reception, and running costs are considerably more expensive compared to those for radio and as a result television diffusion in Africa is a much slower in pace compared to the popularity of radio. Furthermore individuals can afford to purchase a radio set much more easily than they can a television set because of the difference in cost. Television in Africa is essentially an urban phenomenon; many rural areas that constitute majority of the continent of Africa have very little to no access to the medium. Television is, however, an essential tool and component in a growing and developing media industry as such the slow growth of this component within Africa's media are a major concern especially when we talk about children's media (Hawak 1992).

Research. Both academic and audience research in Africa is rare and is largely one of the reasons for the stifling environments existing in many media systems across the continent of Africa. Studies show that successful media organizations and systems around the world invest significant amount of time and resources into research to develop new efficient and effective technologies, program content, and genres that appeal to their target audiences. The African Media Development Initiative report states "there is a lack of robust research, on a continental scale, demonstrating what is and is not working in the attempts by many players to strengthen African media. Another constraining factor working against private and public funding of the media are the lack of reliable information in media industries in many African countries" (AMDI 2005). It is widely accepted that formal educational structures in countries around the world speak to children's cognitive processes and television plays an important role in children's informal learning. Media programs also teach social skills and cultural identity and educate children about current events. This access to education and information by children in advanced countries is well documented (Lemish 2006; Livingstone 2002). However, very little research has been done on African children and the media[6]. In addition, as stated earlier, what has been done is rarely disseminated in the Western academy.

Changing media environment

It is however important to note that the media in Africa have gone through significant growth and development as a result of changes in government and political challenges. As much as there are continuing unrests and new conflicts brewing in countries such as Kenya in recent months, many countries have taken strides in the development of their media industries. Countries like South Africa, Ghana, Nigeria, Zambia have media industries that are worthy of standing as reputable models for other countries in working on making improvements to their media. Other important factors reflecting the growth and changes in the media include globalization and the introduction and availability of new technologies (Ahassan 2005).

Political unrests are all too common on Africa's continent and have been identified to a large extent as responsible for many economic, social and developmental breakdowns in the countries that fall victim to such unrests. Research shows that political unrests are closely connected to lack of economic growth and we argue that lack of economic abilities impact growth in the media and media technologies and content. Government instability drives away investors and creates disruption in the flow of things, creates lack of confidence and uncertainties in the future (Alesina et al 1992). Consistency in media growth, development and expansion are associated with countries that have experienced very stable and democratic governments leading to well developed and stronger economies and as a result growing and well established media systems because of the consistent political stability they have enjoyed over hundreds of years. The United States and the United Kingdom among others in Europe and Asia have one of the most developed and multifaceted media systems in the world along with others in their company like Australia, Japan and Canada who also boast of thriving and well established media industry. These countries have also had very stable and consistent democracies and governments for hundreds of years.

None the less, these limitations are surprising considering the rapid growth of media industries globally and the penetration of these corporations on a transnational level; however, more and more transnational and multinational media conglomerates are entering developing countries and their media markets are influencing programming for children. The entry of more companies into the market impacts the creation and availability of local children programming in third world countries and also influences the availability of foreign imports into the market.

> *States Parties recognize the important function performed by the mass media and shall ensure that the child has access to information and material from a diversity of national and international sources especially those aimed at the promotion of his or her social, spiritual and moral well being and physical and mental health.*
>
> Convention on the Rights of the Child: Article 17 (1989)

Children's television is a fast growing industry in advanced countries around the world. US children's production and distribution companies such as Sesame Workshop, Disney, Nickelodeon, and the Cartoon Network are all well-established in the international market. As one of the fastest growing areas within the Viacom franchise Nickelodeon's consumer-products division brought in sales of $3 billion in 2003 and in 2001, Nickelodeon was received in ninety million households in more than seventy countries (von Feilitzen and Bucht 2001). With the advent of satellite, the mass entertainment for children in most of Africa, and certainly in Sub-Saharan Africa has come to be defined by this western entertainment – Nickelodeon was first available in 1999 to 48 African countries via satellite (Everything Nick 2008) and Disney in 2006 (Clover 2007; Disney Channel 2006). According to analysts from Time Warner, the world's largest media business. In 2004 the BBC announced plans of launching new international pay-TV channels for children with the hope of achieving the kind of success Time Warner has with its Cartoon Network Station (*Too much of a good thing* 2004). This world-wide expansion of western corporations means that African children have access to programs like *SpongeBob* and *Sesame Street* – while we fully recognize these programs represent a range from the educational (Sesame Street) to the merely entertaining (SpongeBob) the argument here is on access not quality.

> *To this end States Parties shall encourage the mass media to disseminate information and material of social and cultural benefit to the child, encourage international co-operation in the production, exchange and dissemination of such information and material from a diversity of cultural, national and international sources.*
>
> Convention on the Rights of the Child: Article 17 (1989)

As international markets expand, many African governments are providing the political and economic framework for the establishment and expansion of broadcast services in Africa. Countries like Ghana, Nigeria and South Africa have allowed the establishment of commercial broadcasting stations to increase access to broadcasting services by their citizens. South Africa's public broadcaster, the South African Broadcasting Corporation and the commercial satellite channel M-NET both provide children's programs. These include educational, entertainment, and entertainment education programs on radio and television targeting children within and beyond the borders of South Africa (Conradie 2000; Cowling 2005). This is the opportune time for examining the changing nature of public service broadcasting, which served as the sole provider of children's programming, as it faces challenges from commercial broadcasters (Blumler and Biltereyst 1997).

The history of children's television in Africa like the media industries in general shows very little development since the introduction of broadcasting by colonial masters in most cases across the continent. The children's media industries in Africa are trailing behind within the present global media context. The growing development of new media such as cable, satellite, computers, Internet and record high profits going into media companies are predominantly developed world focused (Williams 2003). The slow development that the media in Africa has suffered especially in reference to children's programming on television and on radio is quite astonishing taking into consideration the rapid growth of the media industry globally. The state of a broadcasting system on the African continent is an important determinant of the nature of its children's media. The state of a broadcasting system on the African continent is an important determinant of the nature of its children's media. On a continent where children and their needs are largely marginalized, consistent strategic advocacy is necessary to create policies that ensure the media meet the social and developmental needs of children. While a public service broadcasting system may seek to serve the interests of all minorities including children the resources may not always be available to do so successfully. On the other hand, a privatized/commercialized broadcasting system opens the door for capital to flow in from the private sector. However, serving the best interest of children is not always considered as commercially viable.

Media in Africa have been and continue to serve as a propaganda tool for people in power, for nation building and development. Nation building in this case helps to create a single identity for people from these countries to prevent conflicts and unrest in developing countries. However, nation building in our opinion should also involve the development of the mass media and technology that is accessible and available to children and youth because in the current global state of the world it is an essential assert for growth and development and the ability to compete with other countries excelling in this role (Ansah 1985).

In recent years many have called attention to the strengthening of Africa's media arguing that the media are an important tool for education and development of Africa and its people. The 2006 African Media Development Initiative

Report (AMDI) states "fostering a stronger media in Africa is an indispensable part of tackling poverty, improving development and enabling Africa to attain its development goals". In their study of the state of the media in 17 sub Saharan African countries, AMDI researchers found that the media was going through very significant changes as a result of factors like positive and stable changes in government, globalization, economic stability and growth and the introduction and availability of new media technologies (AMDI 2006). As much as Africa is saddled with overwhelming challenges, problems and issues, the need to strengthen the media and its accompanying technology and function is essential if the goal and objective is to get directions for meeting those challenges head on because history shows that the media can help lead the way forward.

Broadcast television can be empowering to the children. Mandates such as the African Charter urge broadcasters to advance the development of children by engaging in productions and documentaries that draw attention to the plight of children; thus children's development is advanced by producing children's programs that both teach and entertain (UNICEF 2006; Jempson 1999) and that reflect the problems and successes of their world – not those of SpongeBob. For example, UNICEF's International Day of Broadcasting brought light to the efforts of broadcasters to promote children's rights and children's participation in broadcasting and in the process also promoted quality programs developed and created by children.

There are success stories – *Curious Minds* (a radio program in Ghana); Voices of Youth (a UNICEF sponsored website); *Soul Buddyz* and *Club Soul Buddyz* (a youth program on SABC in South Africa); *Club Kiboko* (a weekly program on KTV-Kenya) – but they stand as a minority among the Disney, Nickelodeon, and Cartoon Network programs available[7] If we are truly to serve the rights of the child as shaped by the Convention on the Rights of the Child, the Children's Television Charter, or the Africa Charter on Children's Broadcasting and to give them access to the information that helps them to become citizens in a global economy then surely we can do better than SpongeBob.

Notes

1. Media can encompass many forms but for this essay we will focus on television because it is the most ubiquitous and it has come to define 'children's media'. Recognizing that radio is also very important in the lives of African families it is not included because it lacks the global reach. In Africa, according to ARTICLE 19, "a majority of Africans get their information, education and entertainment from primarily radio and then television" (2003, p.1).
2. Article 17 reads:
   States Parties recognize the important function performed by the mass media and shall ensure that the child has access to information and material from a diversity of national and international sources, especially those aimed at the promotion of his or her social, spiritual and moral well-being and physical and mental health. To this end, States Parties shall:
   (a) Encourage the mass media to disseminate information and material of social and cultural benefit to the child and in accordance with the spirit of article 29 [the education of the child];

(b) Encourage international co-operation in the production, exchange and dissemination of such information and material from a diversity of cultural, national and international sources;
(c) Encourage the production and dissemination of children's books;
(d) Encourage the mass media to have particular regard to the linguistic needs of the child who belongs to a minority group or who is indigenous;
(e) Encourage the development of appropriate guidelines for the protection of the child from information and material injurious to his or her well-being, bearing in mind the provisions of articles 13 [freedom of expression] and 18 [parents' rights]. (http://www.unchr.ch/html/menur3/b/k2crc.htm)

3. The Children's Television Charter reads:
   1. Children should have programs of high quality which are made specifically for them, and which do not exploit them. These programmes, in addition to entertaining, should allow children to develop physically, mentally and socially to their fullest potential.
   2. Children should hear, see and express themselves, their culture, their language and their life experiences, through television programmes which affirm their sense of self, community and place.
   3. Children's programmes should promote an awareness and appreciation of other cultures in parallel with the child's own cultural background.
   4. Children's programmes should be wide-ranging in genre and content, but should not include gratuitous scenes of violence and sex.
   5. Children's programmes should be aired in regular slots at times when children are available to view, and/or distributed via other widely accessible media or technologies.
   6. Sufficient funds must be made available to make these programmes to the highest possible standards.
   7. Governments, production, distribution and funding organizations should recognize both eh importance and vulnerability of indigenous children's television, and take steps to support and protect it.
   (http://www.philonline.com.ph/~pctvf/charter.html)
4. Africa Charter on Children's Broadcasting states:
   We, the delegates of the Africa Summit on Children and Broadcasting, Accra Ghana 8-12 October 1997, affirm and accept the internationally adopted Children's Television Charter that was accepted in Munich on 29 May 1995. In addition, we amend the SADC Children's Broadcasting Charter (June 1996) to read as the Africa Charter on Children's Broadcasting.
   Without distracting from the International Children's Television Charter, we further adopt in line with the said Charter and in the spirit of the said Charter, our Africa Charter on Children's Broadcasting, which takes into consideration the needs and wants of children in our region.
   1. Children should have programmes of high quality, made specifically for them and which do not exploit them at any stage of the production process. These programmes, in addition to entertaining, should allow children to develop physically, mentally and socially to their fullest potential.
   2. Whilst recognizing that children's broadcasting will be funded through various mechanisms including advertising, sponsorship and merchandising, children should be protected from commercial exploitation.
   3. Whilst endorsing the child's right to freedom of expression, thought, conscience and religion, and protection against economic exploitation, children must be ensured equitable access to programmes, and whenever possible, to the production of programming.
   4. Children should hear, see and express themselves, their culture, their language and their life experiences, though the electronic media that affirm their sense of self, community and place.
   5. Children's programmes should create opportunities for learning and empowerment to promote and support the child's right to education and development. Children's programmes should promote an awareness and appreciation of other cultures in parallel with the child'

won cultural background. To facilitate this there should be ongoing research into the child audience, including the child's needs and wants. (AMDI, 2006).

6. Children's progammes should be wide ranging in genre and content, but should not include gratuitous scenes, and sound of violence and sex through any audio or visual medium.
7. Children's programmes should be aired in regular time slots at times when children are available to listen and view, and/or be distributed via other widely accessible media or technologies.
8. Sufficient resources, technical, financial and other, must be made available to make these programmes to the highest possible standards, and in order to achieve quality, setting codes and standards for children's broadcasting must be formatted and developed through a diverse range of groupings.
9. In compliance with the UN policy of co-operation between states in the international community, the Africa Children's Broadcasting Charter recognizes all international covenants, conventions, treaties, charters and agreements adopted by all international organizations including the OAU and the UN affecting children, but with particular reference to the UN Convention on the Rights of the Child.
(www.afrchild.ohio.edu/Broadcasting%20Charter/index.html)

5. For example, television ownership ranges from 97% in Senegal to 47% in Ghana and 6% in Uganda (AMDI, 2006)
6. For a review of some of this research see Strelitz and Boshoff (2008).
7. Although *Club Kiboko* is a successful locally-produced children's program, all other children's programs on KTV-Kenya were from Disney, Nickelodeon, or the Cartoon Network. (www.ktnkenya.tv/mod.php?topic=50&style=news&ud=1)

References

Alesina, A. and Rodrik, D. (1992) 'Distribution, Political Conflict and Economic Growth: A Simple Theory and Some Empirical Evidence', in A. Cukierman, Z. Hercowitz and L. Leiderman (eds) *Political Economy, Growth, and Business Cycles*. Boston: MIT Press, pp. 23-50.

AMDI. (2006) *African Media Development Initiative*. London: BBC World Service Trust.

Ansah, P.A.V. (1985) *Broadcasting and National Development*. Accra: Ghana Broadcasting Corporation.

ARTICLE 19. (2003) Introduction. *Broadcasting Policy and Practice in Africa*. London: ARTICLE 19. Retrieved 9 October 2007. http://www.article19.org.pdfs/publications/africa-broadcasting-policy.pdf.

Ashford, L.S. (2007) *Africa's Youthful Population: Risk or Opportunity*. Bridge: USAID. Retrieved 10 October 2007. http://www.prb.org/pdf07/AfricaYouth.pdf.

Biz-Community (2007, August 2) South Africa; Study Highlights Youth Tech Use Across Cultures. *Africa News*.

Blumler, J. and Biltereyst, D. (1997) *The Integrity and Erosion of Public Television for Children. A pan-European Survey*. London: Broadcasting Standards Commission.

Clover, J. (2007) Disney Channel Africa goes 24/7. Retrieved 25 August 2008. http://www.broadbandtvnews/?p=405$print=1

Conradie, P.D. (2000) 'Reactions to Globalization by the Television Industry in Post-apartheid South Africa', *Electronic Journal of Communication*, 10(1, 2).

Convention on the Rights of the Child (1989) Office of the High Commission for Human. Rights. Retrieved 22 June 2007. http://www.unhchr.ch/html/menu3/b/k2crc.htm

Cowling, L. (2005) 'South Africa', in Anne Cooper-Chen (ed.) *Global Entertainment Media; Content, Audiences, Issues*. Mahwah, NJ: Lawrence Erlbaum Associates.

Curran, J. and Park, Myung-Jin. (2000) *De-Westernizing Media Studies*. London: Routledge.

Disney Channel Expands to South Africa. (2006) *Mickey News*. Retrieved 25 August 2008. http://mickeynews.com/News/PringStory.asp_Q_id_E_8106Expand_A_cat_E_TV

von Feilitzen, C. and Bucht, C. (2001) *Outlooks on Children's Media. Children and Media Violence: Yearbook 2001*. Göteborg: Nordicom, The UNESCO International Clearinghouse on Children, Youth and Media.

Götz, M. et al. (2008) 'Gender in Children's Television World Wide', *Televizion,* 21/2008/E. pp. 49.

Hamlink, C. (2008) 'Children's Communication Rights: Beyond Intention', in Kirsten Drotner and Sonia Livingstone (eds) *The handbook of Children, Media and Culture*, pp. 508-517. Los Angeles: Sage.

Hendershort, H. (ed.) (2004) *Nickelodeon Nation: The History, Politics and Economics of America's Only TV Channel for Kids*. New York: New York University Press.

Jempson, M. and Searle, D. (1999) *The Media and Children's Rights: A Handbook for Media Professionals*. UNICEF PressWise.

Lemish, D. (2006) *Children and Television: A Global Perspective*. UK: Blackwell Publishing.

Livingstone, S. (2002) *Young People and New Media*. London: SAGE Publications.

Lustyik, K. and Pecora, N. (2005, September) The World According to Nick. A paper presented to The Society for Cinema & Media Studies conference; Vancouver Canada.

McConnell, B. (2001) *Fighting Over the Children*. New York: Broadcasting and Cable.

McMillan, D. (2007) *International Media Studies*. Malden MA: Blackwell Publishing.

Moran, K.C. and Chung, L. C. (2008) 'Global or Local Identity? A Theoretical Analysis of the Role of Viacom on Identity Formation among Children in an International context', *Global Media Journal,* 7(12) Spring. Retrieved 5 May 2008. http://lass.calumet.purdue.edu/cca/gmj/sp08/gmj-sp08-moran-chung.htm

Osei-Hwere, E. (2008) Children's Television in Ghana: History, Policy, Diversity, and Prospects in a Changing Media Environment. Ohio University, Unpublished dissertation.

Pecora, N. (2004) 'Nickelodeon Grows up; The Economic Evolution of a Network', in Heather Hendershot (ed.) *Nickelodeon Nation: The History, Politics and Economics of America's only TV Channel for Kids*, pp. 15-44.

Pecora, N., Murray, J.P., Wartella E. (2007) *Children and Television: Fifty Years of Research*. Mahwah, NJ: Lawrence Erlbaum Associates, Publishers.

Straubhaar, J. (1997) 'Distinguishing the Global, Regional, and National Levels of World Television', in A. Sreberny-Mohammadi, D. Winseck, J. McKenna and O. Boyd-Barrett (eds) *Media in a Global Context: A Reader*. London: Arnold, pp. 284-298.

Strelitz, L. (2004) 'Against Cultural Essentialism: Media Reception among South African Youth', *Media, Culture & Society,* 26(5): 625-641.

Strelitz, L. Boshoff, P. (2008) 'Children's Communication Rights: Beyond Intention', in Kirsten Drotner and Sonia Livingstone: *The Handbook of Children, Media and Culture*. (eds) Sage: Los Angeles, pp. 237-253.

The Economist (2004) 'Too Much of a Good Thing?' 373(8406), 97-98.

UNICEF (2006) Children's Broadcasting. Retrieved February 18, 2006 from http://www.unicef.org/videoaudio/video_children.html

Williams, K. (2003) *Understanding Media Theory*. London: Arnold.

World Youth Report (2004) *World Youth Report 2003: The Global Situation of Young People*. Retrieved 10 October 2007. http://un.org/esa/socdev/uryin/documents/ch12.pdf.

World Youth Report (2005) *World Youth Report 2005: Young people today, and in 2015*. Retrieved 10 October 2007. http://www.un.org/esa/socdev/unyin/wyr05.htm.

World Population Prospectus (2007) *World Population Prospectus, The 2006 Revision: Executive Summary*. Department of Economic and Social Affairs (Population Division). United Nations. Retrieved 10 October 2007. http://un.org/esa/population/publications/wpp2006/English.pdf.

Children, Media and Globalisation

*A Research Agenda for Africa**

Francis B. Nyamnjoh

If globalisation is a process of accelerated flow of media content, to most African cultures and children it is also a process of accelerated exclusion. For the entrepreneurs who own and control the global cultural industries (i.e. transnational media, record, publishing, film, news, information and entertainment corporations), whose principal purpose is the pursuit of profit, investing in cultural diversity beyond tokenism is too risky to contemplate. Instead, they are more interested in unregulated commercial exploitation and concentrated ownership and control of the cultural economy. In the interest of the predictability that enables profitability, they aim to streamline, standardise and routinise global cultural production and consumer palates. They are keen to slim all differences down into Barbie-like proportions, on behalf of an idea of culture devoid of complexity, richness and diversity. In the light of such obvious poverty of difference, the tendency is to mistake plurality for diversity, oblivious of the possibility that an appearance of plenty could well conceal a poverty of perspectives.

A consequence for cultures and communities that fail the profitability litmus test is reduced recognition of the world's rich creative diversity making the phenomena of cultural imperialism, trivialisation and misrepresentation increasingly likely (Oguibe 2004). A parochial Euro-American culture, purportedly global and globalising, is disproportionately nurtured by the creativity of a particular place, class, gender, generation and language to the detriment of all others amongst whom Africa and Africans occupy the bottom rungs. In this way, culture becomes more contrived than negotiated, and more localised than universal in origin, content and articulation.

Inspired by narrow, individual-centred philosophies of personhood, agency and property rights, this neoliberalism is aggressive in its sacrifice of community rights and group interests, as it pursues profit through the illusion of promoting the interests of the autonomous individual as a consumer (Brown 2003; Rowlands 2004). Old patterns informed by more inclusive philosophies of ownership and control are increasingly giving way to new configurations with a focus on the individual, consumerism and exclusion. National state-owned or public creative industries are yielding to commercial pressure and its emphasis on profit over culture and the vision of cultural institutions as public goods that guarantee cultural pluralism and diversity by providing for groups and social categories that otherwise would be ignored or marginalised by the market is losing currency. This leaves ordinary consumers, marginal communities, and whole cultures literally at the mercy of the McDonaldised cultural burgers served them in the interests of profits. It is only natural for content to be uniform regardless of the nationalities or cultural identities of shareholders, as the global cultural entrepreneurs are keener in advancing corporate and commercial interests and values than in valorising creativity and values that do not guarantee profitability (McChesney 1998; Thomas and Nain 2005).

While African cultures are marginalised by the streamlined information and entertainment menu served by global media conglomerates, the bulk of African children are only spared by the fact that global availability is not synonymous with global affordability. Given Africa's marginality in global economics, given the limited resources of most African states, and given the enormous costs of cultural production and dissemination, even elite African children who can afford access to national and global media content, are often reduced to consuming media burgers conceived and produced without their particular interests in mind, as even their national media are forced to rely on cheap imports as alternatives to local production. The children are often victims of second-hand consumption even as first-hand consumers, since the media content at their disposal seldom reflects their immediate cultural contexts. They may have qualified as global consumer citizens thanks to the purchasing power of their parents and guardians, but culturally, they remain consumer subjects, and must attune their palates to the diktats of undomesticated foreign media dishes. This is generally the case, despite national and regional broadcasting charters that stress the need for African children to 'hear, see and express themselves, their culture, their language and their life experiences, through the electronic media which affirm their sense of self, community and place' (SADC 1996). Most of the contributions in this volume present and discuss such national and regional efforts at children's media within the confines of global consumer capitalism and the hierarchies that shape and are shaped by it.

African cultural production does not attract sufficient attention from cultural entrepreneurs who are mostly white and located in the global North, unwilling to risk profitability through investing in cultures that are largely perceived to be socially inferior, economically uncompetitive and located in 'hearts of darkness' difficult to penetrate. Even when it ventures into Africa, foreign capital dares not go beyond stereotypical representations. Nor are African investors, intellectuals and political elites, schooled in such negative representations and debasement of Africa, all that keen to develop these sectors in ways that capture their creative encounters with cultural others. Indeed, as part of a global ecumene for 'the transnationalization of … a supremely local and parochial set of images and values' from the West (Golding and Harris 1997: 9), the power elite in Africa cannot afford to pay more than lip service to local cultural production and reproduction. Their daily activities and behaviour undermine the very doctrine of the importance of upholding African cultural values (Soyinka 1990: 114-120).

The identity and power conferred by joining the global consumer club explains why, despite much rhetoric about cultural renaissance in many African states, the ruling elites continue to acculturate themselves. They 'progressively take on the look of strangers in their own country due to their daily lifestyle, modeled on that of *homo consumens universalis*' (Amin 1980: 175; see also Onyeani 2000). With a ruling elite whose weakness and marginality *vis-à-vis* global capitalism and its institutions of legitimation have been certified, consuming streamlined global cultural products becomes a major way of staking claim to power locally and of further mystifying the disaffected populations with whom they have lost credibility. At best, these elites commission 'traditional dances' and 'praise singing' and other forms of cultural production – poetry, music, art, books, etc. – which they can use for their personal amusement or to entertain foreign friends and visiting counterparts. As Wole Soyinka laments in the case of Nigeria, complex, enriching dimensions of culture are often 'relegated to token, or symbolic, expositions, starved of funds and given scant coverage even in the media' (Soyinka 1990: 110). In general, performances that were reserved for solemn occasions in the past have been trivialised and in certain cases commodified for consumer tourism, partly for the gratification of the local elite but also because of the desperate quest by side-stepped cultural communities to survive in a global economy.

Often in their capacity as local subsidiaries or representatives of global cultural entrepreneurs, such 'capitalist niggers' (Onyeani 2000) are all too keen to jump on the global consumer bandwagon – a situation not helped by the draconian conditionalities imposed by the Structural Adjustment Programmes of the World Bank and IMF since the 1970s. They thus seek to streamline the consumer palates of their fellow Africans in tune with cultural menus produced in or inspired by the West. They are ready to entertain African creativity only to the extent that such creativity reproduces stereotypes and internalises western inspired consumer cultural aesthetics. Such mimicry is as true of education, art, writing, cinema, fashion and journalism, as it is of scholarship and publishing (Nyamnjoh 2004).

Given their tender ages and given the dearth of counter powerful local messages at their disposal in national media, African children are more vulnerable to uncritical internalisation of the explicit or implicit ideological content of the media they consume. The fact of the media not being about or for African children as primary consumers is in a way an implicit statement on the dispensability of their local cultures. An invitation for them to join the consumer bandwagon on its own terms can only entail an invitation to self-denial, self-evacuation, or self-devaluation, and the glorification of the creativities and mediocrities of others.

But whether or not these invitations are actually taken up by African children, and in what ways, is often more assumed than proven, even when research has been done. The tendency in research has been to mistake labels for contents and exposure for effects, as if the African children involved have lost all agency to the dominant structures of capital. While such assumptions may be commonsensical and understandable, only meaningful research can draw attention away from grand-narratives that either tend to celebrate the illusion of unregulated flows or the victimhood of those at the margins of global abundance. If our modest research in a related area among Cameroonian youths is anything to go by, the reality may be more nuanced than usually depicted. Not only do young Cameroonians appropriate media representations never intended for them, they use these representations to construct fantasies about whiteness, which in turn serve as a standard of measure in encounters with actual whites. The media reinforce ideas of western superiority and allure, thus buttressing fantasies that deny the reality of actual experiences with the modest circumstance of the white tourists, volunteers, researchers or clergy often encountered by the Cameroonian youth. Sometimes the latter would rather believe that the white he or she knows was pretending to be poor, than deny media representations of white opulence. Daily contact with whites can leave young Cameroonians baffled and disappointed. Real experience is dismissed in favour of mass-mediated fantasies. And any white who is reluctant or unable to live up to this representation has no business to be white (Nyamnjoh and Page 2002).

Media globalisation

This paper seeks to draw attention to the sort of research questions that could meaningfully challenge simplistic assumptions about children, media and globalisation in Africa. But first an understanding of changing mediascapes under globalisation is in order. Propelled by 'the incessant pursuit of profit', global media entrepreneurs appear to settle for little short of the total 'relaxation or elimination of barriers to commercial exploitation of media and to concentrated media ownership' (McChesney 2001: 1-4). This craving for profit has negatively affected the traditional emphasis on public service media that guarantee cultural pluralism and diversity regardless of the market. In Europe since the 1990s, market-driven ideas of public service broadcasting serving the interests and preferences of individuals as individuals have become more popular (Syvertsen 1999; Søndergaard 1999). Seen as individual consumers, even children are treated as autonomous agents glued together by a selfless market slaving away for their cultural freedom, development and enrichment as global citizens with power to arm-twist parents and guardians to service their consumer instincts. This development blurs the traditional distinction between public service and commercial broadcasting, and passes for public service even the greedy and aggressive pursuit of profit.

The shift makes a virtue of consumption, presenting it as the ultimate symbol of civilisation. If consumption is the supreme indicator of cultural sophistication, then the media could dispense of traditional ideas of quality educational programmes, and still be of tremendous service to children as budding consumers. Hence the sacrifice of conventional educational content in favour of a plethora of mass and often cheaply produced alternatives, aimed more at forging consumer zombies than developing rounded and critical citizens of the children they target. The profit motive dictates that various media content are conceived, produced, and disseminated with the primary objective of maintaining economic, political and cultural privileges and advantage, while thwarting any attempt at the social shaping or domestication of media technologies and content that could abolish or overturn such privileges. It is precisely in this way, Schiller (1977) perceptively argued way back in the 1970s, that America used the rhetoric of 'unregulated flows', as a 'highly effective ideological club' to promote its political, economic and cultural values by whipping 'alternative forms of social organization' into a ridiculous defensiveness.

However, far from leading to a presupposed convergence, globalisation appears to accelerate the production of differences, heterogeneities or boundaries through the structures of inequalities inherent in global capitalism (Chomsky 1999; Comaroff and Comaroff 2000). As Bill Clinton has very aptly pointed out, the 'abject poverty' which is part of our globalised world, 'accelerates conflict', 'creates recruits for terrorists and those who incite ethnic and religious hatred', and 'fuels a violent rejection of the economic and social order on which our future depends' (Clinton 2001). Globalisation has only intensified age-old boundaries and divisions. 'It looks as if, in a world characterised by flows, a great deal of energy is devoted to controlling and freezing them: grasping the flux often actually entails a politics of 'fixing' – a politics which is, above all, operative in struggles about the construction of identities' (Geschiere and Meyer 1998: 605).

Not only is the traditional idea of public service media fast becoming outmoded, calls for some ground rules to protect cultural diversity have simply been greeted with the rhetoric of free flows at worst or with token concessions to 'cultural minorities' at best. What is more, the corporate media are in a particularly powerful position, given their dual role as players and umpires (McChesney 2001: 3-9). They 'enjoy an enormous leeway to negotiate and protect interests from the vantage of prior monopoly positions', and 'do not have to bend over backwards to strike deals' (Thomas and Lee 1998: 2). Given their freehand and reluctance to invest in diversity, the global corporate media have tended to downplay creativity and variety in children's media in the interest of standardisation, routinisation and profitability.

With such premium on profit, the global media corporations that target children are hardly about the 'unregulated flows' of the world's cultural diversity. Relegated to the margins even in African countries, are what Fayemi (1999) has termed 'voices from within'. That is, 'the lives of ordinary children and their everyday life: how they are nurtured and reared, the games they play, their adolescence and growing up years, their education and their role within their families and immediate environment.' As Soyinka puts it, African children are thus lured and/or coerced 'to develop an incurable dependency syndrome and consume themselves to death', as feeding the global consumerist machine becomes a way of life for them. Caught in the global web of consumerism, 'the self-respecting youth dare not be seen without a Walkman', with often devastating consequences (Soyinka 1994: 209-210). By focusing on more of the same, the global media tend to mistake plurality for diversity (Murdock 1994: 5). The result is globalisation as a 'deeply and starkly inegalitarian' process (Golding and Harris 1997: 7), a one-way flow in cultural products that favours a privileged minority as it compounds the impoverishment of the rest. As 'empires of image and of the imagination', the corporate media control global markets and global consciousness (Murdock 1994: 3), mostly by denying access to creativity perceived to stand in the way of profit, power and privilege.

This literally leaves children and marginal cultures in Africa at the mercy of the McDonaldised, standardised or routinised information, education, games and other entertainment burgers served in the interest of profit by the global corporate media. Because the latter 'advances corporate and commercial interests and values and denigrates or ignores that which cannot be incorporated into its mission', content becomes uniform, regardless of the nationalities or cultural identities of shareholders. This is hardly surprising since wanted are passive, depoliticised, unthinking consumers more prone 'to take orders than to make waves' by questioning the 'light escapist entertainment' menu presented them (McChesney 1998: 7). In this regard, it could be argued, as McChesney (1998: 6; 2001: 13) has done, that the basic differences are not between nation-states as such, but between the rich and the poor (whom I term 'consumer citizens' and 'consumer subjects' respectively), across national borders. However, the fact remains that the investors, advertisers and affluent consumers whose interests the global media represent, are more concentrated in and comprise a significant proportion of the children of the developed world, than is the case in Africa where only an elite minority are involved and hardly any local cultural products are competitive globally.

Research questions

This scenario invites some interesting research questions into assumptions about globalisation of media content as a process of cultural homogenisation. How true are such assumptions of children in Africa, where only an elite few qualify to consume global media first hand? To what extent, for example, is there cultural imperialism, in the sense of a systematic penetration and domination of cultural life on the continent by the globalised western children's media content? How are the elite few among African children, affected by global media content? Is it scientifically adequate to assume cultural homogenisation from such exposure alone? If not, what other indicators are to be used? When is measurement to start and end for a final conclusion on homogenisation to be reached?

Is it possible that African children might desire and consume the same media content as Western children for example, yet read entirely different meanings into that content? If yes, how are we to explain such differences? How do the structurally excluded bulk of ordinary children in Africa react to their predicament? Do they simply celebrate victimhood? Or do they seek to manoeuvre and manipulate themselves into inclusion, even if only at the margins? How does this enrich understanding of the hierarchies of consumption made possible by globalisation? What creative strategies are employed by African children, both elite and marginalised, to appropriate, gatecrash, cushion, subvert or resist the effects of their cultural exclusion by the global structures of inequality evident in global media? How do African children reconcile otherwise conflicting cultural influences in their daily interactions with one another and with others? What accounts for refusal or reluctance to internalise and surrender to marginalisation? How, when, and why do Africans and their children draw from the sociality and conviviality of their cultural communities? In short, to what extent could it be claimed that African children 'may welcome, accept or collude in some cases, but in others they may ignore, select, reshape, redirect, adapt and, on occasions, even completely reject [media content?] Even when the same material is available to all and widely consumed, the eventual outcome, may vary considerably both within and between countries' (Halloran 1993: 3).

Within the context of globalisation and postcoloniality, it is possible for children to assume multiple identifications that draw from different cultural repertoires, depending on the context (Warnier 1999). If cultures prescribe behaviour and beliefs, and if children are exposed to competing cultural codes or styles in this way, should we talk of identity in the singular in relation to those children – especially as every culture takes much time to be transmitted, assimilated or undone? What do we have to say about children's actions and identities inspired by drawing from multiple cultural repertoires? How do children come to terms with the fact that identity in the age of intensified globalisation is not determined solely by birth, or entirely by choices made by them? How well these questions are answered would depend on how sensitive one is to local predicaments methodologically, and also on what meaning one gives 'Africanity' in relation to children in Africa.

Methodology

First on methodology, if we recognise cultural diversity, we must be ready to question theories and methods built under the assumption of a universal culture; and we must be ready to question research on or about African children undertaken from the insensitive position of assumptions about an objective social science. For, every culture generates for itself its own 'thinkability' and 'unthinkability' (Surin 1995: 1183). If arguments to the effect that only someone 'raised and nurtured in the cultural environment of a linguistic group' can 'capture all of a culture's subtleties and complexities' (Grinker and Steiner 1997: 684) are to be taken seriously, then the best way to go about researching any culture is to seek as much as possible to be an insider even as an outsider, to be predicament-oriented. Attitudes of arrogance and condescension towards the cultures in question can only result in knowledge pregnant with prejudice, stereotypes and dogma.

A 'predicament-oriented' approach should seek first 'a local understanding of the nature of given predicaments among those actually facing these predicaments in their everyday lives', and then an understanding of 'the broader historical, structural and/or ecological causes generating such predicaments', with the aim of feeding such understanding 'back to the local level to illuminate the understanding from below of the predicaments confronted there, and to provide guidelines for local actions and struggle' (Himmelstrand et al. 1994: 4-8). This means that social research should not be divorced from its ethical and political implications. Although the debate on 'objective' social research is dated, not enough social researchers are assuming their ethical responsibilities for one to stop flogging a dead horse. Some still believe that social phenomena can be understood, controlled, manipulated and exploited, independent of human intention and expectation. This largely accounts for the tendency to celebrate impersonal and insensitive methodologies that only exacerbate the misrepresentation of the powerless. Such strict adherence to dominant research models has usually precluded the asking of the really important questions of why and how.

Halloran echoes this point with the example of comparative international research, which is quite common in the study of children and media. Such research is by nature very difficult to conduct, but certain assumptions in conventional research traditions have made it even more so. 'At the heart of the problem is the failure to recognize that social research is embedded in cultural values and that the fundamental differences … which obtain in different societies preclude the use of carbon copy survey or interview methods which assume that genuine comparability can be achieved only by administering the same questions in the same way in all participating countries. One has only to take note of the relationship between language and culture to realise that this approach is patently absurd' (Halloran 1981: 9). Like media content, methods of data collection no matter how appropriate in the West are not always adapted to the realities of children in Africa, and a deliberate effort must be made to domesticate them. In certain cases, nothing short of a cocktail of theories, methods and approaches would suffice to take care of the many-sided-ness and particularities of real life in Africa.

Being African

This leads to the second point: the 'Africanity' of children in Africa. What does it mean to be an African child? Who qualifies to claim Africa? Is being African or claiming Africa an attribute of race and skin colour (black, white, yellow), birth (umbilical cord, birth certificates, identity cards, passports), geography (physical spaces, home village), history (encounters), culture (prescriptive specificities), economics (availability and affordability, wealth and deprivation), sociology (social configurations and action, inclusion and exclusion), psychology (mind sets), philosophy (world views), politics (power relations), collective memory (shared experiences and aspirations), or a category through which a world that is not rigidly geographical, racial or cultural is constructed, to name just a few of the many possibilities that present themselves? These are questions which have deep roots in debates on citizenship, identity and belonging – and, therefore, in the definition of rights, entitlement, duties, and responsibilities. The questions are, of course, not uniquely African – indeed, similar issues have been posed and debated with considerable passion in other parts of the world both historically and currently, and contestations around them have also often been played out in violent communal confrontations, civil wars, and inter-state conflicts. And while they may seem straight forward to answer, the questions have been rendered much more complex by the dynamic inter-play of race, ethnicity, gender and religion in the structuring and exercise of power and opportunity. Precisely for this reason, they are not questions that can be addressed in the abstract.

How one answers the questions that are generated by any attempt at grappling with Africanity is not only situationally determined, but is also a function of how selective one is with regard to the various indicators available. Some individuals and communities on the continent and elsewhere might claim Africanity or have it imposed upon them for various personal, collective, historical and political reasons. But it is not always straight forward to say which of these claims may be legitimate and why, especially as identity is not only how one sees oneself, but also how one is seen and categorised by others, particularly where the absorption of new populations is involved. This is all the more so as identities are themselves always in mutation, shaped as they are by changing historical contexts and circumstances, such as internal and international migrations, shifts in social power relations, and articulations of might and right.

It is, however, safe to say that to most ordinary people in Africa, Africanity is more than just a birth certificate, an identity card, or a passport – documents that many of them may not have, even as others coming from elsewhere and waving the flag of Africanity may have all of these documents and more. For the ordinary person, to be African is not simply to be labelled or merely defined as such. It is to be a social actor/actress enmeshed in a particular context that has been and continues to be shaped by a unique history that, among others, is marked by unequal encounters and misrepresentations often informed by the arrogance and ignorance of the economically and politically powerful who take the liberty also to arrogate a cultural superiority to themselves. For the masses of Africans, Africa is above all a lived reality, one that is constantly shaped and reshaped by their toil and sweat as subjected and devalued humanity, even as they struggle to live in dignity and to transform their societies progressively. For these people, the fact of their Africanity is neither in question nor a question. And the least they would expect from concerned scholars, advocates, media practitioners and cultural industries (both mainstream and alternative) is to refrain from adding onto their burdens in the name of a type of media content which, in being ahistorical, also trivialises their collective experiences and memories (Olukoshi and Nyamnjoh 2004).

Different people have different answers to the question on Africanity, but no research can yield adequate results, that failed to problematise this issue. A researcher who assumes or proceeds as though being African is an attribute of birth, transmitted through the life essence of a black African father, and to be protected from contamination by the products of other life essences, is likely to contaminate his or her research with indicators that are short on scientific rigour. Social science is compromised by analysis that confine being African to a birthmark and a geography taken together. It makes much more analytical sense to seeing the Africanity of children as a process. To those who proceed thus, although there is reason to lament the marginalisation of cultural identities from the African continent in today's McDonaldised media content, it would be quite misleading to assume from this a counter notion of a geographically confined, patriarchal, essentialist and frozen understanding of being African. This idea of Africanity is rich, flexible and relevant to researching children and the media in Africa under the current context of accelerated flows of people, cultural products and the fascination by youth with modelling themselves after celebrities – be these Hollywood, Bollywood or Nollywood stars or any other highly mediatised personalities, real or imagined.

Child and youth identities, whether African or otherwise, 'are complex and multiple and grow out of a history of changing responses to economic, political, and cultural forces' (Appiah 1992: 177-178). In our conception, design and implementation of research on children's media in Africa, it is paramount to build in and stay conscious of the fact that identity, far from being 'innate in consciousness at birth', is rather 'something formed through unconscious processes over time' (Hall 1994: 122). As such, identity is always work in progress, subject to constant and often unconscious renegotiation with changing encounters with other ways of seeing, doing and being. As Stuart Hall has so aptly put it, identity 'always remains incomplete, is always "in process", always "being formed"', and therefore, 'rather than speaking of identity as a finished thing, we should speak of *identification*, and see it as an on-going process' (Hall 1994: 122). In cultural identity two phenomena complement each other: 'an inward sense of association or identification with a specific culture or subculture' on the one hand, and 'an outward tendency within a specific culture to share a sense of what it has in common with other cultures and of what distinguishes it from other cultures' on the other (Servaes 1997: 81). There is therefore the need to treat children's identities in Africa as 'a dynamic reality ... that moves forward daily but knows no end' (Mveng 1985: 68). This, and this alone, would ensure that we avoid asking the wrong questions even when we have identified the right problem.

For, although African identities have had a raw deal in relation to other identities, and there is certainly a need to create greater room in children's media for African philosophies of personhood and agency (Nyamnjoh 2002), Africa has been subjected to certain influences through slavery, colonialism, and by interaction with other cultures, that have affected African identities in no small way, and that cannot simply be brushed away like one brushes dust off one's coat (Appiah 1992; Nyamnjoh 2006). Abhorrence for Western colonialism and consumerism notwithstanding, marginalised Africans cannot afford to dismiss as non-Africans those children of the elite few who – as Sarah Akrofi-Quarcoo, Patrick Osei-Hwere, Tewodros Workalemahu and Beatrice Boateng observe of Ghana, Ethiopia and South Africa in this volume – have found attraction in and can afford the current globalised Western media culture (*Sesame Street*, *Sponge Bob*, *Dora the Explorer*, *The Simpsons*, *Scooby-Doo*, *Tom and Jerry*, *Swatcats*, etc.) for purposes of prestige and power; not only because these are the children of those who preside over their destinies, but also because even the elite few often domesticate in most creative and original ways their consumption of foreign media. Nor should black Africans dismiss as non-Africans children of European and Asian descent, born and brought up in Africa, with some of who have never lived outside of the continent, nor are they interested in migrating from Africa. How can such children be denied their Africanity, simply because their ancestors can be traced back to Europe or Asia, while at the same time we are eager to confer Africanity to diaposric Africans whose idea and experience of Africa might sociologically be less real? As researchers, we must therefore be creative, negotiating, dynamic and realistic in attributing Africanity to the children we study.

As researchers, we must come to terms with Africa's negotiated identities in recognition of ongoing processes of 'sorting out, selection, choice, and finally *voluntary* adoption of some ideas, values, outlooks and institutions' that have resulted from encounters with other forms of identity (Gyekyre 1997: 25-26) either directly or through media representations. Studies have evidenced that even in precolonial Africa the idea of a fixed *cultural identity* is more romantic than real (Appiah 1992); rather, ethnic groups have tended to have 'a constant flux of identities' depending on political expediency and other factors (MacGaffey 1995; Nyamnjoh 2007a, b). The children, whose relationship with media is of interest to us, may well straddle multiple identity margins in most fascinating and creative ways, and seeking to pigeonhole them into single identity margins could subtract from rather than enrich understanding of the complexity of their life experiences.

We need therefore, as social scientists, to take seriously arguments against the temptation 'to celebrate and endorse those identities that seem at the moment to offer the best hope of advancing our other goals, and to keep silence about the lies and the myths' in such identities. Our duty as social scientists is to stay committed to the truth about children's identities in Africa. For, although "We cannot change the world simply by evidence and reasoning, ... we surely cannot change it without them either" (Appiah 1992: 173-180).

Homogenisation, conflicts or heterogeneity?

Recognising indigenous African forms should not be mistaken for throwing the baby of adaptability out with the bathwater. African popular musicians for example have evolved and continue to develop musical idioms that capture ongoing processes by Africans at modernising their cultures and traditionalising their modernities. Indeed, the mechanisms developed by Africans in response to the above scenarios are complex, fascinating and informed by ideas of person hood and agency that simply refuse to be confined to the logic of, dichotomies, essentialism, the market and profitability, as the rich personal account of one of Africa's leading contemporary musicians, Manu Dibango, demonstrates (Dibango 1994). As an African musician who has lived the best part of his professional life in Paris and whose music has been enriched by various encounters, Manu Dibango describes himself as "Négropolitain", "a man between two cultures, two environments", whose music cannot simply be reduced to either, without losing part of his creative self (Dibango 1994: 88-130). It appears that no one is too cosmopolitan to be local as well. We only have to note the creative ways Africans have harnessed the cell phone to interlink town and home village, to know how disinterested in a culture of winner-takes-all Africans are.

Equally, to recognise the cosmopolitan nature of African children and their identities, does not necessarily imply to argue in favour of cultural homogenisation implicit in the rhetoric of globalisation. Although globalisation is homogenising consumer tastes, the same globalisation, through the unequal relations it generates, provides consumers (big and small) with the means to create individual and social identities, which are variant and diverse in a way that speaks less of a synthesis of cultures (Appadurai 1996; Warnier 1999). Not even in USA, where much has been achieved in the area of the 'McDonaldization of Society' (Ritzer 2000), is that synthesis possible. It is more a type of unity in diversity, where the fact of children belonging to the same consumer club (wanting the same toys, computer games, television programmes, books, animated cartoons, films, music, fast foods and soft drinks) does not guarantee cultural synchronisation (Lapham 1992).

As Halloran puts it, quoting a cynic, in reference to warring Serbs, Croats, Slovenes, Bosnians and Macedonians of the former Yugoslavia, all watching the same television for years did for them was that they could 'march to fight each other wearing the same T shirts whistling the same pop tune and with a can of coke and a mars bar in their packs.' They had little else in common 'other than a tribally based hate and a need to "cleanse"' (Halloran 1993: 2). This is analogous to the situation between African and Western children, where there is generally very little else in common linking them, than the pool of media products and consumer items into which they read different meanings as first or second-hand consumers, depending on their cultural and social backgrounds. Thus, despite the increasing synchronisation of their tastes and habits, the cultural heterogeneity of children as consumers of similar media contents seems to get deeper instead.

Children everywhere may appear to be chasing after the same media products, but they bring along with them specific cultural traits that lead to diversity in their consumption of those products. It thus appears unrealistic to assume from mere exposure cultural synchronisation as if children had effectively become the consumer zombies intended in the standardised and routinised media content served them. Creative responses by African children may well mean that the final outcome is neither a victory for 'African cultures' nor for 'western consumer values' as such, but rather, a creatively negotiated blend of both to enrich their personal and collective cosmopolitanism. In this way, African children are active agents in ongoing processes of simultaneously modernising African traditions and Africanising their modernities. The outcome is neither triumph for 'culture' nor for 'globalisation' as distinct entities, but rather for the new creation to which a marriage of both has given rise: African children as repertoires, melting pots and negotiators of conviviality between multiple encounters or competing influences.

Researching African children as active agents

How does one meaningfully conceptualize and research agency amongst Africa children as active and passive consumers of global and glocalised media fodder? What basic assumptions must one make? What accumulated personal and collective prejudices must one check against to ensure that the trade of researching agency by African children and amongst those who purport to produce media content informed by their interests or targeting them is sufficiently conscious of context and the interplay of both local and global forces, and adequately participatory to yield innovative results? How often do we reflect on the relevance of our research for the lives of those African children whose agency we seek to understand? In other words, are the issues we seek to research of importance to these children who 'innocently' allow us into their lives – just as they do the media content fed them, and to what extent have they consciously or unconsciously shaped our theoretical and methodological trajectories? Does it make sense, and, if so why, to ensure that African scholars and indeed the African children or communities whose agency is of interest are actively involved from the outset in the research design and implementation? And what, in concrete terms, is required of various actors in the knowledge production and dissemination chain to accomplish this? Is it useful or not to have a negotiated and nuanced understanding of agency based on the literature (orthodox and alternative) and, even more importantly, on the life situations and social positions of African children in and beyond the confines of a place called Africa?

How does one research agency amongst children beyond the bandwagon of intellectual and political fashions or 'correctness' of the times? The current tendency is for researchers to assume that the only agency which matters is that of the purportedly autonomous individual actor, whose assumed autonomy is defined fundamentally in opposition to local and national communities. But this same literature is silent on the impact of external or global forces on internal or local agency. To what extent can individuals, even where creditable with agency, move beyond the bounds of state and sub-national structures with the support of exogenously induced ideas of social change and development by objective and benevolent outsiders?

Is it possible that such enthusiasm to celebrate without problematizing the rights of the choice-driven individual *vis-à-vis* local state bounded structures overlooks some perennial hierarchies and power dynamics within and between states that make agency possible for some only at the best of times? Do African scholars, governments and advocacy groups, for example, have a point when they vehemently argue against the World Bank, the IMF, the WTO, global multinational cultural industries and related institutions for crippling the agency of African states, institutions, communities and individuals with draconian neoliberal policies and stubborn insensitivity to alternative ways of thinking, seeing and doing? If so, how does a researcher on agency meaningfully factor in these concerns without, of course, throwing the baby out with the bath water?

What do Africans, in their world views and dynamism, perceive agency to consist of for the individual (child and adult alike), group, institution and community? How do these African perceptions of agency cope with social change informed by unequal encounters fed by local and global hierarchies of humanity dictated, amongst other factors, by race, place, culture, class, status, gender and age? If unequal encounters are possible and if African ideas of agency have not necessarily always coincided with competing ideas of agency by others encountered by Africans from positions of relative weakness, how have these dominant others set about imposing constrictive perceptions of agency informed by the arrogance and ignorance of power and privilege on Africans, in principle and in practice, and with what consequences? And how does one design and implement research on children's media in Africa, in such a way that these unequal encounters are captured in their fullness and depth, highlighting the limits and possibilities of agency for the one or the other at the level of individual children, whole communities and cultures? Even more importantly, who decides, and when, that it is time to move on from using the past to explain the present and inform the future? This is especially relevant in a context where the wounds of the past are still so fresh, a context where Africa remains a scar on the conscience of the world, to quote British Prime Minister Tony Blair. And what power dynamics and interests are at play to belie the apparent objectivity/neutrality of such choices in scholarly, political, cultural, social or economic circles?

If one assumes an interconnected world of ever-accelerating techniques of inclusion and exclusion, how realistic is it to seek to understand African agency in isolation from the agency of non-Africans, the not-yet-Africans or the Africans-plus – if I am permitted this coinage to refer to those in and outside of Africa who claim African and non-African identities (for example, Africans in the diaspora, and European and Asian diasporas in Africa)? If not, what are the various forms (individual and institutional) and vehicles (political, cultural, economic, social, etc.) that such non-African, not-yet-African or African-plus agency assumes, and with what consequences for Africans and their agency? If the comforts of power tend to blunt one's sensitivity to the predicaments of others, how do researchers, who are relatively better placed than the African children they study, ensure that the assumptions natural to their social positions and cultural palates (race, ethnicity, class, status, gender, generation, etc.) do not influence the research process and its outcome? In a continent starved of basic research funding within universities and research institutions, and where the bulk of research-related activities are funded and controlled through consultancies by NGOs and grants by foundations with pre-conceived ideas of what is relevant rather than in critical scholarly research, how does one provide for the type of critical predicament-oriented research that does justice to children's agency as a scholarly theme?

Which approaches to the study of children's agency are likely to yield the best results? Is it those wherein the research is designed with agency as a primary focus, or those in which structure and agency are seen in interplay? But then, is this question worth posing in the first place for those to whom agency is as much a possibility open to individuals as well as to the groups, communities and structures that they produce, reproduce and transform? When does it become necessary to talk of domesticating or harnessing agency? Are certain cultures and material conditions more predisposed to the one than the other? What experiences and possibilities does Africa have to share in this regard?

What methodologies or methodological cocktails and buffets would best suit the sort of accounts craved to ensure a comprehensive understanding of the agency of African children in all its social and historical complexities and trajectories? If it is not sufficient to be passionate about researching children's agency in Africa without being equally compassionate about the children and communities studied, how does one avoid this methodologically? Is it by emphasizing intersubjectivity and conviviality between the researcher and the researched? Is it by ensuring that researchers take up community membership amongst the researched beyond the participant observation of anthropologists that lasts only as long as it takes to complete their research and unturn-native? And shouldn't the merits of ethnography be pushed beyond anthropology to influence other disciplines that inform policies on Africa disproportionately, despite their tendency to celebrate economic, political and cultural snapshots that reproduce problematic images of Africa and its children? In this regard, shouldn't a systematic effort be made to review methodology courses in view of the fact that the data one collects and the interpretations one brings to bear on children's agency or whatever other phenomenon can only be as rich as one's research questions? How can one make a culture of the fact that children's agency research in and on Africa can only be as good as the questions interested researchers are willing and ready to ask, and how open-minded and ready are they to go beyond rhetoric?

If agency is almost always negotiated, what are the local and global structures that African children have, at different points in time, negotiated or at least attempted to negotiate themselves out of or into, and with what outcomes? What are the current structures African children would want to negotiate themselves into or out of, and with what prospects and challenges?

If agency among African children is not homogenous, as both African and external agents (re)acting on, in and to or interacting with African children are differently positioned in tune with the hierarchies that govern their worlds, how does one avoid a monolithic discourse on the media, agency and African children without falling into sterile relativism? Similarly, what form would empowering the agency of African children take in knowledge production *vis-à-vis* non-African structures and scholarly agents? Who defines which literature available to African researchers, in a context of unequal global flows and the exchange of knowledge products, is credible? Are African scholars involved as co-producers with equal say or as research assistants, 'shoe-shine' collaborators, and other passive presences to be acknowledged in footnotes and appendices or simply ignored? What would guarantee the sort of collaboration that minimizes prejudices, stereotypes, ignorance and opportunism both ways?

It is true that even when we as scholars are predisposed to addressing these weighty questions, constraints of time and money may prevent us really squaring up to them. However, this should not subtract from the fact that in researching agency amongst children in Africa, it is only proper for us scholars to be conscious of (and even to question) our instinct by training to seek to ensure that established scholarly traditions and expectations are maintained. In a world heavy with economic, cultural and political hierarchies informed by, for example, race, place, class, gender and age, such instincts beg a few questions: Whose traditions? Whose scholarly yardsticks? Why traditions and yardsticks? Hence the importance of yet other questions: Who has the power to define, enforce and manage these traditions, tastes and standards? How feasible is it to promote scholarly or research traditions and ideals when they are at variance with dominant economic considerations or with the ambitions of dominance of those who have the means and power to determine the rules of the game with scant regard for participatory democracy? If he who pays the piper calls the tune, then the research and scholarship most likely to inspire investment are those familiar to the paymaster's race, place, class, gender or generation; those into which s/he has been schooled to the point of second nature and which, instinctively, s/he expects every piper worth the name to internalize and reproduce. Yet pipers are just as shaped by their race, place, class, gender and generation as those who pay them. Inviting them to internalize and reproduce tunes at variance with their own traditions and tastes is to devalue and marginalize their own human experience. Over time, in the interests of convenience and material comfort, many a piper yields to the whims and caprices of the wallet and reproduces the research and scholarly expectations of their paymasters. This, in a way, makes all research and scholarship (non-African and African alike) a very conservative industry where, despite rhetoric to the contrary, the emphasis is less on creativity than mimicry, and less on production than reproduction.

Thus, socialised into these hierarchies, researchers of Africa and African researchers operate in scholarly contexts where it is normal to minimize the scientific and creative capabilities of the African mind. Increasingly, for reasons of political correctness, this is true in practice even when it remains unstated. It is hardly surprising then, on the one hand, that African social scientists continue to face an uphill task convincing their non-African counterparts about the maturity and validity of their scholarship. Similarly, it is not surprising that non-African counterparts face a Herculean task to convince African social scientists about the integrity of their research ventures in the context of such inequalities and prejudices. The time has come to pay greater attention to changing not only what is produced as knowledge on Africa but, even more importantly, the institutional cultures within which that knowledge is produced, in view of encouraging greater and more genuine collaboration between African, non-African and African-plus scholars. We need to redress the inequalities, prejudices and tensions that continue to stand in the way of meaningful research on children's agency in Africa. The contributions in this volume offer useful building blocks in this connection.

References

Amin, S. (1980) *Class and Nation: Historically and in the Current Crisis*. London: Heinemann.

Appadurai, A. (1996) *Modernity at Large: Cultural Dimensions of Globalization*. Minneapolis: University of Minnesota Press.

Appiah, K.A. (1992) *In My Father's House: Africa in the Philosophy of Culture*. New York: Oxford University Press.

Brown, M.F. (2003) *Who Owns Native Culture?* Cambridge, MA: Harvard University Press.

Chomsky, N. (1999) *Profit Over People: Neoliberalism and Global Order*. New York: Seven Stories Press.

Clinton, B. (2001) *The Struggle for the Soul of the 21st Century*, http://bbc.co.uk/arts/news_comment/dimbleby/print_clinton.shtml

Comaroff, J. and J. (2000) 'Millennial Capitalism: First Thoughts on a Second Coming', *Public Culture*, 12(2): 291-343.

Dibango, M. (in collaboration with Danielle Rouard) (1994) *Three Kilos of Coffee: An Autobiography*. Chicago: The University of Chicago Press.

Fayemi, A.O. (1999) *Voices from Within*, http://www.fayemi.com

Geschiere, P. and Meyer, B. (1998) 'Globalization and Identity: Dialectics of Flows and Closures: Introduction', *Development and Change*, 29(4): 601-615.

Golding, P. and Harris, P. (eds.) (1997), *Beyond Cultural Imperialism: Globalization, Communication and the New International Order*. London: Sage.

Grinker, R.R. and Steiner, C.B. (eds.) (1997) *Perspectives on Africa: A Reader in Culture, History, and Representation*. Oxford: Blackwell Publishers.

Gyekye, K. (1997) 'Philosophy, Culture, and Technology in the Postcolonial', in Emmanuel Chukwudi Eze (ed.) *Postcolonial African Philosophy: A Critical Reader*. Oxford: Blackwell Publishers, pp. 25-44.

* An earlier version of this article was published in Cecilia von Feilitzen and Ulla Carlsson (eds) *Yearbook 2002: Children, Young People and Media Globalisation*, The UNESCO International Clearinghouse on Children, Youth and Media, Nordicom, Göteborg University, pp. 43-52.

Hall, S. (1994) 'The Question of Cultural Identity', in *The Polity Reader in Cultural Theory*. Polity Press: Oxford.

Halloran, J.D. (1981) *The Context of Mass Communication Research*. Singapore: Asian Mass Communication Research Information Centre.

Halloran, J.D. (1993) *The European Image: Unity in Diversity – Myth or Reality*. A Presentation at the IAMCR Conference, Dublin, June 1993.

Himmelstrand, U., Kinyanjui, K., Mburugu, E. (eds.) (1994) *African Perspectives on Development: Controversies, Dilemmas and Openings*. London: James Currey.

Lapham, L.H. (1992) 'Who and What is American?', *Harper's Magazine* (January 1992), pp. 43-49.

MacGaffey, W., (1995) 'Kongo Identity, 1483-1993', in V.Y. Mudimbe (ed.) *The South Atlantic Quarterly. Nations, Identities, Cultures* (special issue). Durham: Duke University Press, pp. 1025-1037.

McChesney, R.W., (1998) 'The Political Economy of Global Media', *Media Development*, XLV(4): 3-8.

McChesney, R.W. (2001) 'Global Media, Neoliberalism, and Imperialism', *Monthly Review* 52(10), http://www.monthlyreview.org/301rwm.htm.

Murdock, G. (1994) 'The New Mogul Empires: Media Concentration and Control in the Age of Divergence', *Media Development*, XLI(4): 3-6.

Mveng, E. (1985) 'Is there a Cameroonian Cultural Identity?' in Ministry of Information and Culture (ed.) *The Cultural Identity of Cameroon*. Yaounde: Cameroon Government, pp. 65-69.

Nyamnjoh, F.B. (2002) "A Child is One Person's Only in the Womb': Domestication, Agency and Subjectivity in the Cameroonian Grassfields', in Richard Werbner (ed.) *Postcolonial Subjectivities in Africa*. London: Zed, pp. 111-138.

Nyamnjoh, F.B. (2004) 'From Publish or Perish to Publish and Perish: What 'Africa's 100 Best Books' Tell Us About Publishing Africa', *Journal of Asian and African Studies*, 39(5): 331-355.

Nyamnjoh, F.B. (2006) *Insiders and Outsiders: Citizenship and Xenophobia in Contemporary Southern Africa*. London: CODESRIA/Zed Books.

Nyamnjoh, F.B. (2007a) "Ever-Diminishing Circles': The Paradoxes of Belonging in Botswana", in Marisol de la Cadena and Orin Starn (eds.) *Indigenous Experience Today*. Oxford: Berg, pp. 305-332.

Nyamnjoh, F.B. (2007b) 'Culture, Conflict, and Globalisation : Africa', in Anheier, H.K and Isar, Y.R. (eds.) *Cultures and Globalisation : Conflicts and Tensions*, London: Sage, pp.121-132.

Nyamnjoh, F.B. and Page, B. (2002) 'Whiteman Kontri and the Enduring Allure of Modernity Among Cameroonian Youths', *African Affairs*, 101(405).

Oguibe, L. (2004) *The Culture Game*. Minneapolis: University of Minnesota Press.

Onyeani, C. (2000) *Capitalist Nigger*. Johannesburg & Cape Town: Jonathan Ball Publishers.

Olukoshi, A. and Nyamnjoh, F.B. (2004) 'Editorial', *CODESRIA Bulletin*, 1, 2.

Ritzer, G. (2000) *The McDonaldization of Society*. London: Pine Forge Press..

Rowlands, M. (2004) 'Cultural Rights and Wrongs: Uses of the Concept of Property', in Verderey, K. and Humphrey, C. (eds.) *Property in Question: Value Transformations in the Global Economy*. Oxford: Berg, pp. 302-319.

SADC, (1996) 'The SADC Children's Broadcasting Charter', http://www.sosparents.org/sadc%20children-html.

Schiller, H.I. (1977) 'The Free Flow of Information – For Whom?', in G. Gerbner (ed.) *Mass Media Policies in Changing Cultures*, John Wiley and Sons: London, pp. 105-115.

Servaes, J. (1997) 'Mass Media and Fragmented Identities', in Jan Servaes and Rico Lie (eds.) *Media and Politics in Transition: Cultural Identity in the Age of Globalization*. Leuven: ACCO Publishers: Leuven, pp.77-88.

Søndergaard, H. (1999) 'Some Reflections on Public Service Broadcasting', *Nordicom Review*, 20(1): 21-28.

Soyinka, W. (1990) 'Twice Bitten: The Fate of Africa's Culture Producers', *PMLA*, 105(1): 110-120.

Soyinka, W. (1994) 'Culture, Memory and Development', in Ismail Serageldin and June Taboroff (eds.) *Culture and Development in Africa*. Washington: The World Bank, pp. 201-218.

Surin, K. (1995) 'On Producing the Concept of a Global Culture', in V.Y. Mudimbe (ed.) *The South Atlantic Quarterly*, 'Nations, Identities, Cultures' (special issue) 94(4): 1179-1199.

Syvertsen, T. (1999) 'The Many Uses of the 'Public Service' Concept', *Nordicom Review*. 20(1): 5-12.

Thomas, P. and Lee, P. (1998) 'Editorial on Migrants, Refugees and the Right to Communication', *Media Development*. XLV (3): 2.

Warnier, J.-P. (1999) *La Mondialisation de la Culture*, Editions La Découverte: Paris.

SABC's Programming for Children

Charles Owen

Nelson Mandela once said that a nation that takes care of its children invests in its future.

Any nation that fails to invest in its very young is building on an insecure foundation and cannot expect to produce a strong nation that will take its place amongst the nations of the world. The aim of the South African Broadcasting Corporation (SABC) is to carve a place for South African children within national broadcast services in order to contribute to nation building, democracy and development of a healthy society. To achieve this dream, in 2004 the SABC established a children's unit whose main aim is to ensure that there is a comprehensive and holistic approach to developing children's content across all SABC channels and, in the near future, radio content for children This enables the SABC to create meaningful strategic relationships with other stakeholders involved in the development of the African child with the aim of building cohesive platforms that transmit integrated messages that are effective and influential to our viewers.

According to Ghandi, "you have to reflect the change you want to see" and this statement is very close to my heart considering the struggles that our country has with dealing with the HIV/AIDS epidemic.

As reported by the Global AIDS Epidemic report of the UNAIDS, Africa is still the global epicentre of the AIDS epidemic, with South Africa being the worst hit showing no decline in the rates of infections. The report indicated that in 2005, an average of 5.5 million people where living with HIV. The effects of AIDS related deaths that our country has experienced, has had a great impact on our children, those affected and infected. The epidemic contributed to a high rate of orphans in the country and therefore created a high number of child-headed households. This break down in families which is important in imparting values, morals and social development of children has affected the healthy development of children.

Poverty has escalated the rate of the deaths of parents infected by HIV, living a lot of infected children orphaned and lacking parental care. The impact of this has been a lot of sick children who might have other wise continued to have a healthy life style had they head proper nutritional, parental and health care. The continued status quo in our country can be attested to many socio-political and economic issues and fingers can continue to be pointed, however it is a duty of each an everyone of us to curb the rate of infection and to work together in meeting the country's pledges in the UNAIDS declaration. The SABC as a public broadcaster has a crucial responsibility in this regard especially to our young viewers who are the future of our country.

The SABC and its partners (government, civil society and the public) have defined the role of public broadcasting in South Africa in terms of the needs of society, and not the needs of the shareholders. This was the definition crafted for the broadcaster to enable it to evolve from its colonial heritage and from being a government propaganda that served the needs of individuals and the ideals of apartheid. The restructuring of the SABC which took place at the turn of the democratic dispensation in 1994, saw the SABC having to play catch up with strides that have been set by its counter parts around the world as well as creating a new image as a service provider to the nation. This restructuring took place at the time that the country was trying to redefine itself, setting new political agenda and crafting its new constitutions. It took place during a process of healing political wounds of South Africans and a process of reconciliation. This clouded the health picture of the ravages of HIV/AIDS statues in the country which were bubbling under the new political dispensation.

Governed by the South African Constitution on which the broadcasting Act and regulations are based, the SABC was tasked with the responsibility to educate, entertain and inform. Added to these responsibilities the SABC were to be a service to all communities equally, promote gender equity and uplift the disabled. To do this the SABC had to be accessible to the majority of the population were for so long denied access to participation in the development of their communities.

These responsibilities included aspects such as promoting health, cultural identity, and a host of other things that together add up to what we call "nation building", a way of creating unity out of the nurturing of diversity. As can be imagined "nation building" can not be achieved in a society that is being ravaged by an incurable epidemic. The SABC as part of its responsibilities created a series of programming that addressed the issues of HIV/AIDS.

Educational programming that deal specifically with HIV/AIDS programmes were produced for children aged 13 to 16 with the aim of creating awareness amongst children. Our content gradually matured to programming that was aimed at influencing behaviour and changing attitudes but still educational in nature. From 2001, SABC recognized the need to talk to even younger children who were experiencing the loss and impact of AIDS with the aim of capturing their minds and influencing behaviour at an early aged. SABC Education commissioned 20 x 5 minute HIV/Aids awareness inserts for the 6-9 year old age group, for use in School TV and was produced in various South Africa languages for wider reach. As sex and HIV/AIDS education is often considered a taboo subject for children, the subject matter has been handled with sensitivity and honesty and in the manner that was nonthreatening to cultural beliefs and to parent-child relationships. Our content was designed to encourage dialogue between the child and his or her educator and caregiver.

Our content gradually increased over the years as it was no longer sufficient to create awareness and change attitude by talking about it, but was crucial to start modeling behaviour. Through the process of trail and error, we also learned that the didactic educational messages did not work so well as viewers' perceived messages and content as separate from their lives. This content was seen as designed for people that were HIV positive or who had AIDS. This alienated both the infected and affected viewer. One such programme was *Hi Thanu* (Hi V) which dealt solely with HIV/AIDS issues.

The SABC had to find creative ways of crafting content that the viewer could identify with, and the best way of doing thing was to model behaviour and integrate HIV/AIDS content into all our programming instead of making them stand alone programmes. To achieve this SABC got into partnership with Soul City to produce *Soul Buddyz* whose aim was to model healthy lifestyle behaviour which addressed the development of a child holistically. The drama series was initially designed for 8 to 12 year olds but was later designed to include care givers and educators of this age group. The programme was subsequently scheduled in a prime time slot in the early evening.

***Soul Buddyz** drama concept is around a group of children who started a news letter at the school and made it their business to help their school mates and children in their communities who had troubles ranging from with issues of puberty, to a child who is orphaned by AIDS to families that needs social grants because parents were bedridden due to HIV/AIDS. The newspaper was used as a means to communicating issues of health related awareness, the importance of friendship and communal support.*

This award winning drama series which started in 2000 was in 2004 supplemented by an actuality series called *Buddyz on the Move*. This actuality series profiled the work ordinary children did around issues of HIV/AIDS and promoting the importance of a healthy lifestyle. The Buddyz Clubs was started to support a number of group of children around the country who were inspired by the Soul Buddyz drama and started their own clubs.

***Takalani Sesame** debuted in South Africa in 2000, introducing preschoolers and their families to a new brand of educational programming with a focus on basic education, literacy, numeracy and life skills. In 2002, the Takalani partners developed an age appropriate curriculum addressing HIV and AIDS to help children better understand and cope with the ravages of the disease in South*

Africa. This programme focuses on three main themes; knowledge, attitudes and practical skills.

The program uses a multi-media approach to address HIV/AIDS education. In addition to integrating the topic into the television and radio studio scenes *Takalani Sesame* presents HIV/AIDS messages through live action, animation, and outreach materials. One of the most innovative steps by *Takalani Sesame* was the creation of "Kami", a lovable 5 year old Muppet who is HIV Positive. Kami is an orphaned girl, designed to provide age-appropriate messages to pre-school children about HIV/AIDS. In November 2003, UNICEF formally appointed Kami as a global "Champion for Children".

In partnership with SesameWorkshop, the SABC also produced a campaign called *Talk to me*. This campaign aims to create a national day of awareness on issues surrounding HIV and AIDS across South Africa. The campaign encourages a national, open and honest dialogue amongst parents, caregivers and children – whether or not they are infected or affected by HIV and Aids. The series culminates with Prime Time television specials on HIV/AIDS aired on December 1 – World Aids Day. The series is reality-based that follows the courage, hope and drama of real South African families coping with and confronting the disease through dialogue with their children.

Content on HIV/AIDS is also incorporated in most of our content such as:

Thetha Msawawa a children's drama on SABC and one of SABC 1's top 10 programmes also addressed issues of HIV/Aids. The drama series focused on children's rights and the encouragement of a healthy lifestyle.

Zonke Rules, a series on law that address children's rights and what they mean in terms of the South African law. The series would for an example have an episode that deals with HIV positive children and their rights to education.

Healthy Medics Mag (Triple M) a health series that deals with all aspects of health including HIV/AIDS

Precious, a children's talkshow that deals with every day difficulties of being a child in a developing country that also celebrates children and offers them life skills to cope with life. It also gives a platform for children to raise their views and concerns abut HIV/AIDS issues.

Fundani Nathi the series focus on literacy, numeracy and life skills. The series is based on reading and in some episodes addresses HIV/AIDS related issues for children aged 6 to 9.

The aim of integrating HIV/AIDS content was to make it relevant to all viewers and reflect how the epidemic may affect them even thought they were not infected, but most of all the aim was to:

- Reducing stigma by fostering respect and caring for people who are infected and/or affect by HIV/AIDS;
- helping children to build self esteem and develop coping mechanisms;

- breaking the cycle of silence through a better understanding of the disease and its effects on individuals and communities; and
- to improve the lives of children and families affected or infected by HIV/AIDS.

Even though SABC has done great work in addressing HIV/AIDS issues, there is clearly more that needs to be done to ensure that we are able to reduce the levels of infections especially amongst the children, if we are to have a better tomorrow. To do this the newly established children's unit aims to build relationship with those already actively involved in the new South African struggle. The SABC a few months ago signed a memorandum of understanding with UNICEF to partner in producing health series programmes that are of good quality, entertaining and informative. The corporation is also a key player championing the 20 country declaration on the fight of HIV/AIDS funded by the Kaiser Foundation. In addition the SABC's CEO is also playing a crucial role the UN AIDS programme. These activities highlight the importance of partnership and the role and the responsibilities of the SABC in South Africa and the continent. These great strides made by the SABC support the creation of good informative content for SABC viewer both children and adults.

The effectiveness of the content for children however relies on good research in order to carve relevant effective messaging and to measure the levels of impact of the content produced the capacity which the SABC is unable to achieve if it works in isolation. Partnerships are very crucial as they enable cohesion, reinforced messaging and avoid mixed messages being transmitted to our young minds. This also would enable the country to maximize the use of its minimum resources and help achieve a wider rich. It is also important to start creating continuous dialogues between ourselves and countries that are winning the battle as there are valuable lessons that can help steer our country on the road to victory.

The 2006 report on the Global AIDS Epidemic states that "ending the AIDS pandemic will depend largely on changing the social norms, attitudes and behavoiurs that contribute to its expansion" This is a notion that we as the Children's Unit at the SABC subscribe to, and have in the past advocated in our content for children.

With our quest for celebrating childhood and realizing children's dream we aim to deliver full spectrum of high quality accessible content that allows children to celebrate their lives through learning, loving, playing, laughing and dreaming. To develop a healthy society we need to affirm children's identity, culture, aspirations and their holistic development. By achieving to offer an African child this rooted grounding and well being, we would be starting to win the battle against HIV/AIDS. This step enables us to nurture children that are active participants in society with the ability to make critical choices regarding their lifestyle and future dreams, ensuring that the ideals of a democratic society a carried on for centuries to come.

Children and Media in Muslim Africa

Senegal, Sudan, Nigeria

Steve Howard

The *Moulud* season in Kano, Nigeria, the largest city in the Muslim north of Africa's largest country, features all-night celebrations from community-constructed stages where children recite Islam's Holy Scripture, the Qur'an, in its entirety and sing popular songs in tribute to the Prophet Mohamed. Kano radio station technicians travel around the city in the middle of the night to record the children's performances in honor of the Prophet's annual birthday celebration, an important element in the practice of Islam across Africa. The birthday of the Prophet Mohamed (b. 570 c.e.) is an occasion that brings together members of the Sufi orders that are common to the African practice of Islam, a mystical tradition with emphasis on ritual. The children's songs come from the "Islamiya" schools in Kano which have opened in recent years to bring a more Muslim curriculum into to contemporary education. As the songs reach the radio more children learn them and sing them in the streets, spreading intertextuality through a mass media – popular media convergence[1].

The importance of literacy in the practice of Islam – the root of the word *Qur'an* is the same as the one for the Arabic verb "to read" – and the essential proselytizing nature of the religion are aspects of the faith's relationship to children and youth. The Muslim community, the *ummah* in Arabic, very much includes children, and across Muslim Africa steps are taken to ensure that children grow up in an atmosphere enriched by faith. Media today are used by children to learn about Islam and are ubiquitous in African Muslim societies' plans to instruct their children in religion. Islam is the faith of about half of the people of the African continent and is the dominant religion across Africa's north and in an arc from Senegal in the West along the Sahara down to the southeast to northern Mozambique and along the East African coast and the Horn. Twenty-three of Africa's 54 countries have Muslim populations of 70% or more. In this chapter we focus on the experience of children and media in the Muslim cultures of Senegal, Sudan, and Nigeria, in order to understand how three societies communicate Islamic messages to children, how children use those messages, and how children in Muslim Africa are exposed to media for social change. The data are drawn from study of the live media in the three countries, interviews with African media professionals, and in Nigeria, focus groups of children organized off the streets to study the impact of media in political campaigning. The intense recent academic and press focus in the West on the uses of media to propagate Islam have neglected how media may affect children in Muslim societies[2].

As Islam spread from the Arabian Peninsula to Africa from the 8th century c.e. it developed institutions which endure today as centerpieces of African communities. The communicative imperative of the Muslim's faith has been the engine of its dissemination throughout Africa and Muslims continue to derive scriptural and literacy-based means for evangelizing the continent. The Muslim community is ideally a religious community, where faith defines gender roles, the process of education, marriage, family organization and work, and how community members should treat each other. Early Muslim social institutions included the Islamic teacher and the school, *madrassa* or *khalwa,* where families could send their children to learn to read the Qur'an. There were also community organizations like the Sufi sect, founded upon the teachings of a particular learned man, to which many members of the community would belong and which would develop specific rituals, cultural sharing such as poetry and song, and many opportunities for group prayer. The contested terrain that has developed in Muslim Africa is largely between this Sufi orientation to ritual and tradition in Islam that extends from the time of the Prophet Mohamed, and the religious orthodoxy that promotes a strident Islam with conformity to ideals set in the urban central Islamic world. Children and youth are key audiences for the messages that emanate from the rapidly emerging media from Islamic organizations in Africa. Some of those media are state-sponsored where Islam has an officially-sanctioned role as in Sudan or in many of the northern states in otherwise secular Nigeria. And some media are financed by private Islamic organizations with local or international connections in the Middle East.

Radio Sufis in Senegal

Islamic media for children in Senegal are largely produced by the Sufi-based organizations which dominate Muslim life in this West African country. Sufism, as described by Chittick[3] emphasizes the search for a direct experience of God. About 80% of Muslims in Senegal espouse allegiance to a Sufi *tariqa* (sect) with the Tijaniya sect constituting nearly half of Senegal's population of 12.5 million[4]. The Sufis with their rituals, open ceremonies, and strong basis in community life have an impact on the religious atmosphere of the country which always includes children. Indeed, the intention of the high level of religious activity is to promote seamless transitions for all between spiritual life and that of *al-*

duniya (the material world). At the same time there is a strong effort in Senegal to preserve the secular nature of the state. As Villalon recorded a local religious leader ("marabout"), "Senegalese Muslims are not only Muslims. They are also the citizens of a republic, the activists of a party. They are also good Africans. And that which Islam requires of them is that they be at the same time very good Africans, very good citizens, and excellent activists"[5].

Senegal's contemporary dilemma is to meet the aspirations of a population accustomed to the conduct of one of Africa's oldest democracies (since independence from France in 1960) while addressing the needs of a strong Muslim community increasingly aware of developments in the Muslim world beyond Senegal's borders. A desire to improve the educational opportunities of children and youth – inspired by the political will of their parents, has caused broadcasting administrators to include children's programming across the media spectrum. The government published a magazine for children, *Sabian* (youth) which focused more on Senegalese national identity issues, culture and the arts than on the dominant Islamic religious scene[6].

State radio limits its weekly religious programming due to the ostensible secular nature of the state. There are Islamic programs following the evening news broadcast on Thursday through early Friday morning, the Muslim Sabbath. There is Christian programming as well on from 9 am to 2 pm on Sundays for Senegal's Christian minority, who live primarily in the capital, Dakar, and in the south of the country.

Islamic radio programming for children is primarily broadcast by the three privately financed stations that are backed by large Sufi organizations. The Mouride network, out of their headquarters in Touba, provides programs for "all the generations"[7], with individual hour-long programs dedicated to children's comprehension of the Qur'an and other religious texts. Some of the radio stations have adopted popular call-in formats for Islamic programs with Marabouts (religious leaders) answering calls from a wide range of listeners, including children, with questions about proper Islamic behavior in the modern world. One of the Islamic stations is financed by foreign Islamic sources and the state has halted further licensing of private radio and television stations as journalists are perceived by President Abdoulaye Wade as too oppositional in Senegal's fragile democracy. Youth are demonstrating enormous support for the religious radio programs, however, indicated by the large number who listen in groups to follow their favorite Marabout's advice sessions[8].

Family viewing in Sudan

In Sudan, Africa's largest country geographically and most religiously divided with the peace following a 50 year North-South civil war only barely observed, radio and television are used in creative ways to entertain Muslim children, youth and families. Sudan has the advantage of its official use of Arabic as a national language which helps provide access to the diverse children's television productions available in the nearby Middle Eastern Arabic-speaking countries.

Islam came to Sudan's Nile Valley in the 16th century. As in Senegal, the dominant expression of the faith in Sudan is Sufism and Sudan, along with Egypt and India, has one of the world's strongest Sufi identities. But Sudan's proximity to the Middle East has also promoted a recent line of Islamic orthodoxy, characteristic of Saudi Arabia and the Gulf, which today defines Sudan's government and produces tension with the country's traditional Sufi mores. Sudan's children and youth go to school and university under the rules of a declared 'Islamic State' and return home to their families where Sufi sensibilities are the norm. Under these circumstances there is limited freedom of expression in Sudan's media, but the country's unique culture, an amalgam of rural agrarian Africa and Islamic/Arab details, does shine through in poetry recitations, music, songs, dances, and theater which are a large part of the national television programming, a service of the state. The family is central to Sudan's culture and children's media are largely family media in Sudan. A common sight in villages which are not yet on the electrical grid or where service is sporadic is a large extended family and neighbors' children gathered to watch an evening of programs on a television plugged into a car battery outside of the house.

Values are inculcated in Sudan television, and there is a deliberate effort to counter on state television the perceived negative images that anyone may pick up from the videos widely available for rental or purchase. The government's efforts to promote top-down "moral renewal" in Sudan, an effort viewed with some degree of skepticism by many, find its most important venue on television. War, murder, death and violence are not portrayed on Sudan television which instead has a full schedule of cultural programming, interview shows, soap operas (produced both in Sudan and imported from other Arabic-speaking countries) and cartoons. Sudan television seeks to transmit morals, education, and science to families and children[9]. Stories in Sudan, which are the foundation of all the television productions, so often told by grandmothers to their grandchildren, always have morals. But these lessons are delivered in entertaining and performative ways to make the morals easier to remember[10]. The transition from grandmother to teacher is an important one in Sudan's Islamic heritage as well, as teachers are respected for the role they had in spreading the Sufi-influenced Islam up and down the Nile Valley in Sudan's religious history[11].

Sudan approaches the current demand for more interactivity in media through the conventional approach of much live audience programming. We see families with children watching a live performance – usually of a well-known singer with orchestra – as the performer makes efforts to catch audience members' eyes or dip into the audience with a *shabbaal*. This is a dramatic and laugh-producing mild flirtation by a female singer with her long hair as she brushes it across the face of a male audience member. The songs are generally of two or three generations' vintage; everyone knows them and children leave the studio singing as well. The songs have lyrics as homage to the nation's geography, dominated by the Nile, or of light tributes to God. Everything in the media links back to faith, filling the children's senses and memories with its role in their young lives. A recent development in Sudan is the creation of a private network, Blue Nile Television, a pay TV arrangement whose big hit is an *American Idol* imitator, *Tomorrow's Stars*, (*nejum al ghadr*). The show features young children performing songs, religious poetry and the like in front of a panel of judges for prizes. Some see this program as a relatively progressive development for children expressing themselves in an otherwise repressive state.[12]

Poetry plays an important role in these family viewing programs as well. Knowledge of Arabic and knowledge of its correct grammar and pronunciation are highly valued and poetry is an excellent medium in which to display those skills. Much of the poetry is onomatopoetic, full of sounds to thrill the children and which can be imitated, extending its instructional value. The Sudanese poets on television or radio always commit their long odes or *qasaid* to memory, bridging oral and digital communicative processes. These music and poetry programs on television are interspersed with "Sesame Street advertising-style", short interludes of children dressed in adult ethnic costumes from different parts of the country, singing and dancing traditional songs. In many cases, television is the only place where these cultural traditions may be seen by today's general public. Programming in Sudan is also always interrupted by the televised call to prayer, *azan*, which children are already accustomed to from the neighborhood mosque. The message from state television is one of peace and spirituality for all of Sudan in an actual atmosphere of considerable tension as the nation contemplates whether or not it will remain a unitary state following a United Nations backed referendum scheduled for 2011.

Some tension is derived from the proximity of East African countries such as Sudan, Ethiopia, Eritrea, Djibouti and Somalia, all with large Muslim populations, to the wealthy states that lie just on the other side of the Red Sea. Television for children in the Gulf States is marked by high production values, game shows with relatively luxurious prizes, and competitions staged on expensive-looking sets or even exotic locations like islands in the Indian Ocean. It is not difficult for viewers in East Africa to pick up these programs which fuel in part the quest for "Muslim modernity" as the Gulf region has also represented "Muslim orthodoxy" for African Muslims. The great income disparity between the two regions is not necessarily comprehensible to children and is avoided as a school discussion topic in education systems where dissent is not encouraged. The point is that the high production values of children's television from the Gulf, such as from the al-Jazeera Children's Channel in Qatar (affiliated to the al-Jazeera Network), can inspire producers in Sudan and its region but may frustrate its children without the means to imitate what they are viewing.

Nigerian media: Children learning democracy

This section of the chapter takes a different perspective from the descriptions of children's media in Senegal and Sudan by looking at the perspectives of children and youth on media produced for adult voters in Nigeria's most recent political campaigns, for local, state, and national office in early 2007. The section also provides original data for the consideration of the interactions between children and media in Muslim Africa. While it is critically important to ensure step-by-step vigilance of Nigeria's hard-fought – for democracy – carefully monitoring the process as it rumbled along towards its third election cycle since 1999 – the assessment of democracy in Nigeria takes on a future cast when we consider the fate of children within it. Let us imagine how Nigerian democracy would unfold if our primary concern was for the impressions that children and youth have of our current electoral habits and practices. We take very seriously the idea as parents that we are role models for our children. Should we not consider how to extend that idea from parents to voters? The purpose of this section of the chapter is to provide some preliminary thoughts on young people and their engagement with media in the historic elections that took place in April, 2007 in Nigeria.

I undertook this small study to raise issues in relation to the impressions that children and youth may take from media (television, radio, newspapers, public speeches, and wall posters) that are assembled in the process of the political campaigns at the state and national levels in Nigeria. I sought to describe the reaction of young people to these media as they interact with them in their daily lives, at home, in school, work or play. Ya'u writing in 2000 provides background important to understanding the wider context of the lives of these youths. Widespread unemployment, the commercialization of education, the contraction of higher education, the deterioration of the environment and the collapse of many social services have contributed to the difficulties facing families throughout Nigeria[13].

A small survey and focus group discussions were organized to generate larger questions of the differential impact on children of political campaigning in the media. The research was conducted among young people in the immediate area around Mambayya House, the Centre for Democratic Research and Training at Bayero University Kano, a mixed middle class/working class neighborhood in Nigeria's second largest city. Mambayya House is located within the old city of Kano and is surrounded by homes and businesses in the informal sector, car repair, tailoring, fresh produce vending and food processing, furniture making shops, and many schools and institutions of Islamic education. In that Mambayya House plays a national and international role presenting conferences, seminars and public lectures featuring well-known political and academic figures, the area also has a cosmopolitan atmosphere that we found was recognized by the children and youth of the neighborhood.

I wanted to understand if children and youth have a specific or unique view of the political process derived from media that may be different from that intended by its purveyors. What messages are being communicated about politics to children and youth in the media? In a media saturated Nigeria, how do children and youth view media about politics- are they paying attention? How do children and youth learn about politics and what is the role of media in that learning? Which media do children and youth have most access to and what are their media preferences? Where/how do children squeeze media exposure in to a busy life that includes school, perhaps work and chores, and play? Conversations with youth between the ages of 10-19 yielded some answers to these questions. This was a very local study – taking place just outside the walls of the Mambayya House compound – but the articulate voices of these young people suggests the local as an "arena for engagement with the larger world"[14].

Malam Aminu Kano (1920-1983), whose home was Mambayya House, was an early post-independence and largely pre- mass media political leader and champion of the Nigerian poor. He spoke about youth at a conference in Lagos in 1969 and his words remain instructive on the issue of children and politics today.

> Today all over the world young men and women are meeting to decide not only for themselves but for their respective communities what they want their lives to be and the kind of world they want to live in.
>
> There is nothing new in this, except that the youth of today (Nigerian youths are no exception) are impatient and in a hurry. The new rising tide of this impatience on the part of the Nigerian Youth Thinkers Club must be regarded as an integral part of the global youth revolt against society. This is because the youth of the world have suddenly discovered that all social, economic and political systems have not measured up to their expectation and the kind of dynamic world they want to see. They see around them nothing but contradictions in all departments of life. Here in Nigeria, the youths revolt against these contradictions for around them are on the one hand display and concentration of wealth in the hands of the few, and on the other stark-naked poverty, illiteracy, unemployment, unhealthy surroundings, slums, primitive living and all other things that shame the conscience. The Nigerian youths of today are fed up with everything, they are fed up with pomp, waste, inefficient public services, corruption, illiteracy, begging in the street, inadequate facilities for education, lack of proper direction in economic and foreign intervention, deceit and hypocrisy[15].

There are issues larger than politics at play here, the awareness of children of the circumstances of their lives, public consciousness of that awareness, and the participation of children in making their communities and the world. What Nigeria chooses to do with their participation, to engage it or ignore it, will have an impact on the future.

A brief examination of Nigerian media over the 2007 campaign period – primarily a selection of newspapers and a small amount of television news viewing – reveals a paucity of children and youth issues addressed in any social arena, let alone the political one. Politics of course fills these newspapers from front to back, but there is little of voter education content and certainly nothing in terms of suggested issues for parents to discuss with their children at home. Finding a way to promote an awareness of children's issues in the media – particularly in the country with the largest population of youth in Africa – is a hoped –for outcome of this discussion. The findings in this study indicate that the young are watching adults as they engage in politics. The question remains, to what extent are adults watching back? What does the public know about what their children are thinking? And what steps are being taken to shape that thinking in democratic directions? Of course, what is abundantly clear from the results of this study is that plenty is happening to influence young people in the area of politics without much awareness of the power or the impact of how influential these actions may be.

Boys' life in Kano is street life in the neighborhoods and major thoroughfares of the city. Playing football, returning from school, working at petty trades, it is easy to find kids on the streets. Kano itself is a highly stratified metropolis with residents ranging from long-term, multi-generational families to rural migrants, refugees and displaced persons. About 30 youth were interviewed in Hausa, the dominant lingua-franca of the region, in three focus group sessions and then in-depth interviews with 10 more youth were conducted, all in the streets immediately surrounding Mambayya House. It was not ascertained if the youths were actually resident in the area. The "hanging-around" nature of the recruitment process for the study would suggest that most if not all of the boys were from the neighborhood. About 19 of the participants were currently students and the rest were engaged in trade, or employed in business centers or as laborers. The focus groups lasted about an hour and the participants were recruited with snacks. I felt that the focus group dimension was very appropriate in that it replicated an important aspect of the radio call-in programs which have become so important to Kano media life. These programs are building democratic awareness in the community by instituting measured and relatively fair back-and-forth discussions across the region.

Boys remarked in the course of discussions that they appreciated the presence of Mambayya House in their neighborhood for the bore-hole water it makes available to the community and as a source of generator-powered light in an area where state-supplied power is erratic. Several of the participants also remarked that Mambayya House was a source for them of *turawa* sightings[16]. The sample did not include any girls. Locating the appropriate cultural circumstances to add girls to such research in an African Islamic setting is an important goal for further study. The questions and discussion topics for the focus groups included issues such as 1) participants' access to different types of media, 2) their knowledge of politics in general and the on-going political campaigns specifically, 3) the messages picked up from the different types of media, and 4) the specific venues where political messages are viewed.

In order to get a sense of what messages may be specifically communicated to the young interviewees; I asked them questions such as 1) Who is President of Nigeria? 2) What does the President of Nigeria do? 3) Do you watch television and if so, where? 4) Do you listen to the radio and if so, where? 5) What do you hear about the President on television or radio? 6) How will we get a new President?

In the three focus group sessions I tried to get a sense of the young participants' knowledge of upcoming presidential and state governors' races: what are the sources of their awareness of these events? Depending on the participants' awareness, I then probed these issues superficially or deeply. I sought – simply – to see if children/youth have a media-derived awareness of Nigerian politics. A key question was: if participants were aware of politics in the media (radio, television, wall posters, newspapers, etc.), what did they understand to be happening from what was seen (in other words, what message about Nigerian politics is communicated to children in the media? and/or what message are they receiving?)

Both media and politics are very apparent to this age group, according to the results of this small study. In media saturated Kano, Nigeria it is difficult to sort out which are the strongest influences. Participants indicated that they were aware of the political contests currently underway and that their source of this information included radio, television, their cell phone communiqués, and discussions at home with parents and siblings. The issue of usage of this information presents itself in the finding that many of the participants were still citing various (now defeated) candidates whose names had appeared in the recent round of primaries, as still being part of the campaign. It would be interesting to compare this with an adult group to see if this recognition is a function of the candidate's media campaign, no matter what his/her electoral outcome. Nevertheless, the ability of the members of our group to list candidates' names and their parties is impressive (and far exceeds that ability of a similarly-aged group in the United States, for example) In fact, writing as an American observer of this phenomenon I am impressed with details like the boys knowing the length of various office-holders' terms. And of course, every single participant knew the name of the head of state, at the time President Olesugun Obasanjo.

At the same time, a number (about 10% of the entire sample) of participants expressed opinions about politicians which could be described as visceral reactions based on conversations at home or on the streets, most likely not related to actual experiences of these politicians. Expressions of hatred or even desire to kill certain politicians coming from young adolescents may not be taken completely seriously. But the violence that did occur during the April, 2007 elections, including the deaths of more than 300 people around the country, does suggest that unchecked emotions can have disastrous results. In most cases these reactions were expressed in the comparative sense of "we hate our councilor but we love the governor", for example. A milder version of this type of comment was found in expressions like "our councilor does nothing for us", which echoes many adult reactions to politicians.

The focus group process does stimulate discussion so we were impressed with the variety of responses from the participants. Television viewing is close to a universal with this group, viewing-location providing variety in the responses.

Some view at home, others at viewing centers or at the homes of neighbors. It is common to see clusters of boys gathered in the dark outside of shops selling televisions, watching the sets turned on to attract customers. Radio is popular as well, particularly call-in programs that offer prizes. This medium remains a progressive one particularly in conjunction with the explosion in cell phone use and more research can be done on the issue of cell phone- radio call-in interaction as a building block of democratic attitudes. Broadcasts of Freedom Radio, Pyramid Radio, thc BBC, thc Voice of America, were all frequently mentioned by the boys. Radio's strength as a tool for both information dissemination and democratic empowerment is well known and as licenses are granted and stations established in Kano more young people will have access to the airwaves, particularly if airtime is regulated to provide this access.

Participants had a strong grasp of the process by which candidates reached political office, including the paying of taxes, participation in nomination conventions, and party affiliation. And many of them knew about INEC, the Independent National Elections Commission, an agency which had fallen under intense media scrutiny during the elections process. These young people had a good awareness of what politicians did, or were supposed to do, and how the voting process was an effort to regulate politicians' behavior. Wall posters were mentioned frequently as the source of information about candidates that participants could rely upon, although one did remark that design was important in attracting him. "Put a good picture of yourself up there on the posters", he told me, remaking that a number of the candidates portrayed themselves in less-than-flattering photos or drawings. The color schemes of posters were also critiqued as attractive or not and their production quality was assessed. The wall posters are of course highly visible and accessible to neighborhood youth and compete for attention with a variety of other Kano commercial advertising.

The discussion of school and politics had mixed results with some of the participants saying that political discussion should be part of the curriculum and others maintaining that there were other important subjects to learn about in school. The opportunity for critical learning in the context of political discussion in school does present itself as a possibility, however. In any case, it was not apparent that the participants were acquiring the capacity to evaluate media veracity or to compare candidates' or parties' political perspectives based on media coverage.

Despite the apparent lack of critical political discussion in education, the participants have highly developed views of politicians, even at the local level. The boys rated various figures from national to local level with school-type grades like "40%" or expressing satisfaction or lack thereof in various leaders. Much of this information seems to come from household discussions, which raises the issue of children sharing their parents' voting behaviors.

The participatory elements here have the most relevance for an assessment of democracy and media's role in its sustainability in Nigeria. Phone-in radio programming and candidate debates are attracting the interest of youth and they are learning about civil discourse and give-and-take in the process. Accepting interaction without interrupting each other may seem like a small achievement, but its cumulative effect is the democratic process. The participatory learning that takes place on the airwaves needs to be engaged in face to face settings as well, such as the classroom. But it is clear that Nigerian teachers are not prepared to lead their classes in such discussions, despite the cultural importance of this type of give-and-take in contemporary Nigeria. The teacher training institutions focus on the mechanics of a narrowly-set curriculum with little room for teacher initiative or flexibility and the classrooms under their charge are far too large to permit any kind of free flowing debate.

In that the media are a solid and growing set of institutions in contemporary Nigerian life it may make sense to introduce critical media literacy into both the teacher preparation and primary-secondary curricula. Rather than railing against the cacophony of messages from the airwaves and streets that compete with classroom learning, teachers could then incorporate these messages into their students' learning. Children could learn as part of the curriculum of a democratic nation how to assess differences in politicians' and political parties' messages, how to evaluate the sources of these messages, and how the process of influencing a mass electorate actually works.

The comments of these generally adolescent-aged boys about the Nigerian political process and elections indicate a high level of awareness of both the process and the issues. Taking this information to the stage of informing candidates' campaigns on the concerns of youth and seeking child and youth-friendly government policy could be a positive result. These boys and teenagers are political actors, clearly; their further inclusion in the process of politics presents many possibilities. The American philosopher of education, John Dewey, said that democracy would only take firm hold when it is part of the "blood and bone of the people". Commercial media seek an audience wherever they can find one – it is in their business interest. Our societal responsibility is to ensure that the messages being transmitted promote democratic behavior and that children and youth understand them as such.

As we seek ways to make children's issues to become more visible in African election politics, we also need to assure that children are not made vulnerable to exploitation in the process. The '*almajari*', the young rural migrants sent to town such as Kano in search of Islamic education, and so much a focus of current social science research, could potentially fall into such exploitation. The media exposure of this group is not well known. We also need to protect children from becoming street level thugs, the *Yandaba* mentioned in the Ya'u article above, in the service of corrupt politicians. The threat of this type of violence has apparently lessened in recent years, but given the rise of the cell phone phenomenon and the ease of communication, vigilance and instruction in responsible media use are always appropriate. The young people who were at the center of this study have essentially only known a democratic Nigeria. The views that they expressed in the study of children's media observations in Kano are refreshingly well-informed and not cynical. Maintaining these essential social resources through assisting children and youth in finding their voices through a process of critical instruction in media and making their views known to the wider society can be democracy's dividend with lessons for the entire continent.

Conclusion

Children are contributing to the changes rapidly taking place across the Muslim regions of Africa. Their contributions are being recorded in the burgeoning media outlets managed by states and private companies, and they are learning about the world around them from the media increasingly available in print, on radio, television, film and on their cell phones.

The contemporary understanding of Islam has changed in this process as well. The essential literate nature of Islam suggests that with improved education and increasing levels of literacy in the region, particularly among girls, a greater social awareness of the power of their faith will obtain with the new generation. From the hyper-availability of media's messages, the young will be more aware of the global contestants vying to promote particular views before them, and choice will be a component of Muslim society like never before. The participatory and interactive nature of the new media increasingly available to the youth of Muslim Africa will disrupt the process of progressive social change only if it is not accompanied by critical engagement and regulation by the parents of these children and in their schools with trained teachers.

The search for knowledge in Islam is limitless as is the Muslim understanding of the mind of God. Harnessing the technology of modern media to expand African children's capacity to embrace their faith is a challenging goal pursued by innovators and producers of Muslim media in Africa.

Notes and References

1. Interview with Professor Umar Faruk Jibril, Kano, Nigeria, June, 2007.
2. See Eickelman, D. and J. Anderson, *New Media in the Muslim World.* (2003) Bloomington, Indiana University Press.
3. Chittick, W., *Sufism: A Short Introduction.* (2000) Oxford: One World Publications.
4. Villalon, L. (1995) *Islamic Society and State Power in Senegal.* Cambridge: Cambridge University Press: 71.
5. Villalon, L. (1995) *Islamic Society and State Power in Senegal.* Cambridge: Cambridge University Press: 1.
6. Interview with Monsieur Seydina Ousmane Sene, Athens, Ohio, September, 2007.
7. Interview with Monsieur Seydina Ousmane Sene, Athens, Ohio, September, 2007.
8. Interview with Monsieur Seydina Ousmane Sene, Athens, Ohio, September, 2007.
9. Interview recorded on Sudan television August 27, 2007.
10. See S. Howard, 'Introduction' in *The Clever Sheikh of the Butana and Other Stories*, retold by Ali Lotfi Abdallah, (1999) New York, Interlink Books.

11. S. Howard (1989) 'Mahmoud Mohammed Taha: A Remarkable Teacher in Sudan', pp. 83-93 in *Northeast African Studies*. v. 10 # 1.
12. Interview with Dr. Ismail ElMahdi, Athens, Ohio, September, 2007.
13. Ya'u, Y.Z., (2000) 'The Youth, Economic Crisis, and Identity Transformation: the Case of the Yandaba in Kano', pp. 161-180 in A. Jega (ed.) *Identity Transformation and Identity Politics under Structural Adjustment in Nigeria*. Stockholm: Nordiska Afrikainstitutet.
14. Simone, A. (2001) 'Between Ghetto and the Globe: Remaking African Cities', pp. 46-57 in Tostenson, et.al., (eds.) *Associational Life in African Cities*. Stockholm: Nordiska Afrikainstitutet.
15. Malam A. Kano, (1969) 'Youth as a Progressive Force in the World Today', seminar at University of Lagos, in G. Ejiofor (2002) *Mallam Aminu Kano: A Political Phenomenon*. Kano: Clear Impressions.
16. *turawa* is the plural of the Hausa term *bature,* 'European'.

Engendering Childhood

Concerning the Content of South African Television Fiction

Priscilla Boshoff & Jeanne Prinsloo

Two decades have passed since Postman (1987) provocatively described the media and television in particular as the primary curriculum for young people. While resisting the strong effects tradition that proposes a fairly direct relationship between what children view and their consequent behaviours, now – two decades later – the concern remains about the relationship between texts (both form and content) and child audiences. If we sustain the metaphor of television as curriculum, we need to exercise the same civic vigilance in relation to its design and content as for our formal, school-based curricula. In this case our context is South Africa and in this chapter we are concerned with the nature of the gendered curriculum that inhabits South African children's television.

After political transformation, South Africa adopted a remarkable rights-based constitution which insists on social equalities inclusive of gender[1]. In spite of this, South Africa has notoriously high levels of gender violence with disturbing figures of sexual abuse of children. However, there is little in recent South African media studies research that deals with the ways in which gender is framed in children's media or with its potential link with the gendered dimensions of the violence prevalent in South African society to which all children are vulnerable (Barbarin and Richter 2001). Here we are thinking about the ways in which particular forms of masculinity and femininity are framed and naturalised for children over time through story, contributing ultimately to the wider maintenance of the gender order and its inherent inequalities. For this reason, the research we discuss focuses on the kinds of fiction that are available to children, and pays specific attention to the stories children are told. We consider the imaginary worlds children are invited to enter and the various gender roles they are invited to vicariously occupy in following through the narrative of the story. In doing this, we are in a sense considering the gender pedagogy implicit in these media 'lessons'. It is acknowledged that the media play a crucial role in presenting and validating certain ways of being. Within a constructivist paradigm, 'reality' is said to be socially constituted, and what counts as truth is recognised as contingent and changing (Hall 1997).

> Television introduces children to worlds outside their immediate reality. It expands, interprets, highlights, judges, legitimizes or excludes social phenomena that the viewer encounters in reality and in the other media. ... [It] constantly reinforces certain ideological, mythical, and factual patterns of thought and so functions to define the world and to legitimize the existing social order (Lemish 2007: 101).

Represented worlds can then be conceptualised as spaces where different discourses propose and validate particular ways of being in the material world (as Foucault's (1982) notion of governmentality proposes), and where such discourses simultaneously jostle and contest those that run counter to it[2]. Just as children take on the lessons of the formal curriculum to varying extents, they are not merely passive viewers, but negotiate and mediate television discourses within the discursive frames they have at their disposal.

The worlds constructed on television are very frequently in the form of narrative. Narratives have always played a central role in children's lives, and story is described as both a universal means of making sense of the world and as a vehicle for others to make sense of the world for us (Fiske 1987). Narratives enable children to suspend their disbelief and enter the domains of the televised characters. Through processes of identification (Lemish 2007), children can take on the roles of the protagonists or other characters, and along the way learn lessons about what is constituted as heroic, as appropriate, as socially effective. Importantly, the stories children encounter (and psychically enter) take place in sociocultural landscapes; stories are narrated in particular ways so that certain characters and scenarios are valorised and included, while others are excluded or made "other". Children's experience or access to worlds and ideas is not yet extensive and television is (in Lemish's terms)

> "a peekhole" to roles beyond their everyday reach, particularly to those highly prioritised and stereotyped in dramatic genres. ... Meeting these varied characters on television confronts [children] with value-related issues as they compare themselves with [them]... (2007: 55).

If characters provide points of identification and if the narrative action proposes ways of being in the world, we need to consider the kinds of characters and scenarios they are in a sense invited to inhabit temporarily at least for story serves as lessons about 'the events they will never encounter and the kinds of people [in stories] who may never cross their path' (Meek 1988: 28-29). In addition, as stories have the potential for both empowering voices and constraining them, and of constituting diversity or privileging conformity, concern for the televised narratives and privileged world views, attitudes and behaviours that children experience is appropriate. If certain hegemonic discourses are rehearsed constantly, they form lessons that child viewers are likely to internalise. This is their curriculum design.

Television, children and gender in South Africa

As South African society is indomitably patriarchal, we wish to hold up a gender lens through which to scrutinise children's television narratives. In a sense we wish to directly address that aspect of children's television so neatly erased by the signifier, "children": the construction of gendered subjectivities via the media. In examining the gender dimensions of children's television fiction characters, we wished to tease out consistent ways in which gender is framed within fictional narratives. What gender discourses are children presented with to accompany them as they face the difficult task of growing up in our contemporary society? We also ask what the implications are of such framing being normalised and inculcated in children, the next generations of citizens, in South Africa, a country notorious for its gender violence (see for example Haffejee 2006, Hirschowitz et al. 2000, and Vogelman and Eagle 1991).

Our gendered identities do not suddenly appear in adulthood but are formed gradually and incrementally from very early on in life. Apart from the family and school, the media form the most significant arena in which prevalent discourses of gender are made available to children, repeated and normalised. Connell (1987) reminds us that social institutions such as the media reproduce the relations of power that suffuse our societies. In particular, the media is identified as the institution *par excellence* involved in the production and distribution of symbolic meaning and which unarguably presents us with interpretations of the world that bear the imprint of the social processes in which they were made.

Connell's understanding (1987) of hegemonic masculinity and emphasised femininities is a useful frame to use here. He terms socially endorsed, normative heterosexual masculinity (where men are characterised by particular traits such as aggression, physical strength, ambition, emotional control and self-reliance) *hegemonic masculinity*, which is associated with public spaces. It in turn produces *emphasised femininities* as its necessary complement. For women, the complementary femininities include diverse behaviours and characteristics, ranging from nurturing self-sacrifice and support to feminine attractiveness and sexual availability, all of which are oriented towards accommodating the needs and interests of men. They are frequently enacted in domestic or private spaces rather than public ones. Importantly, this gender order assumes heterosexuality. Central to this understanding is the recognition that hegemonic masculinity and emphasised femininities are not in collision but rather in collusion as they serve to promote the masculinity of heterosexuality:

> By understanding gendered identities as tied together in an unequal yet dynamic relationship it becomes clearer that the achievement of conventional masculinity and femininity are mutually dependent (Holland et al. 1998: 171).

Two cautionary notes need to be sounded here. First, no one encounters a single discourse, and discourses that resist and contest the hegemonic gender order are always also in play. Second, children who have other repertoires of understanding (and who are also subjects of other resistant discourses) can read against the preferred or naturalised gender order. However, the power of the hegemonic (patriarchal) discourse is beyond dispute and is our focus here.

Study of the gendering of children's television fiction

It was noted earlier that gender-focussed studies of South African children's television are scarce. In addition, the absence of policy pertaining to gender representations is also striking, for South African children's television broadcasting policy sets very clear parameters and guidelines for broadcasters to follow in terms of content. In keeping with international trends in this area, much of South African broadcast policy (for example the SABC (2000) policy on programming and the Broadcasting Complaints Commission of South Africa (2003) is intended to regulate depictions of violence[3] and to protect the child's rights as they appear in the Bill of Rights (1996). Ironically, while SABC broadcast policy makes specific provision to protect *women* from violence and guard against gender stereotyping, this provision is not extended to children's programming. This presumably reflects an assumption that children form a group apart from adults, with their own set of interests to be protected and promoted in isolation, as it were, from the adult world. Here then, childhood seems to be assumed to be gender neutral.

In order to get a broad overview of the content of children's entertainment and fiction programming, the authors conducted a Content Analysis[4] of one month of children's television screened on the South African public broadcast services, SABC 1, 2, 3 and the one private free-to-air South African terrestrial broadcast service, etv. As the broadcasters differentiate between entertainment and educational programmes for children, we confined our examination to programmes defined by them as entertainment, acknowledging that this categorisation is imprecise. We thus excluded the variety of educational programming broadcast by etv and SABC as part of their service mandate aimed at children and school-going youth in line with the broadcast regulations.

The sample consisted of children's programmes broadcast over the 32 day period from 15 May to 15 June 2007 which were recorded for analysis. Following a conventional Content Analysis approach, the recordings were coded to establish the type of programme (fiction, documentary, etc), the technical form the fiction took (animation, human action, puppets etc.), country of production and language. Thereafter, in line with the gender concern of the study, particular attention was paid to the roles played by the main characters, and in order to identify who *acts* and who is merely *supportive* (one of the binary oppositions inherent in Connell's gender order discussed above), we employed the character roles identified by Russian formalist, Vladimir Propp, which frequently inform narrative analyses (see Fiske 1987, for example). Thus we considered the extent to which male and female characters acted in the role of hero, villain, hero or villain's helper, etc. As Propp focused on the various spheres of action the characters inhabit, his characters provide a useful approach for analysing the sets of masculinities and femininities inscribed in the text. We further coded the character's nature (whether animal, human, etc.) and physical characteristics (including sex, skin and hair colour, age and body weight). These characteristics were identified as important as they pertain to both a gendered and raced world. The further coding of characters in terms of whether they acted in leadership or follower roles enables exploration of other gender dimensions.

It is striking that of the total 198 hours of children's television recorded, only 64 hours, or just less that one third of the broadcast time was devoted to fiction programming. Twelve hours went to advertising, while the remaining123 hours were made up of children's game shows, documentaries, mixed format shows and trailers and programme teasers.

As our focus is on fiction, we focus on the data relating to the gender dimension of the fictional characters. The first finding of note that the data[5] reveals is that these fictional worlds are populated by fewer female than male characters, clearly a very different world to the material world that the intended audience inhabit, for frequently cited statistics put the South African population at 51% female[6]. Of the total of 1008 characters, 285 (28%) were female, in comparison to 674 (67%) male characters. The sex of 49 characters (or 5%) could not be determined and were so excluded from the following discussion.

This discrepancy is maintained in other startling ways across the variables examined. Let's consider the character roles (see table 1.) In the first instance, the role of hero is played far more frequently by male characters, in that male characters take the hero role 195 times in contrast to the 78 female heroic roles. It is important to emphasise this, as although the *percentage* for each sex (31% female and 33% male) seems fairly even and therefore not significant, the *total number* of female characters is markedly less, and consequently girls have far fewer opportunities of identification with female characters in this role.

Table 1. Analysis of character roles and Proppian character functions

Character roles[7]	Female Number (%)	Male Number (%)
Hero	78 (31%)	195 (33%)
Villain	25 (10%)	114 (19%)
Hero's helper	93 (37%)	187 (31%)
Villain's helper	6 (2%)	30 (5%)
Member of family	20 (8%)	19 (3%)
Princess	23 (9%)	26 (4%)
Dispatcher	6 (2%)	9 (2%)
False hero	4 (1%)	17 (3%)

When it comes to villains, boys also get the lion's share of the action! Here, there are 114 male as opposed to 25 female villains, as well as to the 195 male heroes noted above. In fact this means that for every two male heroes there is at least one male villain! If we extend this comparison to the role of hero's and villain's helpers, there are 93 female hero's helpers and, in contrast, only 6 (2%) help the villains. There were 187 male helpers to heroes and a smaller but significant number, 30 or 5% of male characters were villains' helpers. Thus, in this sample, female characters were significantly more frequently the helper than the hero. The female characters also less frequently inhabit the villainous roles, and, as the table of character functions indicates, are proportionately far more likely than male characters to be in need of rescue and protection (the "princess"), to play a supporting role ("hero's helper") and to appear in private, domestic contexts ("member of the family"). Recalling the earlier discussion on hegemonic masculinity and violence, female characters tend to be aligned with normative social roles, whereas the examples of male resistance to the social order in the form of villainy are comparatively pronounced.

Then, not only do these fictive worlds have a preponderance of male characters and a number of them villainous at that, but they are also suffused with a range of other gendered features (see table 2). First, a form of infantalisation of female characters occurs in that the females are consistently scripted as younger than male characters. Relevant here are the categories of child, youth and adult. 35% or 89 female characters are portrayed as children as opposed to 25% or 148 male children. While the category of youth is more equal with 39% or 100 female and 36% or 207 male characters, there are fewer female adults, that is only 22% or 57 female characters as opposed to 196 or 34% male characters.

Table 2. Gendered variations: age, body weight and leadership roles

Characteristic	Categories	Female	Male
Age[8]	Baby	0 (0%)	4 (1%)
	Child	89 (35%)	148 (25%)
	Youth	100 (39%)	207 (36%)
	Adult	57 (22%)	196 (34%)
Body weight[9]	Very thin	4 (2%)	12 (2%)
	Normal	255 (99%)	491 (82%)
	Overweight	0 (0%)	42 (7%)
	Hugely muscular	0 (0%)	57 (10%)
Leadership[10]	Leader	56 (21%)	210 (36%)
	Follower	59 (22%)	116 (20%)
	Equal/ mixed	148 (56%)	257 (44%)

Female characters thus tend to be confined to younger roles. If female characters tend to be younger they also are smaller as there is an interesting discrepancy that relates to body size. First, most male and female characters fall within the "normal" range for body weight, 99% of female characters and 82% male characters, while male characters are either "overweight" (42 or 7%) or "hugely muscular" (57 or 10%) thereby marking masculine physicality. Finally, the disparity between male and female characters initiating action favours male characters, with female characters more likely to be a follower or taking equal/mixed responsibility for leadership. Table 4 shows that 56 or 21% of females are depicted in leadership roles in comparison to 210 or 36% of males. Female characters are also more likely to be followers (59 or 22%) than males (116 or 20%), echoing once again the gender order identified by Connell which was outlined above. That female characters are as likely to be followers as leaders but males far less so gestures to the role of women in society in their supportive roles and men in leadership positions.

It is important to acknowledge that there has been some change in representations at this level for female characters over time and that they do not automatically fall into subservient roles. It remains crucial, though, to also note that the shift is relative. (Similarly, Thompson and Zerbinos (1995) noted shifts in the gender stereotypes in animated cartoons from the 1970s to 1980s.)

Table 3. Gendered differences in skin and hair colour

Characteristic	Categories	Female %	Male %
Skin colour[11]	Asian	11	3
	Black	12	7
	White	70	86
Hair colour[12]	Bald	0.4	7
	Black	36	26
	Blond	24	20
	Brown	27	26
	Grey	4	9
	Red	7	12

If we move to other physical characteristics such as skin colour and hair colour there are also notable differences (see table 3). Mindful that South Africa has a largely black population, it is significant that the majority of both male and female characters were coloured white. They are, moreover, coloured quite literally as the majority of children's television programming is animated, and the selection and construction of the character demographics are conscious (or unconscious) production decisions. An overwhelming 90% of male characters were white, in contrast to 60% of the female characters, who include 14% Asian and 14% black characters. The hegemony of whiteness that pervades much of global television (see Dyer 1997) inserts itself in this children's domain too, playing its role in preserving hegemonic masculinities. Moving to hair colour, it is interesting that female characters are only slightly more likely to be blonde than male characters. Most female characters (63%) had dark (black or brown) hair in contrast to males at 51%. What is more interesting perhaps than the numbers is that male characters are more likely to be outside the rather predictable brown/black or blond, to include baldness, grey and red hair. The range of appearances – and we must recall the significance of appearance in constituting femininity – rehearsed for girls is therefore more limited and anodyne, we suggest.

Heroes and hypermasculinity

A cause for concern then lies in the kinds of character roles in these fictive scenarios that provide. Male character are overwhelmingly in the majority, and while not more likely to be heroes than female characters in terms of percentages the larger number of representations ensures that male characters are foregrounded in this role. Male characters are more likely to be leaders of groups of helpers (or be lone heroes or villains), and act in public spaces. The hugely muscular and overweight category in the male character data can be explained by the typical appearance in certain animated programmes of enormously strong and athletic heroes. Hugely muscular and supernaturally strong hero figures "are popular among young boys whose bodies are not strong enough to grant them the power that is their ideological requirement, and who also occupy powerless social positions in family and school. The physical strength of such heroes is frequently extended by cars, guns and machinery" (Fiske 1987: 102). Hegemonic masculinity is represented through this "ideal type" of hero as a specialist in violence (Connell 1987: 249), a repeated characterisation that serves to naturalise the symbolic privileges of an adult masculinity yet to be achieved. This narrative of masculinity is of course, worryingly violent in its relations to other men, quite apart from the marginalisation of female characters that its construction automatically achieves.

The limited spaces for female characters additionally tend to propose a less active world characterised by help and support. This echoes the point made earlier about emphasised femininities being in collusion, rather than in collision, with hegemonic masculinity, and thus complicit in violent scenarios of competition and conquest.

South African narratives

Since most of the children's fiction broadcast in South Africa is produced in foreign countries and portrays scenarios and contexts that are distant from South African children's lived experiences, it is useful to consider the local fiction productions separately. As Lemish noted, audiences "express great affinity" for local productions, as their generally high ratings indicate (2007: 124). It could be argued that the familiar scenarios, contexts, ideas, accents and character types enables easier entry into the fictive world and perhaps enable easier 'suspension of disbelief'.

Within the time frame of the research, only five local South African or co-productions which presented a local context were broadcast. Of these, two are co-productions with foreign production companies: *Scout's Safari*[13] (the only drama series with live actors) is a USA/ SA co-production; and *Magic Cellar*[14], an animated Canadian-South African co-production. The other three programmes, *Zaka*[15], *The Adventures of Pax Afrika*[16] and *Jozi Zoo*[17], are half hour cartoon series created in South Africa by South African animations studios. Because of the limited size of the sample, no generalisations can be made and we merely use it to make two observations, one relating to the numbers of male and female characters and the other to a tendency to a particular – and unexpected – narrative form.

It is striking that the conventional patriarchal gendering of the characters is less pronounced in these programmes. To start with, the overall discrepancy between male and female characters is smaller, 42 male characters (55% of the total) to 32 female characters (42%), with two indecipherable characters. However, there is a significant difference in the proportion of heroes, with only 32% of the female characters taking on this role while 45% of the males do so. A single female villain (5%) contrasts again with the more numerous male villains (5, or 16% of males). Then, a further 26% of the female characters were helpers to the hero, while none helped the villains. Male characters took on the mantle of helper less frequently, with 13% aiding the hero and a single character (3%) helping the villain. What we have then is more parity between male and female characters than is apparent in the international figures.

Table 4. Character functions: South African fiction

South African fiction	Female	Male
Total character roles	32 (42%)	42 (55%)
Hero	6 (32%)	14 (45%)
Villain	1 (5%)	5 (16%)
Hero's helper	5 (26%)	4 (13%)
Villain's helper	0 (0%)	1 (3%)
Member of family	5 (26%)	3 (10%)
Princess	1 (5%)	0 (0%)

Another unusual and unexpected feature, as noted above, refers to the form of the narrative and narration. Two of the five series, namely *Zaka* and *Magic Cellar*, are scripted as stories being told to children and many of the characters do not play a role in the narratives other than serving as an audience of the tales told. In this sense, there is a modelling of oral tradition which is consistent with the contemporary advocacy of valuing and preserving cultural traditions. Thus, in line with oral story-telling, these programmes depict the act of narration as much as the narrative. In addition, this mediated re-telling of oral literature is consistent with post-apartheid attempts to promote a unified national identity through the synthesis of various literary traditions (Naidu 2001): unsurprisingly, the audience of children in the *Magic Cellar*, represents a veritable "Rainbow Nation" in terms of race and gender identities. It is also significant that both

Magic Cellar and *Zaka* are broadcast on SABC2 which broadcasts in vernacular languages as well as English and presumes a predominantly black audience.

While the narrative is unusual it also calls for some critical reflection about the kinds of engagement it invokes in its audience. There is a strong imperative within the tradition of South African folk tales to be didactic, and these stories contain explicit morals lessons or messages. These messages call for moralistic judgements rather than an empathetic approach to the circumstances described. They also serve to advocate docility and respect. Folk tales frequently invoke animal characters, such as the lazy hare or the vain (female) leopard. Allow a diversion to make the point, after all this is a discussion of stories. In the synopsis of "The Chief's Bride", one of the episodes on the *Magic Cellar* website[18], two sisters are compared. One is 'naughty' or adventurous, the other docile and obedient. When the king is looking for a wife, the girls' mother sends for them to present themselves to the hero. Predictably the wild one doesn't go directly to the king, and, alas, she loses out, as the obedient sister gets the prize, marriage to a king! The lesson: "respectful and obedient behaviour is rewarded in the end".

Well, the moral of the story might have worked well in times gone by, but one wonders about its reception now. The point here is two-fold. The lesson seeks to be monologic (encourages a single reading of the story) and these traditional stories tend towards conservative patriarchy. Such an approach to texts ignores the importance of developing nuanced and diverse understandings of the world and of making allowances for different ways of being. It speaks neither to critical assessment nor compassion. A dialogic engagement would entail the child engaging with different aspects of the story and weighing up issues with a degree of empathy. That a didactic rather than empathetic or humanistic approach to narrative has been nurtured within, firstly, missionary and colonial education, and subsequently in literacy education for black school children is documented elsewhere (Prinsloo 2002, 2004). The point to be made is that the unlearnt lessons of the past are being repeated in the guise of deference to culture and these have gendered implications.

Urbo: the Adventures of Pax Africa stands in sharp contrast to the conservative (but award-winning) *Magic Cellar*. Broadcast on SABC3, primarily an English channel which presumes an audience of higher economic status generally than SABC2, this series is an unusual tongue-in-cheek animation. With its male hero who has some magical protective link to his ancestors, the script dares to challenge convention. It humorously constructs a futuristic Cape Town, iKapa, where corporate capital has resulted in a dystopian future. This environmental and socialist tale has its ghastly corporate capitalist villain, Maximillian Malice with his two henchmen, and its male hero, Urbo. It does however allow a range of roles for its female characters and because there are more points of entry or identification, it allows a much more dialogic encounter with the text. Its playfulness and self-reflectiveness is in direct contrast to the didacticism of the oral tradition where narrators instruct young people about correct behaviours. This allows empathetic nodes of entry into the fictive world, which shift in different episodes.

This brief discussion of the South African productions provides us with some interesting points to ponder. First, there is overall a pleasing shift to constructing fictive worlds with a more equal number of female characters. This, however, must not be conflated with more active and progressive roles for them. Second, there are the productions like the *Magic Cellar* with its high production qualities rehearsing oral forms of story telling through the televisual medium. While signalling an African identity, it simultaneously rehearses a judgmental response to characters, often within the confines of the gender order. Finally, there is the socially concerned narrative that yet remains humorous and teasing, and allows more entry points for male and female identification.

These very different and indeed contradictory faces of South African children's television programming undoubtedly reflect the wider discursive work taking place in post-apartheid society concerning the nature and form of South African national – and, we would argue, gender – identities. Policy documents explicitly state that programme content needs to protect and nurture national cultures and identities (see for example ICASA 2003: 4, 31); however, these "identities" and "cultures" are not uncontested and form the body of an ongoing debate into the politics of belonging and the ideal character of post-apartheid South African society, whether it be multicultural (the "Rainbow Nation"), Africanist or postmodern cultural melange (see for example Nuttall and Michael 2002). In all, what this discussion makes clear is that contemporary South African children's television productions are an important area for contextualised research.

Conclusion

Moving away from our brief focus on South African productions, we conclude by considering all the findings and the implications of the gendering of children's symbolic worlds more broadly.

The gender dimensions of television fiction present cause for concern. In a recent overview of several studies, it was noted that

> the most predictable characteristic of identification – both similar and wishful – as well as para-social interaction with television characters among children was found to be gender. Boys of all ages almost exclusively identify with male figures, while girls identify mainly with females, but with males as well, particularly during the early years (Lemish 2007: 58).

There are two complementary explanations that may account for this pattern. First, as the data above attests, there is a much wider range of male roles for children to identify with than female roles. Female characters are restricted not only in terms of overall numbers but in diversity of personality, roles, settings, plot lines, appearance and so on. Not only are the numbers of female characters small, but the majority or female roles appear somewhat insipid. As observed by

Lemish (2007: 111), "children's television offers a significant under-representation of female main characters and under-development of female character". In addition, female characters are overwhelmingly represented as physically "normal" (not thin or overweight). Lemish (2007: 111) observes that "attractiveness remains the central criteria for identification with female characters and it is associated with feeling good about oneself". Here, attractiveness again is constituted within reasonably predictable and unadventurous parameters of hair colour. The 'plain Janes' are simply absent here.

Second, our society is more tolerant to girls who take on more typical male role than to boys who "act girly". As noted above, the insistence of hegemonic masculinity on heterosexuality engenders resistance by boys to adopting "feminine" characteristics, and also explains why girls can operate within "masculine" worlds by taking on privileged "masculine" characteristics. A good example of this masculine mode of behaviour is the number of stories in which "brainy" female characters use technology (traditionally a male preserve) to help the hero, especially computer technology (for example, Penny in *Gadget and Gadgetinis*, Rebecca in *Yu Gi Oh* and Keitu in *Urbo: The Adventures of Pax Afrika*). The roles that girls occupy in narrative serve to confirm the prevalence of traditional gender roles for girls and women in South Africa. For example, survey research indicates that, following general patterns for adult men and women, more girl children than boys are involved in household maintenance, and that boys generally have more leisure time than do girls to engage in social and cultural activities outside the home (Chobokoane and Budlender 2002).

We want to argue for an urgency to address these forms of representations. This means that media producers need to be think more about the kinds of identities they are circulating. (They would no doubt protest their concern with the well-being of children and not merely the bottom line.) Perhaps for us the most crucial aspect remains the valorising of hypermasculinity and violence within the existing gender order. The rehearsal of these warring identities is neither innocent nor irrelevant and they certainly are not consistent with the kind of thinking that seeks peace in the world. They are not mindful of the sentiments expressed in the opening lines of the UNESCO (1945) constitution which reminds us

> That since wars begin in the minds of men [sic], it is in the minds of men that the defences of peace must be constructed.

Notes

1. That a state body, the Commission of Gender Equity, was created and tasked with working towards gender justice is evidence of this concern about gender inequality (as a result of South Africa's particular history of conservative colonial, traditional African and Afrikaner masculinities). http://www.cge.org.za/userfiles/documents/finaldraftsubmission7Sept03.doc
2. Such a Foucauldian position sees discourse as productive or constitutive of particular subjects, as a set of rules about what is included and excluded, and which, embodied, enable us to act upon the world in particular ways.
3. SABC policy on programming:

http://vcmstatic.sabc.co.za/VCMStaticProdStage/CORPORATE/SABC%20Corporate/StaticDocument/About%20SABC/program.pdf Pages 14-15 deal specifically with violence in children's programming (in accordance with its general provisions and requirements for the representation of violence), but none specifically address issues of children and gender representation.

4. This Content Analysis was conducted as part of a larger international research project organised by IZI (the International Central Institute for Youth and Educational Television, in Munich) entitled "Children's television worldwide: gender representation".
5. The collated data was analysed by tabulating chosen variables: significance of correlation ($p<0.5$) of chosen variables was indicated after data subjected to Chisquare and Fisher's Exact Test for count data.
6. See the Statistics South Africa website http://www.statssa.gov.za/
7. When numbers show a highly significant relationship ($p<<<0.05$): there is good evidence to suggest a significant relationship between gender and the type of role.
8. P-value=0.00068
9. P-value=4.3e-09
10. P-value=7.9e-05
11. P-value=3.3e-61
12. P-value=3e-04
13. *Scout's Safari* is produced by Discovery Communications for Discovery Kids Channel http://kids.discovery.com/fansites/scoutssafari/scoutssafari.html.
14. Co-produced by Chocolate Moose Media (Canada) and Morula Pictures (South Africa) http://www.sabceducation.co.za/magiccellar/index.html.
15. *Zaka* is an animated "edutainment" programme designed to familiarise children with financial matters.
16. See the programme's official website at www.urbo.co.za.
17. The other South African animated programme shown at time of research is *Cool Catz*. While employing fictional characters and storytelling techniques, it is didactic in intent, employing puppetry and animation to teach various skills. *Jozi Zoo* and *Cool Catz* are productions of Mdu Comics http://www.mducomics.co.za/animation.htm.
18. (http://www.sabceducation.co.za/magiccellar/Cellar.html).

References

Barbarin, O. and L. Richter (2001) *Mandela's Children: Growing up in Post-apartheid South Africa*. London: Routledge.

BCCSA. (2003) Code of the BCCSA. Retrieved 14 November 2007. http://www.bccsa.co.za/

Chobokoane, N. and D. Budlender. (2004) Activities over Time. Further Analysis of the Time Use Survey. Retrieved 14 November 2007. http://www.statssa.gov.za

Connell, R. (1987) *Gender and Power*. Cambridge: Polity Press.

Connell, R.W. (1995) *Masculinities*. Cambridge: Polity Press.

Constitution of the Republic of South Africa (1996) Retrieved 14 November 2007. http://www.info.gov.za/documents/constitution/index.htm.

Dyer, R. (1997) *White*. London: Routledge.

Fiske, J. (1987) *Television Culture*. London: Routledge.

Foucault, M. (1982) The Subject and Power. *Michel Foucault Beyond Structurism and Hermeneutics*. H. Dreyfus and P. Rabinow. Brighton: The Harvester Press, 208-226.

Greene, M. (1994) Multiculturalism, Community and the Arts. *The Need for Story. Cultural Diversity in Classroom and Community*. A.H. Dyson and C. Genishi. Urbana: Illinois: National Council of Teachers of English: 11-27.

Haffejee, S. (2006) Waiting Opportunities: Adolescent Girls' Experiences of Gender-based Violence at Schools. Retrieved 14 November 2007. http://www.csvr.org.za/papers/paphaff.htm#note2.

Hall, S. (ed.) (1997) *Representation: Cultural Representations and Signifying Practices*. London: Sage.

Hirschowitz, R., S. Worku, et al. (2000) Quantitative Research Findings on Rape in South Africa. *Statistics South Africa*. Retrieved 14 November 2007. http://www.statssa.gov.za/Publications/Rape/Rape.pdf.

Holland, J., C. Ramazanoglu, et al. (1998) *The Male in the Head. Young People, Heterosexuality and Power.* London: The Tufnell Press.

ICASA (2003) Regional Television Broadcasting Services Position Paper. Retrieved 14 November 2007. http://www.info.gov.za/documents/otherdocs/2003.htm

Lemish, D. (2007) *Children and Television. A Global Perspective.* Oxford: Blackwell.

Meek, M. (1988) *How Texts Teach what Readers Learn.* Stroud: The Thimble Press.

Naidu, S. (2001) *Transcribing Tales, Creating Cultural Identities: An Analysis of Selected Written English Texts of Xhosa Folktales.* Grahamstown: Rhodes University. MA.

Nuttall, S. and C.A. Michael (2000) *Sense of Culture: South African Culture Studies.* Oxford: Oxford University Press.

Postman, N. (1987) *Amusing Ourselves to Death.* London: Methuen.

Prinsloo, J. (2002) *Possibilities for Critical Literacy: An Exploration of the Schooled Literacies in Kwa-Zulu-Natal.* Unpublished Ph.D thesis. Johannesburg: University of the Witwatersrand.

Prinsloo, J. (2004) 'Examining the Examination: The Wor(l)ding of the Matriculation Examinations in KwaZulu-Natal', *Perspectives in Education,* 22(1): 81-97.

SABC (2000) SABC Programming. Retrieved 14 November 2007. http://www.sabc.co.za/.

Thompson, T. and E. Zerbinos (1995) 'Gender Roles in Animated Cartoons: has the Picture Changed in 20 years?' *Sex roles,* 32(9/10): 651-673.

UNESCO (1945) Consitution of the United Nations Educational, Scientific, and Cultural Organisation. Retrieved 14 November 2007. http://www.icomos.org/unesco/unesco_constitution.html.

Vogelman, L. and G. Eagle (1991) 'Overcoming Endemic Violence against Women in South Africa', *Social Justice,* 18(1:2): 209-229.

Disney Kids

Ethiopian Children's Reception of a Transnational Media Mogul

Tewodros Workalemahu

With the penetration of global media contents particularly Hollywood films in Ethiopia in the early 1990s and afterwards, local audiences have been exposed to American movies. A significant part of these audiences is made up of Ethiopian upper-middle-class children in Addis Ababa who are exposed and attracted to the animation features produced by the all prominent manufacturer of children's films and literature, the American based Walt Disney Company. In the following article, I will discuss how the specified children in Addis Ababa, in the midst of their everyday lived reality, make meaning out of the animation and cartoon films that are produced in another setting.

Globalization, global media, and children

Much alike to the last quarter of the bygone 1900s, globalization still remains – perhaps with even more vigour and presence – to be a concept of enormous interest and debate in the first decade of the 21st century. Not a precise concept to define or describe in the midst of the plethora of its manifestations like global warming, global trade, global terror, global media, etc., the notion of globalization has produced fans and cynics who have approached it according to their outlooks and assumptions. It is to be noted that globalization is the watchword of the day although an uncontested definition for its nature is far from being reached. In his introduction to *A Globalizing World? Culture, Economics and Politics*, Held states:

> There is a widely shared – almost taken for granted – view that the world is changing more rapidly and dramatically at the start of the twenty-first century than ever before. Although it may not be a term we all use, many of the chan-

ges seem to be associated with something that has been called 'globalization' (2000: 6).

If globalization is an engine, then media, especially global media, is the fuel that keeps it going. "[W]ithout mass media and modern information technology," Carlsson writes, "globalization as we know it would not be possible" (2002: 8). One aspect of globalization is media globalization which refers to "the worldwide expansion of media production and distribution companies that trade on the emerging global media market" and is, therefore, "primarily the global proliferation of a small number of media conglomerates" (Hamelink 2002: 36).

At the other end of the global media domain are receivers of the media content – the audience – out of which a good third are children and young people under the age of 18 (von Feilitzen 2002). Although children are often classified as 'special' group for whom we make decisions on their behalf, such thought should not in any way be understood as if it connotes they do not have a say on what their preferences are; neither does it imply that children as a group do not have specific needs and choices. "If children as a social group are not acknowledged as a group with diversity in interests, intelligence, taste, class, race, culture, and religion, as well as age and gender", Keyes and Buckingham write "then the particular and specific needs of children are ignored" (1999: 4). In essence, therefore, if we say that children are significant or potential customers of media, and that media contents should take into consideration the diverse preferences and specific needs of children as a group and as individuals, understanding the roles and operations of the global media in this regard is an indispensable challenge. As such, the intricately interwoven concepts of globalization, global media and children and young people shall be dealt with simultaneously in the light that children are as much potential consumers of global media products and thus make meanings and constructs out of the messages they get.

Walt Disney: animation and beyond

Central to the global media landscape are the major players of the system, the dominant first tier of the global media oligopoly. These are what we alternatively know as global media conglomerates that own an array of vast media production, distribution, and sales outlets. As Herman and McChesney (1997) observe, Time Warner, Disney, Bertelsmann, Viacom and News Corporation are the five largest media firms in the world in terms of sales and are also the most fully integrated global media giants.

An indispensable unit of the global media family, The Walt Disney Company became the world's leading media mogul in 1995 following its takeover of Capital Cities/ABC while at the same time increasing the company's U.S. assets in news and sports programming and adding publishing and multimedia to its area of control (Wasko 2001). Although Disney's global leadership was expelled by the merging of AOL/Time Warner in 2000, the company's brand value remains the leading brand name in the media/entertainment industry today (Best Global Brands 2006). Disney is so big, Demers writes, "that its yearly sales exceed the gross domestic product of more than half of the countries in the world" (1999: 2).

The Walt Disney Company today is far more than an animation factory due to its long standing policies of diversification and synergy which make up part of the reason for Disney's extended and consistent presence in the leading pack of the global media conglomerates. True, synergy – the cooperative action of different parts for a greater effect (Wasko 2003) – is not a new development for the Walt Disney Company. "From its inception", Wasko writes, "Disney created strong brands or characters that were marketed in various forms (mostly through films and merchandise) throughout the world...Over the past few decades, the possibilities for synergy have expanded even further with the addition of cable, home video, and other new media outlets" (2003: 171). The diversification of Disney's venture today has led the company to own multi-faceted media/entertainment industries, thus no longer solely labeled "the animation factory". The influence Disney enjoys across the globe today is very difficult to ignore, if not to take part. As Wasko has noted, Disney has carefully designed a system of controlling its products, characters, and images and built a reputation to itself as "a company that produces positive, wholesome, family and children entertainment" (2001: 70).

The media imperialism thesis

The arguments, perspectives and illustrations presented so far in relation to globalization, global media and the Walt Disney Company culminate to what came to be known as the media imperialism thesis, also alternatively referred as cultural imperialism thesis. The concept of media imperialism has come to the focus of research and debate since at least the 1970s (Galtung, 1971; Schiller, 1976), the same time the New World Information and Communication Order (NWICO) debate started drawing interest. Watson and Hill define media imperialism as a term used to describe "the role western media play in dominating 'Third World' developing countries through communication systems" (1984: 173). They further state:

> Crucial to the notion of media or cultural imperialism is the understanding of the relationship between economic, territorial, cultural and informational factors. In the age of western economic colonialism in the nineteenth century the flow of information is a vital process of growth and reinforcement. Where the trade went, so followed developing media practice and technology, reflecting the values and assumptions of those who owned and manned the service (1984: 173).

Former Ghanaian president Kwame Nkrumah was one of the popular figures who stood against the so called flood of "westernization", "a systematic way of disseminating American values and interests through the likes of the global television music of MTV, the global news of CNN and the global box office hits of Hollywood which conflict with local cultures undermining local values and identity" (Williams 2003: 217). For Nkrumah and his supporters, Williams writes, "if colonialism is a form of imperialism – that is the direct control of one nation by another – neo-colonialism is cultural imperialism, with the media one of the vehicles for the transfer of western values and attitudes" (2003: 217). According to Steven, US political and economic influence has been enormously backed up by US film and music. "Where the marines, missionaries and bureaucrats failed, Charlie Chaplin, Mickey Mouse and the Beach Boys have succeeded effortlessly in attracting the world to the American way" (2003: 23). In essence, the media imperialism theory claims that "authentic, traditional and local culture in many parts of the world is becoming battered out of existence by the indiscriminate dumping of large quantities of slick commercial and media products, mainly from the United States" (Tunstall 1977: 57).

At the heart of the media imperialism thesis are the global media conglomerates which produce the media contents that have overwhelmingly saturated the world's entertainment platform. The headquarters of the world's twenty largest media conglomerates are all located in industrialized nations, the majority of them being in the United States, out of which the focus of this study, The Walt Disney Company, is one of the forerunners of the business along with the likes of AOL-Time Warner and Viacom. In attempting to place Disney in the cultural imperialism theory framework, Steven states:

> In tandem with equally prominent brands, such as McDonalds and NIKE, Disney products are impossible to avoid in any major city of the world. It's this never-ending flow of McWorld values and products that makes a concept like cultural imperialism so compelling (2003: 24).

Although the media imperialism thesis has won an enormous interest among scholars and academicians of the globalization affiliation, it has had its critiques too. The 1980s and the 1990s were especially notable in the rise of criticism against the imperialism theory by scholars (Boyd-Barrett, 1982; Tomlinson, 1991, Golding and Harris, 1997) whose criticism was "influenced by audience studies and cultural studies, both of which gave attention to the independent role of culture…something which media/cultural imperialism theorists had missed" (Rantanen 2005: 78).

According to Williams, "[w]hile the cultural imperialism thesis came to exercise a great hold over the policy makers and peoples of the so-called Third World, many scholars reject the thesis for being too pessimistic" (2003: 220). Advocates of the media imperialism thesis, Tomlinson argues, "simply assume that reading American comics, seeing adverts, watching pictures…has a direct effect" (1991: 45). "By neglecting audiences", Williams states that, "cultural imperialism underestimates the challenges to Americanization or westernization in different parts of the world (2003: 220).

The emergence of global media in Ethiopia

In 1977, the rise of the Derg[1] to take control of the country led to a complete breakdown of relations with the United States of America, Ethiopia's superpower ally of more than twenty years. The detachment of Ethiopia from the U.S., and its coalition with the then Leninist-Marxist Union of Soviet Socialist Republics (U.S.S.R.), had its impacts on the media consumption traditions of Ethiopians. People were hardly able to enjoy the right to own media devices such as satellite receivers and VHS players as these were considered as having western imperialistic tendencies. Individuals with tendencies of extravagant living including owning media gadgets were labeled as *adhari*, which means "opportunist" or "one who lives on the shoulder of others". American made films barely made their way to the public and the national television and the local cinemas which were by then nationalized showed media contents that reflected Marxist-Leninist propaganda.

In the late 1980s Ethiopia lost the support of the Soviet Union, which had become dissatisfied with Ethiopia's political and economic development under Mengistu. And finally in May 1991, the Socialist Derg regime was overthrown after the Ethiopian People Revolutionary Democratic Front (EPRDF) took control of Addis Ababa. This time also marked the collapse of the USSR and the end of the "Iron Curtain", the imaginary line that separated the Capitalist West led by the US from the Communist East led by the former USSR. In October 1992, the proclamation of the Press Freedom Bill by the then Ethiopian Transitional Government was introduced. The proclamation combined with the deregulation programme set in the country saw Western media products, especially Hollywood films make their way abundantly to the Ethiopian audience in the past two decades. The fact that access was accompanied by affordability also made the penetration of Hollywood to local audiences an accelerated exercise. Today, Hollywood films in DVD, VCD and VHS formats are rented in Addis Ababa for as little as 1-3 Ethiopian Birr ($0.1-0.31), the shops being placed in a range of 500 meters. There are about half a dozen agents in the metropolis which offer televised satellite broadcasting subscriptions. In addition, the number of Satellite dishes that receive free channels can be purchased for about 1,200-1,300 ETB ($125-135), a very affordable price for many upper-middle-class families in Addis Ababa which is why it is very common to see these receivers placed over the roofs of many households. More specifically, the animation features of the Walt Disney Company are basically made available to the audience in one of the following four ways:

1) *Video Renting Houses*: These are the most important spots where Disney DVDs, VCDs and VHS cassettes are available along with other Hollywood film products. As pointed out earlier, these houses are densely found in Addis Ababa within a range of about 500 meters and their asking price for the films they rent is very cheap, i.e. 1-3 Ethiopian Birr ($0.1-0.31)

2) *Informal Street Vendors*: These are young boys who sell a variety of films out of which Disney's animation make a good portion. They sell both DVDs and VCDs which are most of the time illegally duplicated. The issue of copyright is yet to be seriously taken in Ethiopia although local productions are better protected.

3) *Satellite Televised Broadcasts*: Disney Animation features also make their penetration to the free and subscribed satellite televised broadcasts through channels like Disney Channel, Cartoon Network, MBC3, etc.

4) *Local Ethiopian Television (ETV) Programmes*: Children programmes in ETV – the bi-weekly Amharic *Yelijoch Gize*; the weekly Tigrigna *Embabatat*; and the bi-weekly Oromiffa *Abdi Bori* – show Disney animation features in many episodes.

The shift to the consumption of global media has also been assisted by the incompetence of local production both in terms of quality and quantity. A good case in point is the major national television station, ETV, which was established in 1964, during the time of Emperor Haile Selassie, with the technical help of the British firm, Thomson. ETV was initially established to highlight the Organization of African Unity (OAU) founding heads of state meeting in Addis Ababa in that same year. Colour television was introduced in 1982 by the military government in order to commemorate the founding of the Workers' Party of Ethiopia (WPE). Since its establishment, ETV has remained in the hands of government, with its operations and content regulated by government. These days the common complaint about ETV is the gradual decline in the quality of its programmes (Simon 2005).

How Disney makes contact with Ethiopian children: a look at the social factors

Homes as perceived safe grounds for children

Like in many traditional societies, the trend of child rearing practices in Ethiopia is basically authoritarian. One such tradition in Ethiopia which brings great esteem to parents is when their children are known by members of the community for being "homely" and not seen wondering around. "Wondering around" is considered as a *durye*'s[2] activity whereas "being homely" is acclaimed as noble and *chewa*[3]. In the interview I had with the children, one of the important revelations that came into my attention was when they reflected how they rarely go out of their homes as their parents strictly forbid them to do so.

> *Interviewer:* Are you allowed to get out of your homes as you like?
>
> *Ruth:* No, not at all. My mother is always worried that I may become a victim of a car accident.

Dawit: I am also not allowed to go out of home.

Interviewer: Why not?

Dawit: So that I cannot be hit by a car or I will not become a durye.

Meseret: My parents do not let me and my siblings go outside of the house. They fear that we may go to dangerous places and meet bad friends who may spoil us and teach us bad language. The times they let us go out of the house, it is only when we are sent to buy stuff from the shops. Even if I am allowed to go at times, they make sure that I am accompanied by someone else.

Delina: I am also not allowed to go out of home. This is because I may face different problems. There are durye men who spend all day sitting in the area I live. If I go out from home alone they say some embarrassing things. My parents are well aware of this and for this reason they want me to stay at home.

An important thing to note from the excerpt is that 'the outside world', the world that is out of the home, is perceived by the community as "dangerous", "durye's place", and the space of the "bad". The recurrent mentioning of "durye" is an indication that the children are set by their parents or their immediate caretakers to recognize people they meet or incidents they face outside their homes as threatening to their welfare and dangerous for their personal growth. In other words, the outside world is seen as insecure, aggressive and threatening, and a zone of "duryes", "bad language", and "embarrassment".

The attribute of the outside as 'the bad' is not limited to certain groups of the society that parents or caretakers of the children identify as *durye*s alone, but interestingly to individuals and contacts the children identify as friends as well. Not only are the children forbidden to visit their friends, but also not to let them come or stay long in their houses. Meseret, 11, says"*...when my friend comes to my house, my mother tells me to talk to her quickly and see her off immediately.*"

Parents as oblivious agents of Disney's penetration

One of the ways parents make sure their children stay at home is by bringing cartoon and animation films regularly at home and by subscribing to televised satellite broadcasts in an attempt to discourage their desire of going elsewhere. This is significant in that it shows the media contents the children see at their homes are important ways of establishing some kind of communication with the outside world which they are denied. The fact that homes are perceived as safe grounds for children prompts parents to fulfill the needs of their children so that they do not develop an ambition to go elsewhere. The parents, in order to maintain their children at their homes and also to respond to the demands of their children make sure that they have something to be engaged with at their homes which usually are films and media products made available through DVDs, video cassettes and televised satellite broadcasts through which the likes of Disney sneak through. As a result, the probability of the children's exposure to Disney is further complemented by the fact that parents prefer their children to see cartoon and animation films which are 'safe' from bad language, pornography and violence. As much as parents exercise a higher degree of control in keeping their children at homes, they understand that this is not enough to avoid their fears of "insecurity". Parents are wary of, consciously or unconsciously, the fact that the media is the children's channel of communication to the outside world and is thus capable of exposing them to "the bad" and "the violent". As a result, parents make sure that the children enjoy a selected exposure of films, the selectors being the parents themselves. What is interesting here and what can be argued is the fact that parents select films that are free from "bad language, nudity and violence", which usually are animation films that fall under Disney's products. In essence, it can be argued that parents view Disney (although without knowing what exactly Disney is) as a safe and appropriate media that their children can come in contact with. What this essentially implies is that parents have become oblivious channels of Disney's penetration to children, the audience. They are not aware of Disney but they transport it and facilitate its contact with the target audience.

How Ethiopian children negotiate with Disney

Disney as an agent of symbolic distancing and fantasy

According to Thompson (1995), a critic of the cultural imperialism theory, local audiences make meaning out of the global media messages they receive within the context of their lived social conditions. He argues that the consumption of global media products by local audiences often provides meanings which enable "... the accentuation of symbolic distancing from the spatial-temporal contexts of everyday life" (1995: 175). Thompson further argues that the experience of symbolic distancing which is motivated by the appropriation of global media messages enables individuals "...to take some distance from the conditions of their day-to-day lives – not literally but symbolically, imaginatively, vicariously" (1995: 175). This in turn makes individuals take a critical look at their local culture which assumes central stage of their social context. This experience of symbolic distancing, he writes, enables individuals "...to gain some conception, however partial, of ways of life and life conditions which differ significantly from their own" (1995: 175).

An interesting aspect of the study is the reflection of children on how they wish to imaginatively, symbolically alter their everyday lived reality fancying the things their favourite characters think and do. Drotner stresses that "[c]hildren's reception is selective and not least with young children it seems motivated primarily by problematics that are focal in their own lives" (2002: 116). For example, Adiam, 7, feels that wearing uniforms everyday at school is boring and envies a particular dress she saw in one of the Disney animations she watched some time ago.

Adiam: I remember that shiny dress the magical old lady gave to Cinderella[4]. You know, her step mother and her step sisters denied her of this dress. It is so lovely. Don't you remember when the old magical lady made it for Cinderella? I wish I could have that

Interviewer: What kind of dress was that?

Adiam: It was a shiny long dress which was very wide down the waist.

Interviewer: Why do you want to have it?

Adiam: [Silence]...eh...you know we always wear uniforms here. At least I could wear that dress on Parent's Day. I am pretty sure nobody else would get that cloth.

Adiam's response signifies a 'problem that is focal in her life' – wearing the same clothes everyday as a requirement of the school – and how she wishes to get hold of Cinderella's dress. Adiam singled out the dress as the thing she loves most not because there are other things to choose from, but because the dress represents something that she desperately desires but misses in her everyday life. As a result, by putting on the dress imaginatively, Adiam distances herself from her routine boring uniforms symbolically. Had Adiam had the opportunity to wear whatever clothes she chooses to wear, Cinderella's dress might not have topped the list of her priorities, and thus she wouldn't have distanced herself from her lived reality as there would have been no plight, therefore no reason, to escape from.

A recurring subject that was recited by many children is how the characters of the films they see serve as a fulfillment of how they translate the do's and don't's as put forward by their parents. Thompson (1995: 175) argues that global images provide a resource for individuals to think critically about their own lives and life conditions. In my interviews with the children, a persistent criticism they raised was the way they are kept in their homes all the time despite their desire to socialize and play together with their friends.

Menelik: I am very much fond of Simba[5]. I especially like the time he spent with his friends Pumba and Timon far from his home after being chased away by Scar and the hyenas. He played and enjoyed his time with his friends, and didn't worry about anything. I really envy this most of the time. Whenever I want to go out of home to play with my friends, I have to find ways of cheating my parents who wouldn't let me go out.

Fitsum: I guess I have seen the Jungle Book more than three times now. I like Mowgli[6] very much because he does everything that he wants. When he got back to the human village, there were rules and regulations which he found difficult to understand. He escaped to the jungle to be free again...I understand Mowgli's situation because my father always says I will fail in my exams if I start going out of my home. I think this is foolish because I can be at my home and yet not study. I want to play football just like the other kids but I am hardly allowed to go out.

Both Menelik and Fitsum referred to global media images, Simba and Mowgli respectively, to take a critical look at the confined way of life they are prescribed to practice by their parents. They are symbolically, not actually, transferring themselves from their everyday lived realities to fantasize a life like Simba and Mowgli who for them are embodiments of freedom and happiness. This experience of "symbolic distancing" by Menelik and Fitsum arises from their criticism of their local conditions, i.e. the perception of homes as solitary spaces for children", which, however, doesn't make them rebel from their everyday routines and the norms of the society which they are supposed to keep.

The children understand that the stories and images they see in the movies are not more than mere images and stories. As such, the global image as represented by the likes Mowgli and Simba do make the children criticize their local conditions, but not rebel; makes them wish, but not act; and makes them transfer symbolically, but not realistically. This, in turn, stands against the premise of the media imperialism thesis that local cultures are doomed to homogenization in the scenario of western media dissemination. The children as absorbed and as fantasized as they may be realize that their lived reality, their cognition, and their societal make up can be very different from that of their heroes.

Disney as exporter of 'Americanization', modernity and individualism

Much of the critique of cultural imperialism seems to lie in a critique of modernity, a concept very closely associated with Americanization. The term modernity, as contradictory and complex as it may be, according to Tomlinson, has most often been viewed as the idea of the "most general way in which [people] in the West represent [their] cultural experience to [themselves]" (1991: 140). Berenson in his article *Globalization and Culture: Cultural Imperialism or a Critique of Modernity?* writes that "modernity presents many challenges as the apparent globalization of culture ensues but the debate over cultural imperialism ignores the vitality and inherently assimilatory nature of human cultures" (2001: 1). In other words, Berenson's argument can be interpreted as implying the rather overlooked potential of local communities or the supposed "receivers of culture" in modifying, ignoring or even rejecting the values cherished by the West as "modern".

The pressures of the continually developing nature of the modern world, Berenson argues, force us to exercise our individual freedom to choose our cultural experience, and this very freedom "condemns us to make individual choices that will define our lives" (2001: 4). As such, modernity is not a cultural imposition but rather liberation of the human spirit in the cultural sense (Tomlinson 1991: 149). Taxel attributes the Disney value system to the basic American packages of "individualism, advancement through self help, strict adherence to the work ethic, and the supreme optimism in the possibility of the ultimate improvement of society through the progressive improvement in humankind" (1982: 14). As arguable as they may be, these qualities described by Taxel didn't go unnoticed by the children I have studied. They especially stressed the characters' ability to bounce back from failure and their resilience in difficult circumstances.

> *Liya:* They [the characters] try over and over again and finally succeed. In the course of their actions they repeatedly encounter failure but they never give up. In the end you will always see that they live happily ever after or become kings and queens.
>
> *Dina:* The films taught me not to lose hope in the things I do. For example, if you look at Cinderella, she has finally got the opportunity to be married to the prince. She achieved this because she was tolerant and she did not give up. If she complained or lost hope she might have missed the opportunity to be married to the prince and the old magical lady as well.
>
> *Elsa:* The films always end in joy and happiness. They may make you sad in the beginning or in the middle but the good people always come out triumphant in the end.

Many of the children realize that Cinderella's success came after many hardships and difficult times. Even though there was an element of luck in Cinderella's final triumph, Fikirte, 11, believes that Cinderella was not just lucky: "*The old lady wouldn't have helped Cinderella in the first place had she been lazy. I think she is rewarded for her good ways.*" Fikirte further relates the story of Cinderella to a real life instance by alluding to a story she remembers from the past.

> The story of Cinderella reminds me of a girl in my class while I was in grade two. Nobody liked that girl. They did not like her because they thought the teachers favor her. I know this was not true. They didn't like her because the teachers always told us to be like he. Everybody was saying she would rank 5th from the class but she came up second at the end of the semester. Do you remember? It was the same with Cinderella. Everybody hated her but at the end she came above all of them.

Disney Kids: In defense of the local

Despite the different perspectives and outlooks exhibited by the target children of this study, a definite reflection worth noticing is the kids' overwhelming attraction to Disney animation films who talk of these films. In many instances, they find it very difficult to compare local productions to Western animation features (as represented by Disney in this case) as they convey that there is a huge gap between what the local and the West offer. In comparing the local productions with that of Western ones, Dina gives an interesting illustration.

> *Interviewer:* Have you seen any locally produced films or theatres?
>
> *Dina:* I have seen children's theatre. It is called Doctor Kebero[7]. But I didn't like it.
>
> *Interviewer:* Why didn't you like it?

> *Dina:* It is not like the ones which are produced abroad. You can see that the actors are humans who are dressed up to look like animals. You can clearly see that someone who is supposed to act like a horse is not a horse; it is a human. You can see their human legs coming out of the costumes. But in films like, say, Finding Nemo[8], the fish is a fish and the shark is a shark. They are so real. Even the mouth movement of the fish in Finding Nemo is perfectly matched with what they say. Here, you hear a sound coming out of their mouth but there is no movement at all.

Dina's reservation as far as local productions are concerned, for obvious reasons, is related to standard and quality. When she says "*you can see their human legs coming out of the costumes*" and "*...you hear a sound coming out of their mouth but there is no lip movement at all,*" there is no phrase or word that states she dislikes the story or the plot. These expressions are rather related to quality and techniques of production, which she compares to the characters of *Finding Nemo*, a Disney animated feature, and finds them short.

Samrawit has also similar observations.

> *Interviewer:* Have you seen any animation film that is made here in Ethiopia where the actors talk in Amharic?
>
> *Samrawit:* In Ababa Tesfaye[9] there is a cartoon film called Tsehay Memar Tiwedalech[10]. Tsehay Memar Tiwedalech teaches children to love education so that we can help our country in the future. I have also seen others. But the actors are put on human hands and are covered by clothes. When they sometimes stretch like this (stretching both her hands up), you can see their hands. Then I know it's all fake.

In her case, Samrawit is most probably referring to children films which are made up of puppet acts. Her observation is once again similar to that made by Dina in that there is once again a reference to lack of good technique in production. But this shouldn't be taken as the case for all.

> *Fikirte:* The animation films that are produced here are not as good as those which we rent from the video stores. They always say do this and don't do that. They say the same thing ten times. This is so intolerable. The foreign films don't have such repeated rules and advises. They show you through practicing it. Everybody knows Cinderella is patient. How did we know this? She never said I am patient so be patient like me. She just simply is like that.

Fikirte's dislike for locally produced animation features propped up from an interesting observation she made – an explicit didactic feature of local productions and children programmes. Fikirte's reasoning goes far beyond Dina's and Samrawit's dissatisfaction with regard to format and style.

The mention of 'quality' in the interviews is an important factor towards attraction of films. Strelitz (2004) in his study *Understanding University Student Media Preferences through the Discourses of 'Realism' and 'Quality'* addresses the issue of 'quality' in relation to a theme that emerged in his interviews with

Rhodes University students whose preference for global media was as result of its perceived technical quality (camerawork, scripting, acting, lighting and so on). Strelitz further points out that, for most of these students, it was primarily global media are seen to embody 'quality'. While many students had difficulty in defining what they meant by 'quality', it does seem to mean for them a set of technical production standards inherited from North America. In this regard, it may be argued that both Dina's and Samrawit's perception of how cartoon and animation films ought to be made is set up by Disney's format and style and that any other form of production is unacceptable – thus the effect of homogenization of taste and culture as argued by the cultural/media imperialism thesis. If this is the case and can be deemed plausible, the children are in no way mentally ready to watch and appreciate any locally made animation productions that deviate from Disney's high standard and 'near to perfection' animation features. This, however, is not the case as the children, as contented as they may be with the quality of the films when compared to the Disney counterparts, are regularly watching locally made children shows and short animation productions.

> *Interviewer:* Do you see children's programmes in ETV?
>
> *Nebiyu:* Yes. I always watch Ababa Tesfaye and also Tsehay Memar Tiwedalech on Saturdays and Sundays. I especially like Tsehay Memar Tiwedalech. I never saw an Amharic cartoon film before and I am really excited about this.
>
> *Interviewer:* Why are you excited about Amharic carton films?
>
> *Nebiyu:* Because it's in Amharic. I can't imagine what it would be like if The Lion King was made in Amharic. Our country would have been famous all over the world. Our music teacher once showed us The Lion King in the music room and he told us it was made in Kenya. He also spoke about Hakuna Matata and told us it means "no worries" in a certain African language. If that was Amharic even the ferenjis[11] might have known about us.

Nebiyu's reason for watching Amharic cartoon productions (in this case *Tsehay Memar Tiwedalech*) has got nothing to do with any other thing but language. He is excited about the language of the film being Amharic not because of issues related to language literacy but because of a sense of belongingness. This can be a valid argument taking into account Nebiyu's later reference to his hope that his country can be popular for animation film making. In essence, this brings us back to the criticism of the media imperialism thesis in its failure "to take much more account of the active participation of the audience in shaping any 'meaning' that is taken from mass media" (Liebes and Katz 1990). Nebiyu's sense of nationalism which he learns from his interaction with his community offers a space for him to reason out why he should care to watch local productions. As a result, we can notice that it is not only format and style that may come to the specified children's minds when tuning to their TV sets but also elements of active participation potentials as an audience. Nebiyu brings another instance to the situation.

Interviewer: But some people say local animation films are not as good as the ones from abroad.

Nebiyu: I know they are not equal. The films from abroad are very good in many ways. They are full of colors; their stories are full of capturing moments and really funny actions. But the films I see which are in Amharic are not that bad. I don't know about others but I like them. I think it is because the stories are familiar to me.

From the excerpt, we can understand that Nebiyu watches both local and foreign animation films but for different reasons. It is especially important to note when he mentions why he likes local films – because of familiarity of stories – as this once again alludes to the significance of the capacity of the audiences to evaluate and interact with the media content they see and how they can make meaning out of their lived reality and the social context they are familiar with. In this case, Nebiyu's desire to watch locally produced animation films and children programmes is determined by the stories he knew from the past which are familiar to him. It is worthy noting that these stories make up part of Nebiyu's lived reality, and ultimately they have influenced him in his decision to watch locally produced animation films. What is more interesting is that, there is a tendency from the children that they would be much more interested to see locally produced animation films if they are made in the standard of Disney films which clearly shows that they are not subject to media imperialism's claim of homogenization or any form of identity crisis.

Interviewer: Will you see Amharic animation films if they are made in the standard of the foreign films?

Dina: Definitely. I like Sinzero[12] for example. Although they always show him dancing, I think he is very good. He seems real and Habesha[13] [laughs].

Fikirte: I would like to see quality Amharic films being made. Sometimes my sister takes me to the cinema and we watch Amharic films and I love it very much. It feels good to see a film in Amharic. You see, I don't have to ask the person next to me what the people are talking about if the language is Amharic.

Conclusion

One of the major findings of this study is that although the children identify themselves with the values the Disney animation films represent, it is difficult to conclude that they passively adhere to it. The children are not doomed to a hegemonic dead end as the media imperialism thesis argues but rather interact with global texts and images they come into contact with for reasons of quality and aesthetics. They transfer symbolically to the world they are introduced to through the films but are very much aware of the social values they are bound in. In the abundance of exposure to global media, the children still enjoy local productions and mention issues related to nationalism, local language, and story development for the way they watch local children programmes. As a result, it is, in many ways, difficult to conform to the premises of the media imperialism thesis, as the global media texts' and images' (as represented by Disney in this case) penetration is uneven. The complexity of meanings constructed by the children in their interaction with the global texts and images of Disney makes the task of adhering to or rejecting the penetration of global media messages to the local audience intricate. The nature of other dynamics like societal make up, beliefs and values do not make the task of establishing a relationship that the media imperialism thesis makes between the global and the local easy, and thus any attempt of trying to define such rapport shall take into consideration the interface between text and context.

One of the fertile areas for further research is the issue of media literacy in children's understanding of global media messages. In their comparison of global and local productions, the children repeatedly mentioned issues of language intelligibility and quality of contents. An investigation in this area will have implications for aspects to be reconsidered and revisited in the production of local contents for children.

Notes

1 The Provisional Military Administrative Council set up by the military leadership that overthrew the then emperor of Ethiopia, Haile Selassie I, in a military coup in 1974.

2. *Durye* is a very common Amharic word which is frequently used to refer to young people who are jobless, always seen wondering outside their homes, and disrespectful of community's norms.

3. *Chewa* is the exact opposite of *durye*. It is an Amharic word that designates someone very humble who at the same time doesn't speak much especially in the presence of elder people.

4. *Cinderella* is a 1950 animated feature produced by Walt Disney. In the film, a young girl abused by her stepmother and step-sisters is still able to go the ball and win her prince with the help of a pumpkin, half dozen mice, and a fairy godmother.

5. Simba is the protagonist of the movie and destined ruler of the Pride Lands, an imaginary place where the lions rule the jungle

6. Mowgli is the main character of *The Jungle Book*, a young jungle boy raised by wolves. In the movie, Mowgli is featured as a 10 year old, which is around the age he was in Rudyard Kipling's book when he was first kidnapped by the Bandar Log (monkeys). Mowgli is found by Bagheera the black panther, who would become a good friend later, in a wrecked boat.

7. *Doctor Kebero* which literally translates as "Doctor Fox" is an Amharic children's play which is staged in one of Addis Ababa's cinemas. In the story, Doctor Kebero acts as a villain who treacherously fools and takes advantage of sheep.

8. *Finding Nemo* is an Academy Award-winning computer-animated film produced by Pixar Animation Studios and released to theaters by Walt Disney Pictures and Buena Vista Distribution. In the film, after clownfish Marlin (Albert Brooks) loses his wife, Coral (Elizabeth Perkins), and all but one of his unborn children he promises that he will never let anything happen to the one remaining egg which he names Nemo. Nemo (Alexander Gould) begins his first day at school and is frustrated and embarrassed by his overprotective father, and takes it to such an extreme that Nemo deliberately disobeys his father by swimming out into open water. The rest of the film show's Marlin desperately looking for his son and the adventures he faces throughout his search.

9. Ababa Tesfaye had been a veteran host for the weekly *Yelijoch Gize* (literally "Children's Moment") programme transmitted o ETV on Saturdays and Sundays. Children usually refer *Yelijoch Gize* as Ababa Tesfaye.
10. *Tsehay Memar Tiwedalech* is a weekly 10 minutes animation production that is transmitted through the local Ethiopian Television. It is about a little girl called Tsehay who loves to learn alphabets, words and numbers.
11. *Ferenji* is a commonly used Amharic word which refers to foreign white people.
12. Bringing into action some of the most popular tunes of Ethiopian traditional music, Sinziro is an animated character who is very popular for his cunning and intelligence. Given some background to Ethiopian children literature, one can hardly not identify the legendary character most conspicuous for his trademark haircut.
13. An Ethiopian's reference to his fellow countryman.

References

Berenson, T. (2000) *Globalization and Culture: Cultural Imperialism or a Critique of Modernity?* Retrieved June 14, 2007. http://www.usask.ca/english/frank/cultint.htm

Best Global Brands 2006: A Ranking by Value. (2006) Interbrand Business Week. Retrieved July 10, 2007. http://www.ourfishbowl.com/images/surveys/BGB06Report_072706.pdf

Boyd-Barrett, O. (1982) 'Cultural Dependency and the Mass Media', in M. Gurevitch et al. (eds.) *Culture, Society and the Media.* London: Methuen, pp.174-95.

Carlsson, U. (2002) 'Children, Young People and Media Globalization: Foreword', in U. Calrsson and C. von Feilitzen (eds.) *Children, Young People and Media Globalization.* Göteborg: Nordicom, The UNESCO International Clearinghouse on Children, Youth and Media.

Demers, D. (1999) *Global Media: Menace or Messiah?* Cresskill: Hampton Press, Inc.

Drotner, K. (2002) 'Domesticating Disney: On Danish Children's Reception of a Global Media Giant', in C. von Feilitzen and U. Carlsson (eds.) *Children, Young People and Media Globalization* (pp.111-124) Göteborg: The UNESCO International Clearinghouse on Children, Youth and Media.

von Felitzen, C. (2002) Children, Young People and Media Globalization, in C. von Feilitzen and C. Carlsson (eds.) *Children, Young People and Media Globalization* Göteborg: The UNESCO International Clearinghouse on Children, Youth and Media, pp.13-22.

Galtung, J. (1971) 'A Structural Theory of Imperialism', *Journal of Peace Research*, 8(2) 81-117.

Golding, P. and Harris, P. (1997) *Beyond Cultural Imperialism: Globalization, Communication and the New International Order.* London: Sage Publications Ltd.

Hamelink, C.J. (2002) 'Media Globalization: Consequences for the Rights of Children', in C. von Feilitzen and U. Carlsson (eds.) *Children, Young People and Media Globalization* (pp.33-42) Göteborg: Nordicom, The UNESCO International Clearinghouse on Children, Youth and Media.

Held, D. (ed.) (2004) *A Globalizing World? Culture, Economics and Politics.* London: Routledge.

Herman, E.S. and McChesney, R.W. (1997) *The Global Media: The New Missionaries of Corporate Capitalism.* London: Cassell Publishers.

Keyes, W. and Buckingham D. (eds.) (1999) *Children's Television Policy: International Perspectives.* Sydney: The Australian Key Center for Cultural and Media Policy.

Liebes, T. and Katz, E. (1990) *The Export of Meaning: Cross-Cultural Readings of 'Dallas'.* Oxford: Oxford University Press.

Rantanen, T. (2005) *The Media and Globalization.* London: Sage Publications Ltd.

Schiller, H. (1976) *Communications and Cultural Dimensions.* New York: Sharpe.

Simon, G. (2005) *African Media Development Initiative – Ethiopia: Research Findings and Conclusions.* London: BBC World Trust.

Steven, P. (2003) *The No-Nonsense Guide to Global Media.* London: New Internationalist Publications Ltd./Verso.

Taxel, J. (1982) *A Literature Review of the Impact of Walt Disney Productions Inc. on American Popular Culture and Children's Literature.* Athens, GA: University of Georgia, Department of Language education.

Thompson, J.B. (1995) *The Media and Modernity: A Social Theory of the Media.* Cambridge: Polity Press.

Tomlinson, J. (1991) *Cultural Imperialism.* London: Pinter Publishers.

Tracey, M. (1985) 'The Poisoned Chalice? International Television and the Idea of Dominance, *Daedalus'*, 114(4): 17-56.

Tunstall, J. (1977) *The Media are American.* London: Constable.

Wasko, J. (2001) *Understanding Disney: The Manufacture of Fantasy.* Cambridge: Polity Press.

Wasko, J. (2003) *How Hollywood Works.* London: Sage Publications Ltd.

Watson, J. and Hill, A. (eds.) (2003) *Dictionary of Media and Communication Studies* (6th ed.) London: Arnold Publishers.

White, R.A. (1993) 'The New Order and the Third World', in Gerbner, G., Mowlana, H., and Nordenstreng, K. (eds.) *The Global Media Debate: Its Rise, Fall, and Renewal* Norwood: Ablex Publishing Corporation, pp.21-34.

Williams, K. (2003) *Understanding Media Theory.* London: Arnold Publishers.

Situated Responses to the Digital Literacies of Electronic Communication in Marginal School Settings

Mastin Prinsloo & Marion Walton

In this chapter we examine examples of young children's encounters with computers and the Internet in poorly resourced schools in an African setting. We argue that computerized and networked media resources operate in these settings in specific ways that are sometimes ignored in the discussion of 'digital divides' and the call for the expansion of physical access to computers and the Internet. These local ways of using the digital resources of the media do not always fit with common assumptions about the value of such technology for enhancing learning in otherwise deprived or poorly resourced educational settings.

Globalisation, technology and marginalisation

The information-technological revolution has made possible the new forms of production and organization that have resulted in a global economy. Capital markets are interconnected world-wide and multinational corporations, in manufacturing, services, and finance make up the core of the world economy (Castells 2000). While the electronic media are not the cause of these changes, none of what is commonly referred to as globalisation would be possible without them. It makes sense, then, to think about how these media work in African settings, and with what sort of potential.

Unfortunately, the changes associated with globalization have not improved things for most people in Africa, where many often don't have access to clean water, let alone communications technology. More than ten years ago, Castells (1996: 135) wrote that that the new global economy did not have much of a role for the majority of the African population. Emphasising the relentless logic of the global system he suggested that structural irrelevance was a more threatening condition than dependency might have been for African societies in preceding decades. A sign of Africa's marginal status was the underdeveloped nature of its electronic media. He suggested that Africa (together with other marginal regions in the world) was being left in a technological apartheid. Blommaert (2002) similarly suggested that we were witnessing the widening of the gap between prestige resources and practices at the core (the wealthy parts of the world) and those at the periphery (large parts of Africa, South America and Asia). He pointed out that this was not only something that was happening on a world scale but also happened within most contemporary societies. The electronic media, it can be said, almost certainly exaggerate and extend this gap between the marginalized and included sectors of society because of their technological load relative to print media.

Digital divides

The response to such concerns has been to call for strategies to close the gap between Africa (and other poor regions of the world) and the developed world, and between included and excluded sectors within societies, as far as access to and application of electronic media resources is concerned. One view, which commonly refers to the 'digital divide', has stressed the worth of putting computers and Internet access into poor African settings as quickly and as widely as possible, with the hope that the huge potential of the technology will rapidly connect people to the vast resources of the 'Knowledge Economy', catapulting them towards paths of progress and development. Numerous projects aim to bring information and communication technologies to poor parts of Africa because of the belief in their transformative potential. These include the construction of 'telecentres' and Internet cafés in African villages and urban centres, with Internet-linked computers providing multi-function resources, an initiative supported by the World Bank and UNESCO, reportedly with uneven results (Etta and Parvyn-Wamahiu 2003). A more recent case in point is the aggressively-marketed *One Laptop Per Child* (2007) programme as well as rival programmes that seek to persuade impoverished governments to buy $200 computers for millions of children in countries in Africa, Latin America, and Asia.

In the USA as elsewhere, 'digital divide' rhetoric is similarly invoked when strategies for disseminating skills associated with 'new literacies'. The No Child Left Behind Act, passed by the Bush administration in 2002 and now under attack by members of the Democratic Party for its failures, enacted a wide range of initiatives, many of which were supposed to improve reading outcomes in schools, and to address inequalities in educational outcomes. The Act has a section devoted to technology (Title II, Section D), with the stated goal, "To assist every student in crossing the digital divide by ensuring that every student is technologically literate by the time the student finishes the eighth grade, regardless of the student's race, ethnicity, gender, family income, geographic location, or disability." (discussed in Leu et al. 2004: 9).

At the same time, a more cautious response has been to warn that these new media are no silver bullet, and not instantly able to solve the problems of poverty and skewed development (Warschauer, forthcoming; 2003; Snyder and Prinsloo 2007). Warschauer (2003) developed a model of what kinds of resources are required to help promote meaningful access to and use of technology. These, he said, included physical resources (e.g., computers and Internet access), digital resources (e.g., online content and tools in multiple languages and appropriate to the needs of diverse users); human resources (e.g., knowledge and skills developed through instruction emphasizing critical inquiry and situated practice); and social resources (e.g., enhanced social capital developed through in-person, online, and institutional support).

This expanded model suggests, however, the idea of a divide to be bridged that does not explicitly take account of the social resources, norms, practices and technologies that marginal individuals, groups of people, nation states and regions already hold. As we will argue here, drawing on empirical research, Information Communication Technologies (ICTs), electronic media and digital literacies[1], when they are injected from the outside to bring about certain results, encounter situated social practices that do not simply result in these resources being used in ways that might be expected, and do not necessarily or automatically promote social inclusion or development.

Research in well-resourced contexts

Much of digital literacy research to date has been carried out among those who are either relatively privileged or who are shown to be successful with new digital media. Researchers writing from middle-class contexts around the globe have argued that children's literacy activities involving computers prior to and outside of school are typically more frequent, richer, and more meaningful than those they encounter in school (Gee 2003; Reinking et al. 1998). Clearly, this contrast between in-school and out-of-school experiences with the new literacies only works when such digitally rich, out-of-school encounters with computers are available to children, which is seldom the case in poorly resourced African context. Such research has assumed that one can generalise from middle-class American or European contexts to elsewhere. For example, Reinking writes that:

> By the time many young children begin formal schooling, they are likely to have had countless experiences involving digital forms of communication, for example sitting in the lap of an adult who is corresponding with a relative via email or who is making an on-line purchase over the Internet. Or, they may participate in engaging interactive multimedia stories and games on a home computer… (Reinking 2003: 338).

Reinking contrasts the experiences that children have with computers outside of school with those they have in school, to make the point that schools are not doing enough with the resources of the new digital literacies:

> for many youngsters literacy activities involving computers prior to and outside of school are typically more frequent, richer, and more meaningful than are such activities they encounter when they enter elementary school. (Reinking 2003: 338)

Clearly this contrast between in-school and out-of-school experiences with digital literacies only works when children's out-of-school experiences are 'digitally-rich' in the way Reinking describes. African children in the sub-elite schools and social settings where the majority of people are located, on the other hand, generally only encounter computer-based digital literacies in school settings, if at all, and are probably more likely to access the Internet from a mobile phone than from a computer (Kreutzer 2008).

We examine these concerns and this debate here from the perspective of studies of children encountering electronic media across schools in the Western Cape, South Africa, where a well-funded programme has been rolled out to put computers and connectivity into otherwise poor and under-resourced schools across the region. We argue that computerized and networked media resources operate in these settings in localized ways that are particular to peripheral or marginal settings. These ways do not fit with common assumptions about the value of such technology for enhancing learning in otherwise deprived or poorly resourced educational settings. We develop a theoretical perspective to make sense of these anomalies between the promises in the research literature and our observations of the local situation. We conclude that whether electronic resources offer opportunities for particular users is something that has to be established by situated research, not assumed, in contrast with research models that start from concerns around digital divides and offer solutions along the lines of technology transfer.

Computers in context: Research examples from the Western Cape, South Africa

Until very recently, a large majority of South African children had no access to computers at school. Since the country's first democratic elections in 1994, schools have been under pressure to provide more equitable access to computers and other ICTs. The Western Cape province has embarked on a process of rapid deployment of computers to all state schools (Dugmore 2004). Literacy and numeracy development have been targeted as priority areas for these new computer facilities in Western Cape primary schools. Imported and adapted software is installed in the labs and provides many hours of self-contained 'drill-and-practice' literacy lessons. These lessons, it must be noted, emphasise grammatical and orthographic 'correctness' rather than the sense of the writing. This approach reinforces the prevailing notions of literacy teaching in township schools in the Western Cape, where literacy teaching is most often a drill-and-practice activity (Prinsloo 2005: 7) that focuses on the surface features of text. Commonly, the schools still have little or no library facilities, sports fields, or school hall, and, state schools receive very limited budgets. Consequently, the computers and computer lab are prized acquisitions, and, unfortunately, theft of the computers is a major problem.

We present and discuss three cameos from the wider research in this chapter. Starting at the lowest school level, the first is from a pre-school class at a school in the Khayelitsha township, Cape Town.[2] The dialogue in the fieldnote transcribed below was translated from Xhosa into English.

Example A: Reading readiness?

The children wait outside the computer room in a line until they are shepherded in by the teacher. There are 20 computers in the lab. The children are told to put their hands under the table. The teacher selects a 'pre-reading' programme and calls it up on all the computers. There are 8 balloons, numbered and in a bunch on the screen, and below that a key consisting of numbers in squares from one to ten and below each number the name of a colour. The children can change the colour of the balloons by clicking on the number-colour key.

The teacher asks the children to click on the 1/Red button at the bottom of the screen. One child (Sesethu) holds the mouse and moves the cursor to number one. She places it there but does not click. The children seem confused. The teacher revises the names and places of colours in the sequence again, in case the children do not know the colours by name. He then tells them to click on number 1/Red again. Sesethu says she has clicked, but hasn't. The teacher asks them to find balloon number one and click on it. The teacher comes to Sesethu and her friend and shows them where the click button is. The teacher first asks them to identify the two number ones in the balloons. They identify them and click on them. The balloons become red. The teacher says there isn't a number 2 on the balloons. He asks: "What number comes after number 2?" The children say "Three". Teacher asks, "What colour is number 3?" The learners say "Blue". The teacher asks them to click on number 3. Sesethu identifies number 3 and clicks on it. It turns blue. Teacher says "Good!", and asks for the children's attention. The teacher asks the class to look on the board. He says, "Our four looks like this (4) and their four looks like 4. It is the same thing. Now first click on the yellow and then find the 4 in the balloons". Sesethu clicks on four but it turns blue. The teacher comes over and says she must click on the four first. He helps her to click on number 4 (yellow) and then balloon number 4. The teacher says, "Excellent!" The teacher explained in an aside to the researcher that this was a difficult exercise but a very good one. He said that it taught children fine-motor skills and eye-hand co-ordination. He said that the following term he planned to teach the children how to get in and out of a programme, but now they were started with pre-reading exercises.

The extract shows clearly that the school was using what have been called 'first generation' skill-and-drill computer software, donated along with the computers. The teachers enthusiastically supported the use of this software because it was consistent with their own ideas about how reading as a basic skill should be introduced: as a drill and practice activity (Prinsloo and Bloch 1999). Children encounter literacy in the context of the authority relations and pedagogical practices that characterize schooling in this setting. The enforced passivity of the children (for example, where they sat with their hands under the table while the teacher set up the lesson, and then followed limited procedures in mechanical fashion) is consistent with the way they were expected to behave in school, but contrasts sharply with the often declared potential of ICTs for children's experimentation, self-instruction and individual choices and creativity (Snyder 1997; Gee 2003).

Example B: Cheating literacy

In a related example in a higher school Grade, we see children using 'drill-and-practice' literacy software at a primary school, again in the Western Cape, near Cape Town.

The package the class was using was structured around the United Kingdom's National Curriculum, involving standardised literacy practice and testing, and was adapted or 'localised' for use in South Africa. The software was adapted under license to the UK company that developed it for UK schools, by a South African firm, which translated the English content into Afrikaans, Xhosa, and Zulu, and mapped the word and sentence-based activities onto their equivalents in the local primary school curriculum. In the localisation process, details of content and language were customised, but the coded structure of the package (together with its educational assumptions) remains essentially unchanged. Such educational software typically simulates one prevalent classroom genre of teacher-pupil dialogue, where the teacher questions children, they respond and she evaluates their response against the criteria she holds. The genre has been labelled 'Initiation, Response, Evaluation' (IRE) (Sinclair and Coulthard 1975). Such IRE dialogic interaction in the class has been described as locking children into an activity around learning which can best be summarised as: "Guess what the teacher is thinking". The 'closed' questioning style works to shut down dialogic interchange (Wells 1999), and does not encourage children to provide justification and further information but works well as an attention-focusing strategy for teachers who have limited subject knowledge, pedagogic training and who are dealing with large classes and with syllabus content to cover. The coded structures of educational software often provide an extreme version of this pattern of closed discourse. The software largely comprises sets of exercises that test 'basic skills'. Such educational software creates a representation of the learners and their learning by evaluating answers and summarising them in a score or grade.

In one illustrative example,[3] a child was observed while working alone on an exercise, with headphones on so that he could listen to audio instructions and feedback from the digital tutor as he worked on the exercises: The screen displayed "Grade 7: Punctuation revision". The rest of the text instructed the child to insert commas into the sentences of a paragraph. He read the text on the screen carefully, moving his lips as he read and moving the cursor as he read, word by word. He then added six full-stops to the paragraph and pressed the "Is it right?" button. The programme responded:

> Oops, you haven't found everything yet. [A pop-up displays "You have 0 out of 6 points in this activity".]

The student tried again and again got the same response. He turned to the researcher and then to another student for help. Having been shown that he had inserted full-stops rather than commas, he changed them, but the same response about 0 out of 6 was given again. The other student suggested that he start the exercise again from the beginning. This time he got the response: "Correct. You got it right the very first time."

The software's limited capacity to respond to user actions meant that the negative feedback and low score it first gave the student were based on a simple count of the number of commas inserted, rather than any awareness of what he had been doing. He had found all the places where commas should be inserted in the paragraph but he had inadvertently hit the wrong key on the keyboard. The software was unable to interpret the student's input as a human teacher or fellow student might have. In this case, "drill and practice" meant that the student had to "drill and practice" something he had already mastered. In total he repeated the rather unexciting comma exercise three times over.

In another example, in the same lesson a student showed the researcher how she had figured out how to cheat the programme, successfully bypassing the simulated discourse of an exercise and getting full marks.

> Brenda tugged my sleeve as I was walking around the classroom. When she had my attention, she pointed out that she had full marks for one exercise (46 out of 46). I congratulated her and she shook with laughter. The two girls working next to her quickly explained to me that she had found a way of "cheating" and getting the "high score" for that exercise. I asked Brenda to show me her trick, and she explained her method: "I click all of them, Miss, and then I just go there – Is it right? – and click, and it come all right, Miss."

The exercise in question presented a series of sentences and required the learner to 'click on' the "main idea" in each sentence. Ideas are hard things to 'click on' at the best of times, and the exercise in question in fact required learners to demonstrate their knowledge of sentence structure by clicking on all the words of the main clause of such sentences as 'The girl talks with the man with the red beard'; 'She read the book from beginning to end'. When asked to try the exercise without the "cheat" the student clicked on several of the words in the sentences but did not identify the main clause at all. She apparently attempted to click on words which provided a telegraphic summary of the sentence and she had not identified clauses at all (e.g., she highlighted words as follows: '**She read** the **book** from **beginning** to **end**'; rather than '**She read the book** from beginning to end'.) She certainly was not focusing on sentence structure in the very specifically intentioned but vaguely outlined way that the software programme wanted.

The poor design of the electronic exercise meant that, firstly, it could be "hacked" by a creative student who ignored the sense of the activity and focused directly on its scoring mechanisms and procedures. Secondly, the stated purpose of the exercise ("find the main idea") was a bad surrogate for what it really wanted, which was a grammar-recognition activity – "find the main clause".

As described above, the drill-and-practice exercises of the educational software simulates the interaction patterns of classroom discourse. It does this through rule-governed sequencing of images, text, audio and sometimes video and animation. Notwithstanding the obvious limitations of the software that is used in education programmes, children's enjoyment of the media is notable, but particularly where they can use it to pursue their own interests. The children made their own situated meanings out of the rules of the software programmes, troubleshooting and cheating with pleasure, as they focused on the software's economy of scores and marks, and made these into subversive games of their own (Walton 2007).

The research starts to suggest that computers and software are not simply 'delivering' information to children. Instead, the software is always interpreted in a specific local context. The children are engaged in an active process of sign-making, and their interests often diverge from those of their educators and the creators of the software. The 'drill-and-practice' software makes few concessions to the children's context and does without the reciprocal negotiation of meaning which is fundamental to interpersonal communication. Nonetheless, this study suggests that children use the rule-governed logic of the software as a representational resource and that this is associated with distinctive literacy practices. A similar dynamic is observed with regard to digital literacy practices to do with the Internet as we now discuss below.

Example C: Googling with a difference

Leu, Kinzer, Coiro and Cammack (2004: 15) identify the core skills involved in reading and writing in relation to Internet use as "using a search engine effectively to locate information" and secondly, as "evaluating the accuracy and utility of information that is located on a webpage in relation to one's purpose". These authors take the design of the search engine for granted, and assume that search engine use is a skill that is readily taught through well-designed exercises of a general nature. It seems important, though, to look more closely at what is involved when children in socially marginal settings make use of resources designed at the centre, with different users in mind. The lessons that used the Web usually amounted to "Googling sessions" where the teacher provided a topic and the students were left to use Google to find (and transcribe) relevant results, often working almost entirely independently for most of the lesson. While students saved digital media for their own personal use, the products of the Google lessons were always a hand-written paragraph on a piece of paper – the students seldom had more than thirty minutes per week in the computer lab.

In the following example[4] the teacher initiated the activity by providing the topic for research [apartheid], and suggested Google as a place to find the answer. The transcript from fieldnotes shows two students working together:

The students in this class transcribed the word 'apartheid' into the search engine as their query. The Google interface offered them a small set of high-ranking results (only three displayed above the fold).

> They wait a few seconds for the results to appear, and then click on the first link, which takes them to a page entitled "The History of Apartheid in South Africa". They spend the next ten minutes reading the article. When they are done, they carefully copy down the first two paragraphs of the article on pieces of paper that they brought into the lab with them.

The students selected the top result and treated it as they would treat other authoritative texts, by transcribing it faithfully and returning this answer to the teacher for assessment. The page that the two girls transcribed with such care was written by five second year Computer Science students from Stanford University in 1995. It is a second year student project which exposes the complicity of computer technology and IBM in particular in facilitating the administration of racial classification under apartheid. The irony that these students working in South Africa should be offered, as first choice by Google, on the topic of apartheid, a ten-year old student site from Stanford University, USA, is immense, even more so in that Stanford is the alma mater of the designers of Google. It is also ironic in that South Africa's National Curriculum (Department of Education 2002a: 6) proposes new approaches to history and social science which aims to 'give space to the silent voices of history and to marginalised communities'. The girls' query has powerful local resonances in the face of which Google's localization features are entirely inadequate.[5] The provenance of the information found by the girls suggests that Google is introducing a very different set of values into the South African curriculum.

An early paper written by Google's founders when they were still PhD students at Stanford presents the values which govern its search algorithm. The paper, which introduced the Google PageRank algorithm to the academic community began with the caveat that '(t)he importance of a Web page is an inherently subjective matter, which depends on the readers [*sic*] interests, knowledge and attitudes' (Page et al. 1998: 1). The paper has the subtitle 'Bringing order to the Web', and goes on to introduce the Google algorithm as an 'objective' way of deciding the 'relative importance' of a web page and thus ranking search results. This shift to an automated editorial judgement claims to remove the potential for overt political bias, commercial interests, and the immense labour costs associated with human editorial judgements. (These were the difficulties on which most human-edited web directories such as Yahoo! floundered.)

Current research suggests that search engines are 'gatekeepers' which, contrary to their claims of being impartial and fair arbiters of value, have developed rules or algorithms which accord disproportionate 'visibility' to certain categories of sites. Past research has highlighted search engine bias in favour of commercial sites, popular sites which are heavily linked, and (the category most relevant to the 1995 student site about apartheid), sites from the U.S., particularly those which have enjoyed the cumulative advantages of having been established for longer, and of gaining traffic and better visibility through the benefits of a high Google ranking (Cho and Roy 2004; Vaughan and Thelwall 2004; and Thelwall and Vaughan 2004, Baeza-Yates *et al.* 2002). Such ranking and indexing decisions are hidden behind a veil of secrecy, and are not subject to public scrutiny or any public service mandate (Introna and Nissenbaum 2000; Van Couvering 2004).

The objective counts which underlie the PageRank algorithm thus 'measure' social interests, in a global context of growing inequities in access to social power and resources. The Google ranking algorithm reflects a set of decisions. which without deliberate intention, make it unlikely that schoolchildren in poorer countries will access the local knowledge of the people around them. Google rewards established pages (Baeza-Yates et al. 2002), and these are very seldom African-based. Google is a conversation broker which favours popular sites and sites which get a lot of attention from the other popular sites. African countries struggle to get any attention in the media and elsewhere, except around issues of war and famine. The search engine industry favours those who have the money to buy attention via public relations, search engine optimization and spam (Machill, Neuberger and Schindler 2003). And Google favours topics which interest many web users. There are simply fewer people online in South Africa or elsewhere in Africa than in the U.S.A. By piggybacking on the human intelligence of the creators of the Web, Google was able to shift away from the spam-cluttered nonsense of the early search engines. At the same time, however, Google also piggybacks on the social prejudices and preferences of these early web authors.

The Google interface has been slotted into the existing patterns of classroom discourse, and lab and classroom drill and practice activities in the classrooms studied, so that it comes to function as a kind of "multiple choice" machine. In this way, both teachers and children treat Google like the educational software discussed earlier, although Google (and other search engines) in comparison to the educational software allowed the children a certain amount of space to explore alternative ways in which they could be used.

In a second example of classroom Googling that we examine here, students carried out their teacher's instruction to use the search engine to investigate two topics, electrical safety, and sound energy. The teacher walked around the classroom to check that everyone was on task, and reminded them what she wanted them to do: "Sound energy first. After that you write down safety rules for electricity. See what they say about sound energy and then go to safety rules." Two students working together typed in "Energy. What are the safety measurs". The result to the query generated a set of results that bore very little relation to the topic (see Fig.1 below). Rather than trying another query which better matched their intentions, they scrolled down the list of results, looking for the bolded words by which Google cues a match with their query. They scrolled all they way down the list, up again, and selected the closest match to their keywords, a press release for Massey Energy, entitled "New safety measures for Massey Energy". (Massey Energy is a large-scale coal producer in Virgina, U.S.A.) Both children wrote down the first paragraph of the press release, which they reproduced verbatim: "Massey Energy has announced new safety initiatives designed to help prevent underground mine fires and to improve mine fire response efforts. Massey Energy is headquartered in Richmond, Virginia, USA with operations in West Virginia, Kentucky and Virginia."

Figure 1. Screenshot of Google search results for the students' query 'energy what are the safety measures'

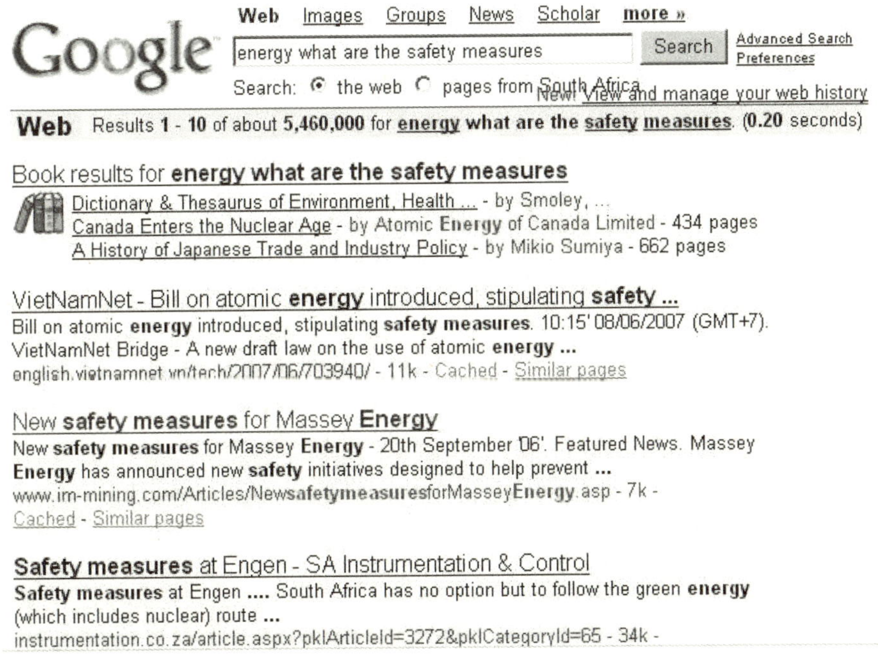
Web Images Groups News Scholar more »

energy what are the safety measures [Search] Advanced Search Preferences

Search: the web pages from South Africa New! View and manage your web history

Web Results 1 - 10 of about 5,460,000 for energy what are the safety measures. (0.20 seconds)

Book results for **energy what are the safety measures**

Dictionary & Thesaurus of Environment, Health ... - by Smoley, ...
Canada Enters the Nuclear Age - by Atomic **Energy** of Canada Limited - 434 pages
A History of Japanese Trade and Industry Policy - by Mikio Sumiya - 662 pages

VietNamNet - Bill on atomic **energy** introduced, stipulating **safety** ...
Bill on atomic **energy** introduced, stipulating **safety measures**. 10:15' 08/06/2007 (GMT+7).
VietNamNet Bridge - A new draft law on the use of atomic **energy** ...
english.vietnamnet.vn/tech/2007/06/703940/ - 11k - Cached - Similar pages

New **safety measures** for Massey **Energy**
New **safety measures** for Massey **Energy** - 20th September '06'. Featured News. Massey **Energy** has announced new **safety** initiatives designed to help prevent ...
www.im-mining.com/Articles/New**safetymeasures**forMassey**Energy**.asp - 7k - Cached - Similar pages

Safety measures at Engen - SA Instrumentation & Control
Safety measures at Engen .... South Africa has no option but to follow the green **energy** (which includes nuclear) route ...
instrumentation.co.za/article.aspx?pklArticleId=3272&pklCategoryId=65 - 34k -

The formal register of the query is partially to blame for the children's lack of success. The phrase "safety measures" (rather than their teacher's suggested phrase "safety rules") and the use of the superordinate category "energy" took them off track. Because they relied primarily on Google's first set of results, and didn't adjust the language of their initial query (beyond correcting the spelling error in "measurs"), the two students didn't find any of the sources their teacher had imagined they could use to complete their first task, and they continued to their next search with only a paragraph from a Mining company's press release, copied *verbatim*. Two neighbouring children had copied the query, received the same results and had also copied the Massey paragraph and so four children in total left the lab with a press release transcribed from a distant American energy company.

The South African National Curriculum for the natural sciences proposes to develop an understanding of science and technology in relation to the local social and natural environment (Department of Education 2002b). It is worth pointing out that in South Africa, and in other parts of Africa, the most prominent dangers of electricity are caused because large numbers of people cannot afford to pay for it. Children are shocked and burnt by wires lying on the ground from illegal connections created to siphon power off the main lines, and by the live ends of wires which have been cut in order to remove their copper. Frequent 'load shedding', or power cuts are problems that have to be dealt with. Finally, the greatest dangers posed to children by electrical power may well be the future environmental costs of climate change. These children's Google search did not take them anywhere near relevant information relating to such issues, underscoring the point again about the bias towards issues affecting well-off countries on the Internet.

The children were considerably more successful at finding materials for "Sound Energy". The first source they came across was written by children and clearly illustrated. It had been created for the ThinkQuest competition. The children read the discussion of sound energy and musical instruments with great attention, and then returned to once again transcribe the first paragraph for their answer. Interestingly, and unlike their previous searches, they continued reading through the Google results even after they had finished their transcription. Although most of the sources they explored were written at a level which was far too complex for them, one student appeared to be trying to make a connection between kinetic energy and sound energy, and continued to try an additional query [kinectic energy].

Overall, though, in the half hour they had in the lab, the students were hardly able to develop their understanding of the set topic in directions imagined by the national curriculum.

Making sense of digital literacy practices in sub-elite school settings

A key insight from the study of literacy as situated practice (also known as the New Literacy Studies: See Street 1983; 2001; Gee 1996; 2003; Prinsloo and Breier 1996; Blommaert et al. 2006) is that literacy is a form of human activity that has to be interpreted contextually, not as an issue of measurement or of skills. The relationship between the practices and norms that shape reading and writing in particular contexts is complex: what counts as effective performance in a setting can be shaped by multiple influences from within and beyond the local setting. The goings-on in sub-elite school settings, such as in the township schools on the fringes of Cape Town that we examined here, have a local distinctiveness in comparison to what happens in well resourced or middle-class schools; yet such settings are often seen only *in relation* to the wider system as 'peripheries' or 'backward areas' and the literacy activities (including digital literacies) are understood as deviant, lacking or deficient. National testing programmes show that the large majority of township children fail at tests of standard orthography, in English and in indigenous African languages; but such tests do not explain what it is that these children do, instead of 'doing things right'. Such tests and assumptions are not much good in giving direction as to what should be done, beyond more testing and more work on 'basic skilling'.

As Blommaert et al (2006: 2) explain it

> The 'margin', so to speak, is not necessarily a space in which people fail to *meet norms,* but it can as well be seen as a space in which *different but related norms are produced*, responding – 'ecologically', so to speak – to the local possibilities and limitations. Such norms, of course, do not matter much in the larger scheme of things. Lifted out of their local context, they bump into the homogenising, singular images of normativity dominant in most societies and get disqualified without much ado.

If these local norms are only seen as lacks, or absences or errors, however, then we fail to take account of how they happen and what to do about them. Approaches to differences in unequal societies that simply see them as errors obscure an accurate view and appraisal of the dynamics in that setting. Strategies for change that don't take account of how local norms are grounded on practices can't deal with the persistence of these 'errors'. Blommaert et al (2006) show this in relation to print literacy 'errors' in their study at one school in Khayelitsha, Cape Town. They show that consistent, patterned and repeated errors in children's writing and spelling display a kind of skeleton writing competence in which acoustic images of words are written that do not match standard orthography. They argue that this displays one particular 'literacy culture' or 'sub-elite literacy economy' (p. 10), with a degree of autonomy in relation to the standardised practices of the mainstream. They argue that the norms or codes of literacy are deployed differently in these settings, in a different system of visualisation of meaning. They constitute a hetero-graphy as opposed to an ortho-graphy.[6] The authors suggest that these literacy practices present a "sociologically realistic" form of literacy in that they mirror the marginalised status of the community in which they occur. The teachers deploy this literacy in their teaching practice, as is clear both in their pedagogy and in the way they correct and mark learners' assignments.

On the basis of this analysis we can go on to examine further how the teaching of literacy and the use of computers and the Internet in classes are embedded in a local economy of semiotic resources. We draw further on the perspective on digital literacies as situated social practice to do so.

Digital literacies as situated social practice

The view on digital literacies that we are applying here conceptualizes literacy as sets of social practices that are contextually embedded and situationally variable, rather than as an autonomous skill, practice or social technology whose forms, functions and effects are unchanging and neutral across social settings (cf. Street 1983, 2001; Warschauer 2003; Snyder and Prinsloo 2007; Walton 2007). Reading and writing, in this view, appear as not exactly the same thing, in their uses, functions, modes of acquisition and status across groups of people and across specific social domains within societies. Blommaert (2002, 3) made this point with regard to language in African settings: "Even if language forms are similar or identical, the way in which they get inserted in social actions may differ significantly and consequently there may be huge differences in what these (similar or identical) forms *do* in real societies". We can say the same about screen-based communication. The transfer of linguistic and semiotic signs across social spaces does not automatically entail the transfer of their functions and values, unchanged.

Following from this epistemological and methodological orientation, digital literacy practices, as one example, have meaning in relation to their contexts of use, rather than having unchanging functions independent of their social location. Reading 'effectively' and 'correctly' does not involve just the finding and decoding of words, images, and multi-media screens but also includes the practices of 'seeing through' the representational resources of the texts to make sense in particular ways, which vary across social settings. Meaning, in this view, is related to the readers' uses of the text. So the same multimedia text on screen is therefore not functionally the same in a different setting. It necessarily follows different meaning conventions, and requires different skills for its successful use, when it functions in different social contexts for different purposes, as part of different human activities. It is no wonder, then, that ethnographic enquiry across multiple sites produces evidence of substantial variety and specificity in the ways reading and writing were embedded in social practices. The particular uses of 'skill and drill' software and 'googling' sessions that we reviewed in this paper are consistent examples of a 'school literacy' culture that is widespread across sub-elite schools in the Western Cape, elsewhere in South Africa (Prinsloo and Stein 2004; Prinsloo 2005) and elsewhere in Africa (Williams 1996)[7]. As Blommaert et al (2006) suggest, this is not simply a restricted or limited literacy whose limits can be seen with reference to 'how things ought to be done'. If we think of digital literacy as an "autonomous" matter of technique ('how to use a search engine to best get the information you need') then we also think that we can "train" people in Internet use as a neatly packaged set of technical skills. We have shown in the data and the arguments above that digital literacies are situated within diverse cultures of reading and writing and need to be addressed as such[8], while tools such as Google are informed by the default values of their designers and users, and these values can and should be challenged.

A key point to recognize in trying to understand these dynamics is that signs of communication (spoken, written, visual, gestural, artefactual) are also and always signs of social value. Bourdieu (1991: 55) made this case with reference to 'linguistic markets' whereby linguistic differences (e.g., of dialect, pronunciation, vocabulary in a common language) in their social uses reproduce the system of social differences, so that particular competencies function as "linguistic capital, producing a *profit of distinction* on the occasion of each social exchange" (p. 3). We can equally think about digital literacy and the new media in similar kinds of ways, as carrying social capital in situated ways within specific social economies, and as working in particular and variable ways depending on how they are inserted in social action in local contexts.[9] When children (and adults, of course) make sense of and interact with particular instances of screen-based, multi-modal writing they always draw on much more than 'purely' linguistic, semiotic and literacy-coding knowledge. An interpretation of any utterance or text always involves an interplay of linguistic, semiotic and social frames of interpretation. So that when children google an answer to a question and faithfully transcribe a paragraph from an obscure foreign web-site, for instance, they are acting consistently with a local cultural understanding of how such literacy acts are and should be done in schools. Such activities both endorse and neutralise (by way of recontextualising processes) the content that they are receiving, giving it an altered and localised significance.

This understanding of how digital literacies work in marginal setting starts to help us understand why, indeed, computers in classrooms are not the silver bullet that will take care of learning problems in marginal African settings. As Snyder (forthcoming: 3) summarises a review of two decades of research on digital literacies and school learning: "there is still no commanding body of evidence demonstrating that students' sustained use of word processing, the Internet and other popular applications has any impact on academic achievement" and she refers to "a growing recognition that computers in classrooms were unlikely to negate the influence of social class on students' achievement" in the context of international research. The earlier research by Snyder et al (2003) studied the effects on academic success that computer access in school and at home had on a range of children from different class backgrounds had on their school achievements. They concluded that such access alone was not enough to enhance young people's literacy achievement at school. They concluded: "Access cannot be seen merely as a matter of having a way to use computers and a connection to the Internet. 'Access' needs to be rethought as a much more complex and multileveled social goal." (Snyder et al. 2003: 381) They conclude that access should be concerned with not only who gets how much of the technology resources but who gets the benefits associated with such resources and how much of them. The work we have presented here addresses the importance of power relations in school-based uses of computers, namely the power differential between teacher and student in classroom discourse, and the power of global software developers in relation to the local educational curriculum. These and other differences in social power should not be overlooked if researchers are to understand the actual practices of people using digital technologies in situated ways.

Notes

1. We talk about digital literacy and digital literacy practices in this chapter to refer to the reading and writing practices via electronic screens on computers (and other electronic devices) and to the linked reading and writing practices that use these electronic media via the Internet and other forms of networked communication.
2. This data and analysis were first presented in Prinsloo (2005).
3. This data is reported on in more detail in Walton (2007).
4. This data is discussed more fully in Walton (forthcoming).
5. Subsequent to this study, localization features have been introduced in Google which ironically, boost the ranking of spam sites which use the keyword 'apartheid', but which exist to sell the African diet drug, Hoodia,
6. The 'errors' are not completely chaotic and display a kind of order. The authors show that many of the (deviant) features that they detected in the learners' writings also occurred in the writing of teachers (One example of teacher writing: "Learners feel shy to speak a minority language. Mostly make use of code switching." Blommaert et al, 2006: 14).
7. Williams (1996) described the dominant pedagogic practice of both trained, experienced and inexperienced teachers in Zambia and Malawi, in the teaching of both first language as well as English reading, as being that of the 'look and say' approach, with no attention to the presentation or checking of meaning.
8. See the papers by Street, Snyder and Warschauer in Baynham and Prinsloo (forthcoming) for further discussion on these conceptual and methodological points.
9. A case in point is the differences in what is considered high status writing amongst academics and amongst cell-phone users. Most older academics identify themselves as clumsy 'digital immigrants' in their 'orthodox' orthography cellphone writing, in comparison to their 'digital native' children.

References

Baeza-Yates, R., Saint-Jean, F., and Castillo, C. (2002) Web Dynamics, Age and Page Quality', in *Proceedings of SPIRE 2002*, September.

Blommaert, J., Muyllaert, N., Huysmans, M. and Dyers, C. (2006) Peripheral Normativity: Literacy and the Production of Locality in a South African Township School. *Linguistics and Education,* 16(4): 378-403.

Blommaert, J. (2002) 'Writing in the Margins. Notes on a Sociolinguistics of Globalization', Unpublished written version of a lecture given at Cardiff University, April 2002, during a workshop of the Leverhulme Trust project on Language and Global Communication.

Bourdieu, P. (1991) *Language and Symbolic Power*. Cambridge: Mass: Harvard University Press.

Castells, Manuel (2000a) *The Information Age: Economy, Society and Culture*, Updated edition, Oxford: Blackwell, 3 volumes.

Castells, M. (1996) *The Information Age: Economy, Society and Culture. Volume 1. The Rise of the Network Society*. Oxford, Blackwell.

Castells, M. (1998) 'Information Technology, Globalization, and Social Development'. Paper prepared for the United Nations Research Institute for Social Development, 'Possibilities for Development in the Information Age'. Geneva, March 22-24.

Cho, J. and Roy, S. (2004) Impact of Search Engines on Page Popularity', in*Proceedings of the 13th international Conference on World Wide Web* (New York, NY, USA, May 17-20, 2004).

Department of Education. 2002a. Revised National Curriculum Statement Grades R-9 (Schools) Social Sciences. Available: http://www.thutong.org.za /resources/ncsdocs/GET/Statements/GET_RNCS_Social%20Sciences_2002.pdf. [11 February 2008].

Department of Education. 2002b. Revised National Curriculum Statement Grades R-9 (Schools) Natural Sciences. Available: http://www.thutong.org.za /resources/ncsdocs/GET/Statements/GET_RNCS_Natural%20Sciences_2002.pdf. [11 February 2008].

Dugmore, C. (2004) 'A New Era in Education', *Khanya: Education through Technology*, 5(3).

Etta, F. and S. Parvyn-Wamahiu (eds) (2003) Information and Communication Technologies for Development in Africa: Volume 2, The Experience with Community Telecentres. Ottowa: International Development Research Centre. Downloaded, Dember 2004. http://web.idrc.ca/en/ev-33004-201-1-DO_TOPIC.html

Gee, J. (2003) *What Video Games have to Teach us about Learning and Literacy*. New York: Palgrave.

Gee, J. (2000) 'The New Literacy Studies: from 'Socially situated' to the Work of the Social', in D. Barton, M. Hamilton and R. Ivanic (eds.) *Situated Literacies: Reading and Writing in Context*. London: Routledge, pp. 180-196.

Gee, J. (1990, 2nd ed.1996) *Social Linguistics and Literacies*. London: Falmer Press.

Kress, G. and T.van Leeuwen, (1996) *Reading Images: the Grammar of Visual Design*. London: Routledge.

Kress, G. (1997) *Before Writing*. London: Routledge.

Kress, G. (2001) Keynote presentation, 'Writing, Knowing, Learning in the Era of Multimodality'. International Literacy Conference, Cape Town, November. Downloaded from http://www.ched.uct.ac.za/literacy/GuntherKress.html

Kreutzer, T. (2008) *'Assessing Mobile Technology Usage in a South African Township School'*, e/merge 7-18 July.

Leu, D., C. Kinzer, J. Coiro and D. Cammack (2004) 'Toward a Theory of New Literacies Emerging From the Internet and Other Information and Communication Technologies', in R. Ruddell and N. Unrau (eds.) *Theoretical Models and Processes of Reading*. International Reading Association. Pre-print copy downloaded, December 2004 from http://www.readingonline.org/newliteracies/lit_index.asp?HREF=/newliteracies/leu

Machill, M., Neuberger, C., and Schindler, F. (2003) 'Transparency on the Net: Functions and Deficiencies of Internet Search Engines', *Info The Journal of Policy, Regulation and Strategy for Telecommunications*, 5(1): 52-74.

One Laptop per Child. (2007) One Laptop Per Child (OLPC), a $100 laptop for the world's children's education. Retrieved July, 2007. http://www.laptop.org/

Page, L, Brin, S., Motwani, R., Winograd, T. (1998) The PageRank citation ranking: Bringing order to the Web, technical report. Available: http://citeseer.ist.psu.edu /page98pagerank.html. [11 February 2008].

Prinsloo, M. (2005) 'The New Literacies as Placed Resources', *Perspectives in Education*, 23(4): 87-98.

Prinsloo, M. and Stein, P. (2004) 'What's Inside the Box?: Children's Early Encounters with Literacy in South African Classrooms', *Perspectives in Education,* 22(2): 67-84.

Prinsloo, M. and M. Breier (1996) *The Social Uses of Literacy: Theory and Practice in Contemporary South Africa.* Amsterdam: John Benjamins.

Reinking, D., M. McKenna, L. Labbo and R. Kieffer (eds.) (1998) *Handbook of Literacy and Technology: Transformations in a Post-typographic World.* Mahwah, NJ: Lawrence Erlbaum.

Sinclair, J. and Coulthard, M (1975) *Towards an Analysis of Discourse : The English Used by Teachers and Pupils.* Oxford: Oxford University Press.

Snyder, I. (forthcoming) Shuffling towards the Future. Draft paper for Baynham, M. and Prinsloo, M. *The Future of Literacy.* London: Palgrave Macmillan.

Snyder, I. (ed.) (1997) *Page to Screen: Taking Literacy into the Electronic Era.* London: Routledge.

Snyder, I. and Prinsloo, M. (eds) (2007) 'Young People's Engagement with Digital Literacies in Marginal Contexts in a Globalised World', *Language and Education,* 21(3) Special Issue.

Snyder, I., L. Angus and W. Sutherland-Smith. (2003) 'Building Equitable Literate Futures: Home and School Computer-Mediated Literacy Practices and Disadvantage', *Cambridge Journal of Education* 32(3): 367-383.

Street, B. (ed.) (2001) *Literacy and Development.* London: Routledge.

Street, B. (1984) *Literacy in Theory and Practice.* Cambridge: Cambridge University Press.

Thelwall, M. and Vaughan, L. (2004) A Fair History of the Web? Examining Country balance in the Internet Archive, *Library & Information Science Research,* 26(2): 162-176.

Vaughan, L. and Thelwall, M. (2004) 'Search Engine Coverage Bias: Evidence and Possible Causes', *Information Processing & Management,* 40(4): 693-707.

Walton, M. (2008) Semiotic Machines: Software in Discourse. University of Cape Town (Ph.D.)

Walton, M. (2007) 'Cheating Literacy: The Limitations of Simulated Classroom Discourse in Educational Software for Children', *Language and Education,* 21(3): 197-215.

Warschauer, M. (forthcoming) Digital Literacy Studies: Progress and Prospects', in M. Baynham and M. Prinsloo (eds) *The Future of Literacy,* London: Palgrave Macmillan.

Warschauer, M. (2003)*Technology and Social Inclusion: Rethinking the Digital Divide.* Cambridge, MA: MIT Press.

Wells, G. (1999) 'Language as Education: Reconceptualizing Education as Dialogue', *Annual Review of Linguistics,* 19: 135-55.

Williams, E. (1996) Reading in Two Languages at Year Five in African Primary Schools, Applied Linguistics, 17(2): 182 – 209.

Celebrating Youth Media and Proposing a Way Forward

Mimi Brazeau

"This will never work". Thirteen years ago, these were the words of one of the national radio station's most influential Directors in West Africa. Plan[1] wanted to initiate the first ever radio show travelling to villages and recording in front a large audience to produce a weekly "live show" exclusively with children. After weeks of lobbying, preparation, training and research, the project was developed and twelve children produced the first Radio Gune Yi 'Youth Radio' show in Senegal. Even the producers had their doubts: can children lead a one-hour show, say interesting things and have a genuine impact on the promotion of their rights? Research done prior to the program's launch revealed that the majority of the population were reluctant to allow children to freely express themselves. However, 1995 seems like many generations ago and Plan West Africa has never stopped producing radio shows and has extended the production and broadcast of youth radio shows to eleven West African countries. Hundreds of committed people and radio stations and thousand of youth have contributed so that children and youth voices can be heard. They even "dared" having an impact on the way people perceived children and youth and on the audiences' intentions (let's be realistic) and actions to respect children's rights.

Plan intends to share the lessons learnt and the best practices through its experience in youth media in West Africa. The vivid testimonies provide undeniable incentives to do more events and the lessons learnt offer a framework to focus on quality both for content and process.

Radio Gune Yi in Senegal

Radio Gune Yi (RGY) is a show produced by different youth each week in a different location and recorded in front of a community. According to the first evaluation made ten years ago[2], the recording of an RGY program is not only a radio broadcast, but a rare local event which has an impact both on the children who participate and their parents, other spectators and decision-makers. Speaking into the mike during a RGY recording is clearly a unique experience for the Senegalese child. It gives them the rare opportunity to express themselves in public, to learn by doing, to show those close to them their capacities and to make themselves heard throughout the country. RGY has also had an impact on parents' attitudes towards their children in communities where the program has been broadcast. The children become not only agents of change, but actors influencing the development of their communities. Children who spoke in the microphone have created a new image for themselves and have earned the respect of the adults in their community. RGY is a project which has obtained remarkable results in terms of promotion of the Rights of the Child. The young traditional chief of Rao said, "Development is done for the future. The future is our children, and if they have knowledge, if they know how to express themselves, it will be good for the village and if things are better in the village, maybe they will stay here."

Radio Gune Yi is still being broadcast today on a weekly basis on Radio Television Senegal. This project has helped set the parameters for more high quality responsible programs produced with youth.

I am a child but I have my rights too! In West Africa

I'm a child but I have my rights too! is an awareness campaign on the rights of the child with a regional perspective created by Radio Gune Y and initiated and produced by Plan and broadcast on radio stations in seven countries across West Africa from 1998 to 2005. With thirty short stories dramatised for radio, the campaign promoted children's right to go to school, to grow up healthy, to have access to potable water and so on. The messages were designed to attract children and their parents by being both informative and entertaining. They defined roles and responsibilities in the defence of children's rights and give concrete advice on child survival issues. Burkina Faso was the first country to launch the radio campaign in 1998. Since then Plan Togo, Senegal, Mali, Guinea, Guinea-Bissau and Benin have produced the drama spots in more than 20 different languages and with the active participation of hundreds of young people.

Presenters, journalists and technicians from more than 90 radio stations have been trained to host the show. 'I'm a child but I have my rights too!' has won several international awards and the evaluation[3] shows that both partners and listeners were very satisfied with the quality of the productions. For the radio stations the involvement in the campaign project often meant that they opened or extended children's slots in their broadcast. The training and the partnership with Plan have built the capacity of the radio stations to improve their programming for a young audience.

Storytelling and educational drama have proved to be effective and popular ways to raise awareness of children's rights in the project countries[4]. The identification factor was high and children could relate the stories directly to their own lives. The messages gave children courage to seek support from adults and to look for solutions to their problems. They gain knowledge, which they also pass on to others by discussing what they heard with their families and friends. Hearing other young people talk on the radio encouraged and motivated children to participate themselves or in other ways make their voices heard.

Children who participate in production and broadcast of such radio program acquired a range of new skills, including communication and vocational skills. They are often empowered to take on new roles and responsibilities in their communities. With this project, Plan demonstrated that children were capable of doing radio shows, giving advice about health issues or creating their own associations. Slowly parents and other adults started to change their attitudes and valued children as actors in the communities.

The campaign contributed to breaking taboos surrounding excision and raised the awareness about issues such as girls' education, discrimination of disabled children and ill-treatment of step-children.

Pape the little hero – a story

Pape is a young boy, handicapped by poliomyelitis. He is often teased by the other children in the village. One day another boy, Boubacar, is in danger and Pape sums up all his courage and manages to save him. Pape shows that he is a brave boy who deserves the friendship of the other children, despite the fact that he is handicapped. Ashamed of his behaviour, Boubacar promises to be Pape's friend and to defend him against the other children. When he proposes that Pape participate in the football game – as a referee – Pape can not hold back his tears of happiness.

This story refers to article 23 of the Convention of the Rights of the Child (CRC): a disabled child has the right to enjoy a full and decent life, in conditions which ensure dignity, promote self-reliance, and facilitate the child's active participation in the community. Its objective is to raise the awareness of problems linked to the integration of handicapped people in their society. This particular story is one of the most popular and became famous in Senegal when it was performed live at the launch of the radio campaign. The First Lady was moved to tears and decided to create a fund for the integration of handicapped children.

Comment from a listener:

> When my mother heard the program on the radio she said that I could start school. She understood that I have to be able to read and write.

In São Domingos in Guinea Bissau 12-year old Genoaria is now about to start her second year in school. She is disabled by polio and her mother "never had the idea to send her to school". Not until she heard the sketch about discrimination of handicapped children on the radio.

The protective star

After the death of her parents, Finda is living with her uncle Abdolaye. Her life is very difficult and her uncle often beats her. One day when she is sent to the well Finda stumbles and breaks the pitcher. When her uncle sees the mess he beats her harder than he ever did before and Finda loses consciousness. In a dream, Finda sees her mother and she begs her to end her misery and suffering. The mother promises to visit the uncle in a dream and tell him to change his behaviour. The next morning the uncle wakes up in anguish, realising how badly he has been treating Finda. He decides to buy her a nice gift and promises not to beat her again.

Article 19 of the CRC gives children the right to protection from all forms of physical or mental violence, injury or abuse, neglect or negligent treatment, maltreatment or exploitation. This is one of the most popular stories. Handling children over to the care of relatives or institutions (child entrusting) is a common practice in West Africa. All too many children have recognised their own fate or that of a neighbour or friend in this story, which seems to have talked directly to the hearts of both children and adults.

Comments from listeners:

> This program is extremely important. Many parents give their children to other adults to raise them and then they are exploited. This campaign tells them that they should treat all children well, not only their own.
> (boy, 15, Guinea Bissau)

> My cousin, who is an orphan, cried when she heard this story. She is not in school and she has to work very hard.
> (girl, 19, Guinea)

Understanding the messages

The weekly and quarterly contests were designed as a game and a distraction for the young listeners but also as a means to verify that the messages were understood. In focus groups and interviews children and adults have proved that they are able to discuss the themes and relate them to their own lives. An issue that has been repeated in evaluations, reports and interviews is a certain reluctance among parents to the notion of children's rights. Rights are perceived to be in conflict with a tradition where children do not question or even address adults unless they are told to do so. Parents have feared that certain messages would "rebel" children and render them impolite and disrespectful. A priest in Sotouboua, Togo, even brought this up in sermon as a potential problem. "Too much talk about rights and not enough emphasis on responsibilities" has been a common remark ever since the first broadcasts in Burkina Faso. Plan has taken this concern seriously and the stories in the second phase of the program clearly accentuated children's responsibilities whereas this was more implicit in the first series. Radio stations have also responded to the reactions with further information and discussion regarding both rights and responsibilities of the child.

This evaluation has found no indications what so ever that an increased awareness of their rights would make children impolite or rebellious. This is confirmed by quantitative data from the mid-term evaluation in Burkina Faso. Out of the 600 child respondents, aged 8-18 years, no fewer than 92% acknowledged that children have duties, such as "doing well at school", "listen to parents and teachers and respect them", "obey the parents" and "help the parents". Asked about a child's responsibilities regarding the right to expression 82% of child respondents answered "to be polite/respectful".

Appreciation of the stories

Earlier evaluations have shown that the stories are very well adapted and appreciated by both children and adults. This can only be confirmed:

> The stories are funny. Sometimes I don't even want them to stop.
> (boy, 11, Guinea Bissau)

> We laughed a lot. It was a very lively program, almost like seeing a play at the theatre. You also had to listen carefully for the question to see if you had captured the answer.
> (father, Guinea)

> Ah, those little stories. Yes, I liked them a lot, especially because children were speaking.
> (Imam, Guinea)

> I have appreciated the fact that even the youngest children are encouraged to express themselves. This is something that has been lacking in our country. We do not foster citizens who know their rights and what they can demand of their authorities.
> (Inspector, Togo)

In the Burkina Faso-evaluation 98% of children found the program "excellent" or "good" and 99% wanted the campaign to continue. 42% of adult listeners expressed strong appreciation of the messages (against 6% who liked it a little or not at all).

Project's impact

> You cannot change people's behaviour just like that. But at least we have tried and I would say that something has happened. Before nobody ever talked about children's rights.
> (Radio director, Benin)

The positive impact on children of meaningful participation in projects that concern them has been repeatedly documented. This evaluation confirms the results of earlier studies: there are many positive changes in the lives of children who have participated in the radio campaign and its related activities.

> The first time I heard my voice on the radio? It was fantastic. The best thing that have happened in my life!
> (boy, 16, Togo)

The first and most obvious effect on children who participated in the project is that they have acquired *communication skills*. This means they can and dare to express themselves, also in the presence of adults.

> I learned how to talk to adults without being afraid.
> (girl, 9, Togo)

> Before I did not dare to talk in front of an audience but now that is as easy as nothing.
> (boy, 13, Togo)

Many parents have appreciated that their children had had the opportunity to learn better French, alternatively to use their mother tongue, during the rehearsals.

Related to this are *technical/vocational skills*; children who participated in the productions worked with professional actors and learned acting techniques and how theatre/radio production works. Children learned to act on stage and in front of a microphone, how to use their voices and how to articulate and interpret their lines.

The participants have also acquired *problem-solving skills,* which are closely related to the increased ability to communicate. Many of the young actors from the productions said that they had changed the way they behave towards siblings and younger children. They have learned to discuss instead of fighting.

> I used to beat my younger brother but I don't do that anymore. I try to talk to him instead. You know, even the youngest children have the same rights as we.
> (girl, 12, Guinea Bissau)

Children have gained *self-confidence*. The theatre activities have helped many children discover their own talents. They have also received the recognition of others. Teachers describe participants in the school theatre groups in Togo as *role models* in the eyes of the other children.

> Through this project children discover what they are able to do. There is now a group of young people who make themselves seen and heard. The other children want to be like them.
> (School inspector, Togo)

Parents often witnessed an *increased dialogue* between them and their children as a result of their participation. With new confidence and an awareness of their right to express their views, children have started to bring up issues that concern them at home. Several other media projects of this type have proved that there is a correlation between the interpersonal dialogue on an issue and a positive change.

Participation in the project gives children *hope for the future*. They have seen that they are able to achieve something concrete. For example, children who participated in theatre activities had the opportunity to see the reactions of the audience and could sometimes witness the direct impact of their work on others. After a theatre performance about child trafficking by Club Anié, Togo, a boy from the audience stepped forward and said that he had his bags packed and was about to leave for Nigeria. Having seen this performance he had decided to stay in his village. The children from the theatre group were very proud of this. They had managed to change something in somebody's life. For them it has been important to help other children:

> If children know their rights they can react when something is wrong.
> (girl, 15, Togo)

Children who participate in this project often become *active in other domains*. Participation gives children a feeling of responsibility and importance and a sense of being useful in the community.

> I remember hearing it [the campaign] on the radio and I wished that everybody would listen so that some things might change in our society.
> (child actor, girl 14, Togo)

Empowerment in this context is about children earning skills and capabilities to take on new roles and responsibilities for the development of their communities and for the promotion and defense of their rights and others. One good example of empowerment is the young people in Britam, Guinea Bissau, who created an association in order to raise funds for a village school (see below).

Case study: Epifanea, child actor (Guinea Bissau)

Epifanea was 14 years old when she was selected to participate to the production of *I'm a child but I have my rights too!*. She had never acted before: "I didn't know anything about children's rights. I learned so much." She played the little girl who does not want to get married to an older man in the story about early marriage:

> When this story was broadcast on the radio I told my father: this is my voice. He listened and I think he understood what it was all about. He said: I will let you wait for marriage until you are ready.

Epifanea thinks that the radio campaign can change things for children in Guinea Bissau. "It can change the minds of parents. I know parents who give their children more freedom because they heard on the radio that we have the right to play." Also for her personally, the campaign has had an impact: "Before I used to fight with other children but now I try to discuss things with them instead."

Impact on families and communities of child participants

A Plan community worker from Togo summarizes the impact that child participation can have on parents and communities: "In our society children are usually considered incapable. With this campaign parents have understood that children have competencies: they can do radio shows and they can give advice about health issues. This is a major step forward! Children are valued in another way – and more and more regarded as useful for the community, able to change something".

Parents have understood the advantages of participation for children. In Guinea for example parents contacted teachers to suggest that they make theatre out of the stories of the campaign.

> Parents appreciated that the campaigned encouraged children to speak out. Some even forced their children to listen to the radio because it made them understand the importance of going to school.
> (Teacher, Guinea)

Impact on listeners

The radio campaign has been heard throughout seven countries with a total population of 60 million people. On its listeners – children and adults – the sketches and the radio programs often made a strong impression.

> This program has been like sunshine in our children's lives – especially for those living in the deep rural areas. It has really mobilised both parents and children.
> (Radio host, Togo)

This and earlier evaluations reveal numerous examples of behaviour change and concrete actions taken by children and adults who listened to the show, notably an increased enrolment of girls in school and better treatment of children.

The baseline studies revealed that the general knowledge about children's rights in all seven countries was very low. There are many indications of an increase in this knowledge, thanks to the radio campaign. In focus groups children say that they were surprised to learn that they not only have duties but also rights. The themes most often cited by children were the right to education, health, leisure and protection against practices such as early marriage and excision. This is confirmed by quantitative data from the Burkina Faso-evaluation, where these were the most frequently mentioned rights. 74% of children were familiar with the right to education (compared to 30% in the baseline study), 34% with the right to health (11% in the baseline) and 20% with the right to rest and leisure (5% in the baseline).

One remarkable difference, according to many interviewees, is that adults have started listening to what children have to say:

> If they talk nonsense three times, maybe the fourth they say something good.
> (father, Togo)

For example, many children (both girls and boys) in interviews and focus groups admit that they did not know before that there were dangers involved or negative effects of excision. With this knowledge they are at least able to try to influence the adults that take the decisions. In Guinea a female teacher tells us how some girls came to her after having heard the story on excision and asked her to talk to their parents. She visited their parents, discussed the preoccupation of the girls and the parents agreed not to excise them.

The campaign has helped breaking the taboos around excision, according to radio journalists. "This had a great influence on people. They have started talking about excision – something that we never did before", says a radio host in Togo, whose radio station broadcast the story on female genital cutting eight times during phase II.

> When people hear about the possible consequences they often change their minds. We invited doctors to the show and now those who say that excision has something to do with religion are losing credibility.
> (Radio host, Guinea Bissau)

There is however a long way to go before certain rights are fully respected. Increased awareness is only the first step.

> Some things are difficult to change. With excision people know it's bad but do it anyway.
> (Zone coordinator, Guinea)

"We children learned a lot, but I think our parents learned even more", says a 12-year old girl in Guinea Bissau. In Burkina Faso, the number of adults who said that they had been informed about child rights through the radio campaign rose from 17 per cent in 1998 (the first year of the campaign) to 60.7 per cent in 2002.

Case study: Child listener: Hawa, 18 (Guinea)

According to Hawa, the rights of young people in Guinea are not much respected. Especially, she says, this is a problem for girls. "You see many girls, young ones, who work in the street as vendors." She insists on the importance of education for girls: "Earlier this year my mother fell ill. My aunt and my father told me that I had to quit school to take care of her." Hawa, who belonged to a listening club at her college, brought home the cartoon book and an audio cassette of the campaign and made her aunt listen to the stories. "Thanks to this program I didn't have to leave school. My aunt decided to take care of my mother until I have finished college."

Empowerment and change

Child listeners in focus groups always stressed the importance of reaching parents with the campaign messages. Many also remarked that it is important for children to know about their rights because with increased knowledge they will be able to defend themselves and others. There are numerous examples of how children, thanks to the radio campaign, actually started to look for solutions to their problems and took the courage to seek support of adults. This was especially evident for radio hosts, since children often turned to the radio for help and advice. Behaviour change in terms of long term changes in social behaviour (such as the practice of excision) is a process which cannot be measured or established in an evaluation of this kind. There are though countless examples of individual change and some strong examples of impact on whole communities. These are without exception villages where Plan is present with committed field workers and where the campaign has been used as a tool in a larger effort to promote children's rights and incite change. Field workers witness about increase in school enrolment and positive effects on hygiene practices and vaccinations.

Other important changes, which children and adults confirm in the focus groups and interviews, are attitudes to equity between girls and boys and a destigmatization of disabled children. After the broadcast of the sketch about "Alpha the little hero", Radio Labé in Guinea received positive feedback from a group of young handicapped bicycle mechanics, who claim that they are met with more respect and friendliness. The impact of information and communication does not end only because the project is completed. It is very likely that the program can contribute to changes quite some time after the end of the broadcast. To create sustainable structures thought, the messages have to be followed up and reinforced. The need to continue with advocacy work related to the rights of the child is repeatedly pointed out:

> Children are still invisible in our society – in spite of campaigns. They might know their rights by heart but they can't apply this in their lives. Which child in Senegal would tell his or her parents what they think about a subject?
> (Radio director, Senegal)

Change is not happening over-night and both children and adults seem to have realistic expectations. "For a long time we have talked about children's duties. Now we talked about their rights. It came almost like a shock to the community", says one radio director in Benin.

The following example from a village in Guinea Bissau highlights the strengths of the entire radio campaign project. Here we see how young people become aware of their rights (to education), organize themselves, seek adult support (the radio station) and manage to mobilise the whole village for their sake:

> Child listener: Lazard, 14 (Benin)
> "I never ever want to go back to Nigeria again". When Lazard was 11 years old his parents were convinced to send him away by a Nigerian friend who lived near their village, in Bohicon, Benin. "He said that everything was better for children there. He gave 20 000 CFA[5] to my parents. I didn't see them again for two years." Lazard discovered that nothing was like the man had promised. He had to work hard at a construction site. One day he fell ill and the people he was staying with hit him to make him go to work: "There was a lot of blood. They didn't take me to hospital. I cried and begged them to send me back to my village but they refused." One day Lazard met a man from his village in Benin at the market. He asked the man to tell his father to come and bring him home. Lazard waited and after three months he saw the man again. This time he hung on to him until he brought him back to the village. Lazard still has scars and a deformation of the cranium from the assault he was exposed to. He often complains about headaches. He has joined a reintegration project by NGO Crap in the village Gbozoun in central Benin.

All children in his class have been trafficked and many share his experiences of ill-treatment and exploitation. NGO Crap has worked with Radio Carrefour and with audio tapes of the *I am a child but I have my rights too!* campaign messages and today these children are well aware of their rights. Some of them say that they would not dare to talk about their rights with their parents, but that they share what they have learned with other children and tell them to listen to the messages on the radio. Lazard insists that the campaign must continue: "Nobody pays attention to us. But when the radio says that we have rights, maybe parents will listen."

> When children know their rights they get confidence. Before in the villages you had to get married once you had reached the age of 17. Your future was determined. But when young people know their rights they might be able to change that, to take their own decisions. This campaign encourages young people to take their future in their own hands.
> (Teacher, Guinea Bissau)

Evaluations have also repeatedly proved the impact of this project on its young listeners, their parents and their communities. Numerous examples show how the increased knowledge and awareness of children's rights have led to a strong mobilization for their defence – which means that the project has reached its global objective. The obvious follow-up question is: how sustainable are these changes? The first step in a social change process is generally recognition of a problem, which can lead to the identification of a solution.

This evaluation of *I am a child but I have my rights too!* reveals important lessons – not only about the campaign, its implementation and impact – but also about young people and their communities in West Africa today. It is clear that children still have very few opportunities to express themselves in the media and that the project therefore is highly relevant. *I'm a child but I have my rights too!* fills a gap and is innovative in terms of radio broadcasting for children in a region that offer little media content, interesting programming or distraction for children.

In many ways the campaign can be seen as a direct response to the Oslo Challenge, which acknowledges that "the child/media relationship is an entry point into the wide and multifaceted world of children and their rights – to education, freedom of expression, play, identity, health, dignity and self-respect, protection – and that in every aspect of child rights, in every element of the life of a child, the relationship between children and the media plays a role". Moreover, by developing partnerships and strengthening the capacity of the partners the radio campaign project facilitates others to be able to live up to the challenge as well.

For Plan in West Africa this campaign is an encouraging experience to draw on in the development of new media initiatives, further exploring how children can be involved and earn the skills and confidence necessary to take on new responsibilities in their communities.

Kids Waves West Africa

Today in West Africa, Plan, partners and youth from 10 countries broadcast radio shows replicating the positive lessons learnt from Radio Gune Yi Senegal and the radio campaign on child rights broadcast in West Africa. New programs have been created involving young artists in creating songs highlighting youth issues and children rights.

In 2006 in Mali, Plan organised the Youth Media Development Forum (YMDF'06) where more than 400 delegates, experts and youth, from more than 60 countries (most of them developing countries), discussed how to do more and how to improve what we do. The 5th World Summit on Media for Children held in South Africa also allowed for fruitful discussions on high quality responsible media. Plan, partners and youth played a major role in arguing media programs with youth should expand in all parts of the world.

Children and youth have to be part of the discussions on matters that affect them. The media have the responsibility to involve them in the social dialogue. The acknowledgement of their potentialities will lead to the recognition of their capacities. Children and youth know best how to reach their peers, and they also attract an 'older' audience interested in knowing what's going on with one third of the world's population who have not yet reached the so called 'majority'. That's two billion individuals with dreams, concerns, aspirations and ideas – most of them desperately seeking for a better world, a better life. Changing things, improving things will happen with them – or will not occur.

Youth need to understand that their voice is of interest to the general public if it raises the debate to better understand what they live and experience; they need to ensure that what they say helps the audience make informed choices. They need to ensure that the messages conveyed are easily digested; they need to influence the audience to ensure they understand the dangers linked to ignorance which leads to mistrust, incomprehension and chaos. In order to succeed – and it is quite a challenge all media makers and youth need to ask themselves every day "How can we do better to reach the audience so that people feel informed, inspired and motivated to change and improve things?"

Talking about youth issues is very important; having youth voices taken into account is vital. But all this has depth and meaning if actions follow the dialogue. Broadcasters and producers should consider this as part of their mandate to produce more high-quality responsible media programs with youth and for youth; to be ethical and child-aware; to assist and put pressure on governments to honour children rights; to share resources and skills with those requesting assistance. The public media should honour their mandate with regards to the UN Convention on the Rights of the Child while the private sector should not hide behind the fact they are profit-oriented and that they themselves did not sign or ratify charters or legal documents stating their social responsibilities.

Ten years ago, the World Bank[6] asked thousands of people what they desired most. Having a 'voice' was one of the most frequent replies; second after to improve income and basic necessities. Not being able to have a say in decisions that affected their lives was identified as a key element of poverty in itself.[7] Today, with new technologies growing and expanding to the most remote areas, the desire to be part of the social dialogue has probably increased. Youth should continue to request to be heard, but they should also ensure they convey their messages with accuracy, in their own words, from many angles; and with the creativity and seriousness needed to reach and convince as many people as possible. Today, youth express themselves as young citizens, demanding their rights and trying to understand why positive changes do not occur as fast as they grow up. The Millennium Development goals and the promised results for 2015 are not close to being achieved. Engaging into the debate those who will be the first target of today's failures is one way of ensuring they will feel not only part of the problem but of the solutions also.

Notes

1. Plan is an international NGO working in 66 countries worldwide to achieve lasting improvements for children living in poverty in developing countries. Plan's vision is of a world in which all children realise their full potential in societies which respect people's rights and dignity.
2. Radio Gune Yi Evaluation, The Centre for Development Communications, Washington, USA, 1998.
3. I am a child but I have my rights too! Evaluation, Rosita Ericsson, 2005.
4. The following text for this section is taken from the evaluation of the project.
5. Approximately 28 Euros.
6. World Bank (1999) Voices of the Poor, Washington, DC, US.
7. Extract from Panos London Illuminating Voices, the Case for Communication in Sustainable Development, 2007, London, UK.

Beyond Child Participation

Tracking Progress of Media Education for Children and Young Persons in Ghana

Sarah Akrofi-Quarcoo

It has been over two decades now since educators and researchers, under the aegis of UNESCO, began advocacy for media education to empower consumers particularly children, to cope with the negative influences of the media's "omnipresence" and engulfing power. Media education seeks to provide consumers with critical knowledge and analytical tools so that they can derive greater benefits from the ongoing technological revolution. Globally, progress is reported to be uneven and incoherent.[1] There is evidence of advancements made in some countries notably, Great Britain, Canada and Australia which have long histories of practice. However, in other regions of the world, practice is yet to move from the experimentation phase to that of widespread use[2]. This paper tracks media education delivery in Ghana, a country that has witnessed immense transformation of its mass media and telecommunication landscape and also educational reforms in the past decade or more. It examines potential sites for media education delivery including school curricula and discusses the children's radio programme *Curious Minds* as a "silent" approach to media education practice in Ghana based on the concept of child participation.

Why media education

International discourses on media education point to a growing need to employ appropriate education strategies to counter negative media influences on society and especially on children and young persons. Media Education experts suggest that such strategies need to blend critical literacy with experiential learning and critical pedagogy (Tyner, 1998). The UNESCO initiated Grunwald Declaration of 1982, issued by 19 representatives from various countries outlined the principles underlying media education in the following statement:

> We live in a world where media are omnipresent: an increasing number of people spend a great deal of time watching television, reading newspaper and magazines, playing records and listening to radio…Rather than condemn or endorse the undoubted power of the media, we need to accept their significant impact and penetration throughout the world as an established fact, and also appreciate their importance as an element of culture in today's world. The role of communication and media in the process of development should not be underestimated, nor the function of media as instruments for the citizen's active participation in society.

In 1999, recommendations at the Vienna Conference on "Educating for the Media and Digital Age", clarified the objectives of media education as: ensuring that citizens learn how to analyse, critically reflect upon and create media texts; identify sources of media texts; understand the media's political, social, commercial and/or cultural interests and their contexts; interpret messages and values offered by the media[3] in all forms – print, symbols, representation, sounds and images. Media education demands that citizens are empowered to "take a certain distance towards immediate pleasures that media can provide" (Waheed Khan, 2008: 15) and appreciate the media's other sides. As Considine (1995) asserts, the greater concern of media educators is about ideology, power, and social relations. Ultimately, media education has a vision of "social justice and critical citizenry" (Prinsloo, 1999: 163) and also "democratic participation" (Domaille and Buckingham, 2001).

From protection to empowerment

The philosophies and ideals of media education represent a paradigm shift from protection against harmful media effects, to that of empowerment. Media consumers both young and old, need media education. However, children and young persons are considered the primary targets, partly because they are perceived to be vulnerable to media effects resulting from their relatively closer association with media technologies. In most countries, the screen media have become a "parallel school" or "surrogate teacher"[4] for young persons and children. A 2003 Kaiser study by Rideout et al reported that children six and under spend an average of two hours a day with screen media mostly television and video. From the protectionist perspective, such intense exposure to media must be controlled in order not to harm children's development. In some countries the media regulation regimes are not the best or non existent. However, there is evidence that regulation and self-regulation measures such as restricted viewing by parents, scrambling devices and the V-Chip have not been quite effective given the fact of media globalisation, the upsurge in interactive media technology and also changing experiences of children and young persons. Media education therefore is considered a response to the search for new approaches to encouraging productive and responsible use of media.

The option of empowerment considers target groups as "sovereign" "lively, street-wise and self confident" (Waheed Khan, 2008: 15) persons, capable of reacting rationally to media content. This is in line with the principles of autonomy as spelt out in Articles 12, 13 and 17 of the UN Convention on children's rights. As Angeles-Baustista (1999) points out, the best investment one can make for children is to support them to be critical media users rather than leave them to be "totally mesmerized and powerless" under media influence.

Who takes charge?

Media education is an "all hands on deck" activity, involving teachers, parents, schools, researchers, and civil society, among others. The decentralised nature of media education also means, there are varied approaches to delivery, and much depends on the social context and cultural context. However, in a majority of cases, teachers have been the primary drivers with the school or educational system, as the host. For example in the UK, teachers of English began the process by engaging with students' experiences of media including cinema and the popular press. According to Buckingham (1999), by initiating this process, "teachers sought to demonstrate what they perceived as the moral or aesthetic limitations of the media."

In Canada, teachers have been in the forefront of media education which started as part of film courses in secondary schools. According to Anderson et al (1999) one of the approaches to media education in Ontario is an "ontological function in which students' relationship with fantasy, reality, one another and the world are sorted out." As part of this function, values of students and media messages are examined and evaluated. By so doing, students are able to prioritise their own values through critical analysis.

Australia is another leader in media education where the concept emerged as a force within the educational system. According to McMahon and Quin (1999), media education has been variously packaged in English courses, Arts programmes and also in a learning area called Technology/Technology and Enterprise.

In the Nordic countries, for example, in Finland, media education has since the 1970s, been a part of primary and high school education. According to Tufte (1999) the subject has been integrated with Finnish art and history. In Sweden, as in the case of Canada, media education is a compulsory subject in schools, Film studies have been taught as part of media studies. Outside the Nordic countries, for example in Germany, media education has been progressing at various levels within and outside the established school system.

Media education programmes have also been driven by parents, activist groups, churches and religious communities. For example, in Latin America, the Catholic Church has been instrumental in training housewives, the youth, community leaders and other social groups to exercise their right to participate in media activities. In the Philippines, Children's Television Foundation (PCTVF) led an initiative geared towards empowering children to understand the media. In 1996, PCTVF designed and implemented a project that involved children in using various forms of media to express themselves and to process their thoughts on their rights (Angles-Bautista, 1999).

Examples of similar school projects are rare in Africa and as Domaille and Buckingham (2001) noted in a global youth media survey, few media education programmes exist outside formal schools. The Catholic Church has been a key initiator of the process on the continent for example in Chad, Zimbabwe and Mozambique. Neighbouring Nigeria with whom Ghana shares cultural and social experiences has recently called for the institution of media education for children and young persons. Significantly however, quite a number of countries on the continent encourage children's participation in media which has implications for media education. The subject is discussed later in the paper.

A case for Media Education for children and youth in Ghana

Kumar (1999: 244) argues, that the "root of media education lies deep in the anxieties of industrialised West to come to terms with the growth of mass media" that are "spawned by the industrial revolution" and "hailed as great progress for mankind" but condemned for the "popular urbanised culture" created as a result. However, beneficiary countries of this technological revolution have their own share of the anxieties. In Ghana, such apprehensions have been nursed since radio was introduced in the Gold Coast in 1935. A primary concern of the colonial government then, was to 'inoculate' citizens against "undesirable ideas which might come from outside" Ansah (1985) especially through radio.

In 1965 when television was introduced, the concern was more urgent given the visual nature of the medium. The mandate of the state owned station, whose transmission then was largely urban focused, was "education and edification' and not to cater for "cheap entertainment" or "commercialism".[5] Accordingly, programming content was projected at 80 percent local productions and 20 percent foreign programmes. But this target has hardly been achieved even after 43 years of television in Ghana.

The uneasiness about cultural adulteration heightened with the onset of media pluralism and the demise of broadcast monopoly in the early 1990s following the deregulation of media and communications technologies. As at May 2007, the National Communications Authority, (NCA) responsible for granting communication licenses and broadcast frequencies, had licensed a total of 167 FM radio stations to operate[6] out of which 130 are on air across the country. Twenty-four private radio stations and five television station are currently operational in the Accra-Tema metropolis, an area with an estimated population of 3 million.

Forty-four paid television services using terrestrial VHF/UHF frequencies as well as one cable television have been licensed to operate. Also granted licenses are over 104 Television Receive Only Stations (TVRO)[7] including satellite redistribution channel stations. DSTV, run by Multichoice Africa is a leading provider of satellite broadcast in Ghana with channels from Africa, Britain and the USA. Across Africa, Ghana is one of the largest subscribers of DSTV[8]. The facility is available largely in hotels across the country but also in elite homes in the cities. The NCA projects that by 2015 television will be completely digitalised making it possible for television stations to operate more than one channel.

While the development has been hailed for expanding children's viewing and listening choices, the uneasiness over what children actually view and hear on radio remain afloat. The growth in the number of radio and television stations, has not translated into expanded space for children on the stations. Few children's programmes are available on local private television stations; all the children's programmes aired on these stations are foreign originated,[9] from the Big Three" producers of American children's programmes – Nickelodeon, Cartoon Network and Disney.

Out of the 130 radio stations currently operational in the country, only a fraction are committed to children's programming. The public service station, Radio Ghana, whose mandate is to cover all marginalized groups including children, airs 7 children's programmes weekly in English and six local languages.

Besides lack of interest in programming for children, television stations have been criticised for displaying poor judgment and taste in the images shown and for bad programming especially broadcasting inappropriate films during hours children watch television (Gadzekpo, 2003). A study on Children's Perception of Cartoon Programmes in Ghana earlier in 2000 showed that 76% of children watch television daily.[10] In addition to animated programmes, Ghanaian children are also exposed to a variety of entertainment genres mainly from the United States, Europe, Latin America, Nigeria and South Africa. These include films, telenovelas, reality shows and music programmes mainly targeted at adults.

Television is also held culpable for the falling standard of the English language – the language of instruction in schools – because children are perceived to spend more time watching television than they do on reading. This appears a peculiar problem for some African countries. For example, a study in Egypt showed that television influences children's reading habits and also their preferred reading materials (Kamel (1995) quoted in Tayie, 2008).

The expansion of Internet services is another cause for anxiety. Although penetration is growing rather slowly, estimated at 2.7 percent as at 2007[11], there are concerns over unrestricted access of the facility to children with particular respect to pornographic content.[12]

Legislation/government action

Sadly, legislation and regulation lag way behind the expansion and transformation of the media landscape. For example, after nearly 15 years of broadcast liberalisation in Ghana, there is no broadcast law to regulate the operations of the expanding industry. The legislative framework for children's programming is also considered weak (Gadzekpo, 2003). The legislative framework of the telecommunication sector is equally poor. A group – Advocacy Committee on Broadcast Law – which has been working on a broadcast law for Ghana, recently submitted to government, a draft Broadcast Bill. Areas covered in the bill include funding, frequency authorisation, programming, ownership and control and as well, human resource development. The bill proposes, among others, that programmes must uphold editorial freedom and independence, strengthen and promote local culture and heritage, and be sensitive to children's programming as detailed in the *African Charter on Children's Broadcasting 1997*. Incidentally, there is little information in the Charter specific to media education.

While post-colonial regimes in Ghana have also not been unconcerned about public anxieties flowing from the media's growth, it is significant to note that much of the expression of concern has been confined to speeches and policy documents. Such documents do not suggest media education but they seem to promote the old thinking that children ought to be protected and defended against media influence based on concerns for nationality, culture and the public good. For example, in the early part of the 2000s a media policy document published by the National Media Commission (NMC) – the constitutional body with oversight responsibility of the media – noted:

> Our culture in all its rich diversity has through our history been the fabric and the product of communication among our people and with others. It is our desire that technologically-mediated communication be similarly interwoven. Traditional and modern communication should interact with our people to build and maintain their own distinctive many–roomed dwelling within the global village. (National Media Commission, ISBN 9988-572-65-4).

In September 2007, the ruling government of the New Patriotic Party (NPP), launched a National Orientation Programme which seeks to re-orient the thinking of the citizens especially, the youth to appreciate their beliefs, culture and values rather than foreign ones. Oboshie Sai-Cofie, then Minister of Information and National Orientation[13] stated:

> The youth, particularly, are becoming alienated from their traditions and culture and are rather increasingly embracing foreign cultures as portrayed in their mode of dressing, exposure to foreign films and their attitude to elders and authority. We as parents, teachers and all who share responsibility for the upbringing of our youth must endeavour to insulate them from negative habits and culture and inculcate in them, a proper sense of discipline and decorum. The media, print, radio and television, need to take a closer look at the language and content of their publications and programmes and endeavour to give greater attention to the promotion of Ghanaian ethical and cultural values. (http://www.ghana.gov.gh)

The statement falls short of calling for media education. Importantly however, it calls for measures to insulate children from negative habits linked to media which implies "protection" but also media education. What then is the status of media education delivery in Ghana? What programmes/approaches exist in schools/curriculum at primary to tertiary levels? What recognisable programmes exist at the civil society level and by youth media groups?

Educational /school programmes

School Curriculum

It has been suggested that since it aims at promoting critical and analytical thinking, media education should become the foundation of basic skills, common to school curricula (Bevort et al; 2008). While in some countries, media education is said to be "struggling for recognition in its own right" (Domaille and Buckingham, 2001), in Ghana the concept appears a 'stranger' even to drafters of the country's educational curricula. Authorities at the Curriculum Research and Development Division (CRDD) of Ministry of Education are unaware of media education delivery in schools as Dr. Ruby Avortri,[14], Acting Director of the (CRDD) and Kwabena Nyamekye[15] in charge of English language curriculum indicated.

Language, film studies, arts and literature courses, are recognised sites for the integration of media education programmes in advanced countries. However information obtained from the CRDD does not suggest that media education has been integrated into any course at the basic and secondary levels.

In 1987, Ghana's education system was reformed for the first time since 1961 to replace the British-based system. The change was in response to criticisms that "the level of education has been overly academic and removed from the country's development and manpower trends.[16]" Consequently, in addition to English, Mathematics, General Science, French, Ghanaian Language and Art, courses such as pre-vocational skills, Pre-Technical Skills, and social skills (later changed to Social Studies) and Religious and Moral Education were made part of the curriculum at the primary and Junior Secondary School levels. Although it may be argued that English Language subjects such as comprehension and also English Literature encourage creative and critical thinking, the teaching of these subjects usually tends not to inspire the kind of competencies required to analyse and interpret other forms of media aside the printed text.

The country's second educational reform was launched in September 2007 and it aims at meeting the challenges of the millennium. Among the challenges of the millennium is the rapid diffusion of media and media technologies with attendant impact on children and young persons' development. Incidentally, in the process of the revision, an attempt was made to drop Religious and Moral Education. The move was forcefully resisted, largely by faith based schools who probably perceived the subject as the only classroom based option to cushion children and young persons against the devouring effects of media content.

Like parents, teachers, moved by moralistic pangs and also the determination to get children committed to their books have maintained a double standard attitude towards media. While admonishing children against watching television (protectionist perspective)[17] teachers tend to complement classroom teaching with illustrations from television programmes, as the medium is perceived to provide easier frame of reference for children. In addition, teachers give assignments that require information from television (cultural perspective).

A junior secondary school pupil intimated that their science class was once assigned to watch various television channels for a month and analyse the trend of weather reportage on the different regions. The point was confirmed by Avortri and Nyamekye who noted that television serves as information sources for science, social studies and English language subjects. Students at the senior secondary school level are encouraged to complement classroom learning of oral English with listening to radio and watching television news programmes.[18] Meigs (2003) observes that the cultural perspective involves critical analysis. However, it may be argued that this analytical capacity resulting from the cultural perspective may be limited and fall short of the expectations of media education principles and goals.

Media and related courses

Formal education on the mass media in Ghana is a phenomenon of the last 40 years, predominantly confined to tertiary or university level as professional disciplines. Generally, Ghanaian children qualify for tertiary education by age 18. By extension, majority of the country's children are completely cut off learning about media until they are adults. And even that, the decision to learn about media is a matter of choice and interest.

Until 1972 when the University of Ghana established the School of Communication Studies (SCS), the Ghana Institute of Journalism (GIJ) was the only media training institution. Later in 1978, the National Film and Television Institute (NAFTI) was established, to train students for the film industry. Since the 1990s following media de-regulation, there has been a growth in the number of institutions that offer media training. None of these institutions offer a specific course on media education.

Generally, the SCS course prepares Masters of Arts and Master of Philosophy students for industry and careers in academia. In addition to core subjects in Print Journalism, Broadcast Journalism, Advertising and Public Relations, other courses offered include communication theories, Media, Culture and Society and Research Methods as well as elective courses in Public Opinion, Telecommunications, Communications Technology and International Communication. Media education does not feature as a separate subject but it is incorporated largely in communication theories and practical broadcasting production classes. Students learn theories such as reception analysis; representation and stereotyping; theories on the political economy of media, media constructions and deconstruction among others some of which are applied in broadcast production and research.

The GIJ offers courses at the degree and diploma levels similar to what one obtains at the SCS. Teaching is directed at building students' professional competencies to function effectively in media industry. Here too, student productions constitute a component of the training. The NAFTI programme which has been upgraded to a degree one offers theory and practical courses in film production, screen writing and directing, acting technology, television, photography and stagecraft. However, the numbers of students who graduate from these media institutions every year do not translate into the quality of productions most children are exposed to. Given the high cost of production, some qualified producers, directors and script writers have left their profession in the hands of untrained and unqualified persons. Therefore it is difficult to pass judgment on the impact of the education received.

Educational broadcasting

Although at independence Ghana inherited a national broadcast institution created for propaganda purposes (Article 19), there was also no doubt about the government's interest in radio as a tool for in-and-out of school education. Right from the onset the adolescent school boy and girl and the "widely scattered and influential body of teachers" were targeted with programmes meant to change their outlook. Direct broadcasting to schools – Schools broadcast – was introduced on radio in 1956, to "supplement and enrich work done in the classroom but not to replace the teacher."[19]

The radio schools broadcast supported the government's Accelerated Development Plan for Education launched in 1951/52. Training colleges and schools, from primary to secondary schools were target beneficiaries. It could be inferred from the lessons, that the broadcasts were meant to improve citizens' ability to read printed text, to appreciate African culture and to speak the English language well. Lessons included English pronunciation, English Literature, African History, English Language and book reviews in local languages. There were also programmes for general listening – "Everyday English" and "Parlons Francais".

Television broadcasting to schools later complemented the radio broadcasts in promoting Ghana's Accelerated Development Plan on Education. In 1973 the educational television service folded up due to technical and economic problems. The radio broadcasts were also discontinued some years later. However, the television programme was re-introduced in the early 2000s as one of several projects under the "President's Special Initiative" with a focus on Distance Learning. Lessons in English, Mathematics and Science are packaged by professional teachers for junior secondary and senior secondary school students.

This instrumental use of broadcasting for education has different objectives from what media education propagates. While the former seeks to support teaching and learning, the latter provides knowledge and understanding and encourages a critical attitude towards the medium, functions, programme content, as well as production issues. The common denominator of the two approaches however, is children's relationship with broadcasting as a source and provider of education and learning. Educational broadcasting is an example of partnership between broadcasters and teachers which could be developed to support media education programmes. With this partnership, some of the challenges that may impede the delivery of media education in schools such as lack of teachers and large classes may be overcome.

Information literacy in schools

The emergence of new information, communication technologies (ICTs) such as the Internet and computers, seem to be opening up opportunities for media education in schools particularly, at the primary and secondary levels through information literacy programmes. Acquiring information literacy skill, as has been explained in various UNESCO documents, means empowering citizens with both the technical skills to use and apply modern ICT such as computers, the Internet to access and create information, to navigate in cyberspace and negotiate hypertext multimedia documents and as well, skills to interpret information. Ghana's ICT policy launched in 2003 has a mission to transform the country into an"information-rich, knowledge-driven high income economy and society"[20]. One of the strategies for achieving this mission is to "promote the deployment and exploitation of information, knowledge and technology within the economy and society as key drivers for socio-economic development".[21] To this end, information literacy programmes are being promoted in schools.

In 2005, the Ghana Associated Schools Project Network (ASPnet) with support from UNESCO's Information for All Programme (IFAD) trained teachers and head teachers of secondary schools in ICT application and skills for twinning among ASPnet schools. The objective is to promote quality education through Internet access. Beneficiary schools in Tamale, the Northern region of Ghana, were provided additional equipment for ICT centres after their training. The ASPnet project currently involves 130 public schools at the primary and secondary levels in Ghana.

In addition to training teachers, about 148 Information Literacy centres are being established across the country for use by people such as out-of-school unemployed and under-employed adults; migrant and refugee populations; disabled. A programme to computerise all public schools is expected to be completed by 2011 by which time computer studies will be an examinable subject for the Basic Education Certificate Examinations (BECE) level.

Child focused Civil Society Group

Among the few organisations that have shown some commitment to children and media in Ghana is Women in Broadcasting (WIB). This is an organisation of producers, reporters, directors, programme makers and editors which engages in women and child advocacy using the electronic media. Its approach to media education has been through training workshops in programme production and presentation. Between 1999 and 2003, WIB provided a series of training workshops for in-and-out of school children across the country. Over 400 school children and 100 out-of-school children benefited from the training programmes.

Those in schools were introduced to skills in production, interviewing, news writing, and presentation. Training emphasised participation in the media as one of the rights to freedom of expression and as well freedom to impart knowledge and ideas based on children's realities. The training for participants outside formal schools targeted "porters" apprentices and street children who were exposed to some films on violence and sex. The viewing sessions were followed by discussion and critique sessions. Their attention was drawn to issues beyond the aesthetic values of the films to image construction, deconstruction, reality and representation as well as audiences and reception issues. Participants shared opinion on how children were portrayed in the films.

Children and Youth in Broadcasting runs similar training programmes for children in media. The do-it-yourself approach enables children to learn about the media. The group produces a weekly programme called *Curious Minds* where the principles of child participation are applied.

Child participation in radio – *Curious Minds*

Radio programmes run by children for children have been a "silent" approach to media education for children based on the ideals of children's participation. The approach is considered 'silent' because of its indirect and informal nature and also because it is not widespread. To a large extent, radio (largely public radio) remains the most reliable and effective medium for children's participation programmes in Ghana. UNESCO figures on population and ICT for Ghana[22] show that there are about 2.5 million radio household as compared to 955,000 television households. Radio is therefore a powerful media for social change. By participating in radio, children "become producers of media in their own right"(Buckingham, (2001). But also they are empowered to use the medium as a strategy to promote social transformation. The example of *Curious Minds* is worth sharing.

Curious Minds

Curious Minds is one of the few locally produced children's radio programmes. The magazine programme is produced by the Children and Youth in Broadcasting – a group that works to support advocacy on children's rights – for children. The hour-long programme is broadcast live in English and Ga[23] on the public service stations, Uniiq FM and Obonu FM, both transmitted from the capital Accra and received across the country (in the case of programmes on Uniiq FM). Production is done under the supervision of a broadcaster known by the group as the coordinator. Two founding members of the club, now above 18 years, assist the coordinator.

The programme has a 15-minute "partnership segment" which discusses topical subjects on children that occur in the media during the week. The segment explores children's role in addressing the issues from a rights perspective. Ten to 15 minutes are devoted to "Letters to the One Who Cares". This segment targets teachers, parents, political leaders and policy makers and solicits their commitment to children's rights. The "facts corner" a five minutes segment on science and general knowledge is followed by a 30 to 35 minute discussion segment that occasionally, includes phone-ins and musical breaks before the discussions.

What makes *Curious Minds* unique as an approach to media education is that it encourages full participation of children at all three levels of production – pre-production, production and post production. For Kingsley Obeng Kyere,[24] Coordinator of the programme and a trained broadcaster, these three stages of the production provide opportunities for learning, analysis, consultation and interpreting media content. For example, at the combined pre-production and post production meetings held prior to the live broadcast days, the group takes decisions on themes, content, format; selection of resource persons and the direction of the programmes.

As well, members evaluate and critique the previous weeks' programmes. Through the various roles, children get a better understanding of theoretical issues such as stereotyping, representation, image construction, and the use of appropriate words and language. Also children offer invaluable perspectives on some of the critical issues of the times such as child abuse, child labour, and affirmative action for girls etc. Full participation at all three stages does not only provide children with enough practical experiences but also equips members of the group with analytical, critical and creative skills to interpret other media content.

Kingsley Obeng Kyere said the process underscores the principles of media education. According to him, children can not go on air if they do not know how the media function, or understand gate keeping process or do not understand some of the factors that go into; for example, selecting resource persons. He believes that this form of education is critical for children who need to understand the media better in order to exercise the right to impart knowledge and ideas to others.

The child to child and also the "self" approach to teaching and learning is equally unique. At the production stage, that is, during the live broadcast, children express themselves freely and play their assigned roles without promptings from adults. Adult presence could be intimidating and usually does not encourage critical debate. Obeng Kyere said the physical context of production involving working in the studio and handling equipment is another unique learning opportunity as compared to classroom learning. Experiences are personal and direct rather than remote. Children get better grasp from practicing how to handle, control and manipulate sound.

Some of the children see participation in media as psychologically rewarding as the process provides them the opportunity to explore their own identities and emotional investments in the media. The absence of adults boosts their self development, consciousness and promotes critical thinking as well as problem solving skills.

Much of the success of the youth media or children's participation approach as shown by *Curious Minds* could be attributed to the roles by the public station (which allows children space to "experiment" with their equipment) and the producer, who gives children the opportunity to explore their talents and creativities. The nature and level of participation that is encouraged is equally significant in order to achieve the ultimate objective of empowering children to be responsible media users and consumers. This level of participation encouraged is possible largely on public stations as a local study has shown[25].

Another lesson from this case study is that much depends on adults to make children's participation in media work so as to realize the principles of media education. Some of the challenges outlined by members of the group that work dangerously against media education include how adult producers perceive children and therefore their preparedness to provide children the opportunity to learn and understand the media.

Conclusion

Ghana is not unchallenged by the issues for which a media education movement is being promoted. Yet, relatively little progress seems to have been made beyond children's participation to encourage media education. There appears a big gap in knowledge and understanding and also in research specifically on media education. The inter-connection between media education and information literacy has not been clearly understood by teachers and some parents. Apart from professional media related courses offered at the tertiary level that integrate theories such as reception analysis, there are no clearly defined pedagogical methods that target children and young persons at any level of the school curriculum.

Although activities and programmes outlined in this paper have implications for media education, the focus on media education is still diffused. The situation might remain so until the future direction and pedagogical issues relating to the introduction of information literacy programmes in schools are clarified. Some educationists however believe that "teaching media education without a responsible media is useless".[26] Avortri[27] suggested that media education should start with media practitioners and their enterprises. Until then, children's participation – the example of *Curious Minds* – remains a unique approach to media education in Ghana.

Notes

1. See *Media Education A Global Strategy for Development*, A Policy Paper prepared for UNESCO Sector of Communication and Information by Professor Buckingham of the Institute of Education, University of London, England, March 2001.
2. See *Empowerment Through Media Education An Intercultural Dialogue* (ed.) Carlsson, Ulla; Tayie, Samy; Genevieve Jacquinot-Delaunay and José Manuel Pérez Tornero.
3. See: 'Media Literacy for Children, Young People, Adults and Media Educators', in Ulla Carlsson (ed.) (2006) *Regulation, Awareness, Empowerment Young People and Harmful Media Content in the Digital Age.*
4. The expressions, surrogate teachers, parallel schools and primary curriculum were variously used by Considine, D.M (1995) www.helsinki.fi/~tella/178 mediaedu.html and Prinsloo, Jeanne (1999) in von Feiltizen, Cecilia and Carlsson, Ulla: *Children and Media Image Education Participation.*
5. Excerpt from the speech of Ghana's first President, Dr. Kwame Nkrumah at the commissioning in 1965 of Ghana Television.
6. The figures were obtained from a statement by Major J. R.K. Tandoh, Director, Acting Director General of National Communications Authority at World Press Freedom Day on May 2, 2007.
7. Ibid.
8. DSTV Guide September 2008.
9. Only the public television station GTV currently runs two locally produced children's programmes targeted at children between 6 and 15 years.
10. Graduate Diploma project by Collins Kyei Boafo (2000) *Study on Children's Perception of Cartoon Programmes on Television* submitted to the School of Communication Studies, University of Ghana.
11. The figure was given by Mr. Joshua Peprah, Director of Operations NCA at the launch of the television station, Fon TV in Kumasi.
12. In 2003, government release expressed concern over easy access to pornography in Internet cafés by children and teenagers. See, Gadzekpo, Audrey (2003) 'The State of Broadcast Regulations on Children in Ghana', in von Feilitzen, Cecilia and Carlsson, Ulla (eds.) *Promote or Protect Perspectives on Media Literacy and Media Regulations.*
13. The Ministry was formerly known as Ministry of Information. The National Orientation component was added in May 2005 with an additional mandate to change the behaviour and attitudes of the Ghanaian and make them more sensitive to the cultures, beliefs and values of the country while instilling in them the values of citizenship.
14. Interview with Dr. Ruby Avortri at Ministry of Education on October 9, 2007.
15. Interview with Kwabena Nyamekye at Ministry of Education on October 9, 2007.
16. http://www.yfughana.byethosst9.com/EDUCATIONAL % 20REFORM%20IN%GHANA.... accessed on 11/2/2007
17. According to Devina Frau-Meigs the protectionist, the cultural and the participatory perspectives are pedagogical stances that co-exist but are not mutually compatible. However, both the protectionists and cultural stances use media in illustrative settings. Quoting Gonnet (1995) Frau-Meigs explains that the latter aims at creating a critical citizenry through content analysis of audio visual productions. See 'Media Reregulation, Self Regulation and Education', in *Promote or Protect Perspectives on Media Literacy and Media Regulation* (2003 yearbook)
18. Interview with Kwabena Nyamekye of the Curriculum Research and Development Division of the Ministry of Education at his office, on October 9, 2007.
19. The year was before Ghana's independence in 1957. The idea for School Broadcasting was however conceptualised in 1951 after the Gold Coast government had launched the 1951/1952 Accelerated Development Plan for Education.
20. The Ghana ICT for Accelerate Development (ICT4AD), 2003 ISBN: 9988-0=1985-0
21. ibid.
22. portal.unesco.org/ci/en/ev.php-URL_ID=20753&URL_DO=DO_TOPIC&URL_SECTION=201.html accessed on September 12, 2008

23. Ga is the language spoken by about 3% of the country's population who are found in the Greater Accra Region.
24. Kingsley Obeng Kyere was interviewed by the writer on phone on October 15, 2007. He is a trained broadcaster and also serves as a supervisor for *Curious Minds*.
25. *Children's Participation in Broadcast Production: A Study of Selected Radio and Television Stations in Accra*. The study is a Master of Philosophy Thesis by Sarah Akrofi-Quarcoo submitted to the University of Ghana in 2004.
26. Interview with Kwabena Nyamekye at his office, Ministry of Education on October 9, 2007.
27. Interview with Dr. Avortri at her office, Ministry of Education on October 9, 2007.

References

Ansah, P.A.V. (1985) Broadcasting and National Development, Golden Jubilee Lectures. Accra: Tema Press.

Anderson, N; Duncan, B and Pungente, John J. (1999) 'Media Education in Canada – The Second Spring', in von Feilitzen, Cecilia and Carlsson, Ulla (ed.) *Children and Media. Image Education Participation*. Göteborg: Nordicom, The International Clearinghouse on Children and Violence on the Screen.

Bevort, E. Frau-Meigs, D; Jacquinot-Delaunay, G; Souyri, C. (2008) 'Why Media Education? The Grunwald Anniversary', in Carlsson, Ulla, Tayie, Samy, Jacquinot-Delaunay, Genevieve and Pérez Tornero, José Manuel (eds.) *Empowerment Through Media Education. An Intercultural Dialogue*. Göteborg: Nordicom, The International Clearinghouse on Children, Youth and Media.

Buckingham, David (2001) Media Education. A Global Strategy for Development, A Policy Paper prepared for UNESCO Sector of Communication and Information.

Buckingham, David (1999) 'The Place of Production, Media Education and Youth Media Production in the UK', in von Feilitzen, Cecilia and Carlsson, Ulla (eds.) *Children and Media. Image Education Participation*. Göteborg: Nordicom, The International Clearinghouse on Children and Violence on the Screen.

Broadcasting Policy and Practice in Africa (2003) Published by Article 19.

Considine, D.M. (1995) Are We There Yet? An Update of the Media Literacy Movement; Accessed on www.helsinki.fi/~tella/178 mediaedu.html

Domaille, Kate and Buckingham, David (2001) *Youth Media Education*. UNESCO (survey report).

Frau-Meigs, D. (2003) 'Media Regulation, Self Regulation and Education', in von Feilitzen, Cecilia and Carlsson, Ulla (eds.) *Promote or Protect. Perspectives on Media Literacy and Media Regulation*. Göteborg: Nordicom, The International Clearinghouse on Children, Youth and Media.

Gadzekpo, Audrey (2003) 'The State of Broadcast Regulations on Children in Ghana', in von Feilitzen, Cecilia and Carlsson, Ulla (eds.) *Promote or Protect? Perspectives on Media Literacy and Media Regulations*. Göteborg: Nordicom, The International Clearinghouse on Children, Youth and Media.

Khan, Abdul Waheed (2008) 'Media Education, a Crucial Issue in the Building of an Inclusive Knowledge Society', in Carlsson, Ulla, Tayie, Samy, Jacquinot-Delaunay, Genevieve and Pérez Tornero, José Manuel (eds.) *Empowerment Through Media Education. An Intercultural Dialogue*. Göteborg: Nordicom, The International Clearinghouse on Children, Youth and Media.

Kyei, B. (2000) 'Children's Perception of Cartoon Programmes on Television', University of Ghana: School of Communication Studies (Graduate Diploma project).

McMahon, B; Quin, R. (1999) 'Australian Children and the Media Education, Participation and Enjoyment', in von Feilitzen, Cecilia and Carlsson, Ulla (eds.) *Children, Young People and Media Globalisation*. Göteborg: Nordicom, The International Clearinghouse on Children and Violence on the Screen.

National Media Commission, ISBN 9988-572-65-4.

Prinsloo, Jeanne (1999) 'South African Media Education in the Late Twentieth Century Rising Phoenix or Dying Swan?', in von Feilitzen, Cecilia and Carlsson, Ulla (eds.) *Children and Media Image*

Education Participation. Göteborg: Nordicom, The International Clearinghouse on Children and Violence on the Screen.

Rideout, Victoria J; Vandwater, Elizabeth A. and Wartella, Ellen A. (2003) *Electronic Media in the Lives of Infants and Preschoolers*. The Kaiser Family Foundation (report).

Tayie, Samy (2008) 'Children and Mass Media in the Arab World A Second Level Analysis in Media Education, a Crucial Issue in the Building of an Inclusive Knowledge Society', in Carlsson, Ulla, Tayie, Samy, Jacquinot-Delaunay Genevieve and Pérez Tornero, José Manuel (eds.) *Empowerment Through Media Education. An Intercultural Dialogue*. Göteborg: Nordicom, The International Clearinghouse on Children, Youth and Media.

Tufte, Birgitte (1999) 'Media Education in Europe with special Focus on the Nordic Countries', in von Feilitzen, Cecilia and Carlsson, Ulla (eds.) *Children and Media. Image Education Participation*. Göteborg: Nordicom, The International Clearinghouse on Children and Violence on the Screen.

Tyner, Kathleen (1998) *Literacy in the Digital World: Teaching and Learning in the Age of Information*. Mahwah, NJ: Lawrence Erlbaum Associates.

Drop It to the Youth

Community-Based Youth Video as a Tool for Building Democratic Dialogue in South Africa

Steven Goodman, Rebecca Renard & Christine Mendoza

For three days in March 2007, media educators from the Educational Video Center (EVC) in New York City taught a documentary workshop for thirty teenagers and unemployed young adults from the Soweto Township in South Africa. Invited to Johannesburg by the 5th World Summit on Media for Children and the United States Consulate General, EVC structured an experiential workshop for the participants to collaboratively plan, shoot, and edit their own short documentaries. They chose to explore three subjects they felt were of critical importance to their communities and to the broader struggle to overcome the legacy of apartheid:

- the public's understanding of human rights as protected by the new South African constitution;
- the low rate of youth learning about their history and culture through visiting post-Apartheid museums and other "heritage sites";
- and the high rate of teen pregnancy and unprotected sex.

Combining street interviews, poetry, photography, and video imagery, as well as popular commercial music, each team crafted a documentary that spoke to public audiences with creativity power, passion and a sense of urgency. After the workshop concluded, the youth screened their documentaries in a range of school and community forums and led discussions about the social issues they explored.

EVC's documentary workshop, screenings, and the community conversations they sparked provide a powerful model for using grassroots youth video as a tool to amplify youth voices and foster informed dialogue and problem solving among youth and other marginalized populations in townships and rural areas. Further scaling up the impact of this approach, one can envision mobile video screenings followed by discussions in schools, and community forums that are in turn videotaped, providing local residents with a voice access and a direct in-person dialogue that would otherwise not be possible. There are many examples

of dynamic and successful community and youth produced radio organizations in South Africa. The conditions are ripe for youth produced video to now be employed as an education, communications, and development strategy given South Africa's inherited problems of high adult non-literacy and inequitable distributions of telecommunications and electric power. In this paper, we will briefly discuss this context, the history of student media activism, provide a narrative case study of the Soweto youth documentary workshop, and propose strategies for moving forward to harness the power of youth media for the ongoing process of building an inclusive and participatory democracy in South Africa.

Snap shots of youth media activists on location

Pearl looks directly into the camera, squinting slightly in the bright sun. She is standing on the grounds of the Hector Pieterson Memorial Museum. Behind her is the stone monument commemorating Hector Pieterson and all those who died in the Soweto uprising of 1976. She speaks with the clear and measured voice of a seasoned reporter:

> *Welcome to the cradle and birthplace of student and youth activism that lighted the spark of the youth contribution and liberation of South Africa during Apartheid with its dark, murky period.*" The camera pans to another young member of her

documentary crew who continues the narration: "*Today we dig deeper into the minds of our youth finding out how the torch of our heritage has been preserved for future generations.*
(Hector Pieterson Museum & US Consulate Johannesburg, Producer, 2007)

Inside the Museum, Mbuso (he goes by the nick name "Ice") records a poem he wrote for his group's documentary on human rights. It's the third take:

In the streets dead bodies bleeding
A sister and a brother carrying a corpse of a dead friend crying
Fumes and bullets all over the road
The road to freedom is over I thought
1994 the dream that was long awaited before

His voice is urgent. The rhythm builds. His head moves back and forth in the low angle closeup frame.

Now the stones are used to build and shape our freedom wall
A sister and a brother, Black and white holding hands
I'm human
What hurts you hurts me too
Respect mine, I respect yours
Let us share our human rights
Ubuntu pambi
Then he pauses, and almost with a loving caress he says:
"*My Africa*"

His fellow crew member shooting the camera knows Ice got it right that time and says, "*Yeah*", forgetting that the camera is still recording. Ice bows his head slightly and smiles (Hector Pieterson Museum & US Consulate Johannesburg, Producer, 2007).

Down the street from the Museum a third documentary team interviews students and teachers from the Orlando West High School about the problem of teenage pregnancy. A young girl wearing her school uniform of maroon sweater vest over a white shirt and striped tie eagerly speaks into the microphone: "*They think pregnancy is a game. They know there is protection. But they are still having sex without it.*" She adjusts her backpack and adds, "*… they should abstain*" (Hector Pieterson Museum & US Consulate Johannesburg, Producer, 2007).

The group ends their documentary with a poem, expressing their mixed feelings of both frustration and hope:

….But motivational speakers speak
Parents talk the talk,
But in the same way, youth walk the walk
They know it all
Yet into this trap they fall
(Hector Pieterson Museum & US Consulate Johannesburg, Producer, 2007)

Shot in a close-up profile, Cello recites the poem facing the left side and then the right, alternating with each verse.

> *They respond*
> *It's a natural call*
> *And what can you say?*
> *Just drop it to them*
> *Drop it to the youth, drop it to them*!
> Then the whole crew joins in and repeatedly chants the refrain:
> *"Drop it to the youth, drop it them!"*
> (Hector Pieterson Museum & US Consulate Johannesburg, Producer, 2007)

Their message is: Teach, guide, help the youth. That is what they intend to do with their documentary.

Taking the means of public communication and cultural expression into their hands, the youth quickly learned how to blend the genres of community affairs documentary, video art, and public service announcement and use them to both inform and transform their community audiences. They seemed to begin the workshop as students and end as civic journalists and activist-teachers.

Each team used their video to pose questions, survey public opinion, and explore a particular social problem. They also sought to use their video to solve that problem by "conscientizing (raising the consciousness of) their audiences. Each video opened spaces for dialogue by presenting historically marginalized audiences of black South Africans from the townships with faces, voices, and perspectives with which they can identify and/or take issue with. With a strong point of view, sense of conviction and purpose, the youth producers conclude with exhortations to act. For example, the last scene of the human rights video shows the youth team shouting directly at the audience with one collective voice: "Know Your Rights! (Hector Pieterson Museum & US Consulate Johannesburg, Producer, 2007)

In the final narration of heritage sites documentary, the youth reporter concludes:

> *I stand next to one of our heritage sites, disappointed at the views of youth with regard to visiting heritage sites. We have discovered that more needs to be done to conscientize young black South Africans about partaking in preservation of our heritage, their heritage.*
> (Hector Pieterson Museum & US Consulate Johannesburg, Producer, 2007)

Before their final "*drop it to the youth* chant, the producers of the teen pregnancy documentary prominently display the following three titles in bold white letters over black:

> "***They say we can not reduce the ever escalating Teenage Pregnancy***."
> "***We say, WE CAN!***"
> "***Play your ROLE!!!***"
> (Hector Pieterson Museum & US Consulate Johannesburg, Producer, 2007)

As video pamphleteers, the workshop participants used a mixture of art, journalism, and activism to inspire and rouse the public to their cause. They are of course not the first youth to use media for this purpose. South Africa has a rich history of youth produced media to draw upon that is rooted in the youth organizations formed in the pre-1994 struggle against apartheid.

Student media production under apartheid

Although they operated under the Nationalist Party's harsh climate of repression and censorship with the constant possibility of fines, closure, banning, and imprisonment, the alternative and underground student press was an especially important tool in the hands of university anti–apartheid activists (Pissarra 1991). (There is little evidence of South African student video at that time.) This was particularly the case in the 1970's with the rise of the Black Consciousness movement and the uprising in Soweto, and into the 1980's as international boycotts and the movement to free Mandela grew. Students depended on underground newsletters to stay informed and connected (and burned them as soon as they finished reading them). And the government fined, banned, and eventually shut down many of them because of that.

In addition to curbing the flow of information through censorship and banning, the racist government practiced a campaign of disinformation. School curricula taught history that was re-written from the white government's perspective. The Nationalist Party outlawed television for fear that, according to Dr Albert Hertzog, Minister for Posts and Telegraphs at the time, "South Africa would have to import films showing race mixing; and advertising would make (non-white) Africans dissatisfied with their lot. (Hertzog, May 4 1967: 4) When they finally allowed it into the country in 1976, only one station was established, the South African Broadcasting Corporation (SABC), and it was often used for propaganda and disinformation by the apartheid regime. This made the alternative perspectives and sources of news and information that the student press provided that much more important.

There were scores of youth and student organizations with regional and national membership (see for example http://www.sahistory.org.za/pages/govermence-projects/june16/organisation-list.htm). Many organizations had their own publications such as the South African Students' Organization's SASO Newsletter, The South African Students Press Union's SASPU National and the SASPU Focus, and the Grassroots which reported on news from over 60 democratic organizations, including the Cape Youth Congress (CYCO). For further information on Anti-apartheid periodicals from 1950 to 1994 see Aluka, Struggles for Freedom in Southern Africa. http://www.aluka.org.

The legacy of these youth organizations lives on in contemporary South Africa. Today, many of the more than three hundred youth based organizations in Johannesburg alone trace their origins to the anti apartheid struggles for democracy.

Now, many of these organizations that have taken up the challenges of public health education in the face of the devastating HIV / AIDS crisis still largely rely on community newspapers to disseminate information. Some use community radio to advance their work.

Our documentary workshop served participants from two youth organizations: the Hector Pieterson Youth Forum and the "Democracy in Dialogue" project at the Constitution Court. Both groups were inspired by the previous generation's student activists. The following section tells the story of the journey we took together, the work that was created and the lessons we all learned along the way.

The narrative

Arriving in Soweto, we couldn't help but be humbled as we stepped out of our van onto the hallowed grounds of the Hector Pieterson Memorial Museum. The name "Soweto" evokes images of the primary, middle, and high school students who dared to raise their voices in a peaceful demonstration for freedom and self determination and were met with a brutal onslaught of police violence. It is the battleground where over 500 people lost their lives in the world historical march for human rights.

The rust red brick museum is a memorial to Hector Pieterson, the first student to die in the Soweto uprising. And so we were reminded of this history every time we walked down the hallways. History came alive all around us through the story-high photographs and newspaper clippings that covered the walls and through the film and television footage that looped in the television monitors lining the ramp up from the lobby. This history that echoed in the halls outside our meeting room was the backdrop and the context for our work, and also gave it its meaning. Almost like ghosts, the black and white images of children marching on the streets thirty years and only two blocks away from where we stood, and the grainy images flickering on the screens were like specters haunting our classes; a constant reminder that nothing is more powerful than organized and unified youth voices calling out for freedom and human dignity. At the Museum we came face to face with the tragedy and sacrifice that youth made a generation ago. But looking out at the faces of the youth in our workshop – young people who were not yet born in 1976 and who were full of so much hope and promise – we also saw the triumph over apartheid the older generation of students helped bring about.

These new youth were ready for us. While we set up our equipment, they sat in the auditorium bleachers with pads and pens poised, as if in a university lecture. To help break the ice for the workshop, we had them play a short game. Without talking, two make-shift teams had to race to line themselves up according to their birthdays. Fingers flew and eyes gestured as they tried to complete the task. When one group bragged that they had finished first, only to discover that some of their teammates were positioned in totally wrong order, they hemmed and hawed playfully. But everyone laughed. They were a fun bunch.

It seemed they were also a diverse bunch. Although we didn't conduct any sort of demographic survey, the youngest that we had in our group was 13 years, and the oldest looked to be in his mid-30s. They ranged the economic spectrum, as well. There were some who were obviously more middle-income than the others, sporting cool shades, name brand jeans, and mp3 players. While others wore the same clothes each day or were swimming in pants that were several sizes too large. As we moved into discussion, we noticed that they spoke English on different levels, too, perhaps indicating their class differences even more so than their appearances.

We brought with us the tools of community-based youth media – a suitcase crammed with video cameras, microphones, headphones, and laptops for editing – to amplify the voices of the thirty young participants. But we also brought an educational philosophy of practice that had been developed and refined working with New York City teenagers over the past twenty-three years at the EVC. Since 1984, EVC evolved from a single video class into an internationally acclaimed non-profit organization with four main programs: a semester-long *High School Documentary Workshop*; a pre-professional paid internship program called *YO-TV (Youth Organizers Television)*; Community Engagement program screening EVC documentaries in local neighborhoods to organize for social change; and an *External Education Program* that provides training institutes and curriculum resources for K-12 educators on a local and national basis as they learn to integrate media analysis and production into their classes.

We began the workshop with a critical viewing activity. We played a segment from a documentary that EVC students in New York had created, called *Patriarchy is Malarkey!*, which explores gender issues and violence against women. (Educational Video Center, Producer, 2004) Despite the foreign accents of the voices on screen, the young people in the auditorium were rapt. From just five minutes of video, fifteen minutes of emotional discussion bubbled forth. Moving from the themes in the video to the way the video was put together, the young people were able to identify some of the essential elements of a documentary. We told them that like the video they had seen, the short documentary they would create over the next two days would: express a point of view; contain multiple perspectives; use visuals or "b-roll"; include interviews conducted with people in the community; have a clear introduction and conclusion; and, if they chose to, could have music.

Then began the arduous process of determining which topics the groups would explore. Since there were three facilitators, there would be three groups, and therefore, three topics. We asked the young people what issues they felt strongly about, and we recorded all of their ideas on poster paper, watching the list grow and grow until more than 25 topics were scrawled on sheets across the room. Some were as general and universal as gender and racial discrimination; some were questions of national concern such as unemployment rates of South African nationals versus immigrants; some were teen-specific questions such as how to get young people off the streets and more involved in school and meaningful activities.

Through consensus, they selected the final three issues they agreed were of critical importance to black South African youth and to the broader goal of continuing to build a democratic South Africa. They would explore: the public's understanding of human rights as protected by the new South African constitution; youth interest in learning about their history and culture through visiting "heritage sites"; and the high rate of teen pregnancy and unprotected sex. Once they chose the team they'd like to be in, each group had to create three questions that they would ask people on the street about their topic. The selection of central questions helps drive and focus the process of inquiry. These questions would provide the general framework for the documentary, so they had to be substantive. The Heritage Sites group decided that they wanted to know the extent to which young people visit museums and other sites of historic and cultural significance and find out what keeps youth from visiting those sites. They wanted to use this information to think about ways the heritage sites could be revamped to attract more people in their own cohort. The Human Rights team was motivated by their concern that too many people didn't really know their rights even though their country had just finished celebrating Human Rights Day. They wanted to make a tape that informed and inspired action.

After testing and revising their questions and getting a quick "camera 101" lesson, we descended upon the streets of Soweto. The three teams spread out to ensure that we weren't covering the same territory. Each team member would have a chance to try various crew roles as they moved through their interviews. They needed a brazen talent scout to find or persuade passersby to be interviewed, a director to help set up the shots and keep people from walking into the frame, an interviewer to get strong responses for the "meat" of the documentary, a sound person to make sure the conversation was audible atop the buzz of Soweto life, and a camera person to capture it all on tape.

On its most basic level, bringing the workshop out to the streets went to the heart of our teaching methodology: put cameras into the hands of youth and have them go out into the surrounding community to collaboratively ask questions about the pressing issues in their lives. In fact, there is a deeper philosophy of practice that grounds this methodology providing a theory and structure which can be described as *critical literacy.* Drawing upon the works of educators Paulo Freire (Pedagogy of the Oppressed), Myles Horton (The Long Haul), John Dewey (Experience and Education), among others, this experiential and inquiry-based methodology, "provides students not merely with functional skills, but with conceptual tools necessary to critique and engage society along with its inequalities and injustices", according to Shor (Goodman 2006: 208). Developing critical literacy skills enables students to investigate power relations within the social and historical context of their lived experience and within the broader frame of their mediated culture. In this way, students build their capacity to understand how media is made to convey particular messages, and how they can use electronic and print technologies to creatively express themselves, and document and publicly voice their ideas and concerns regarding the most important issues in their lives. Learning about the world is directly linked to the possibility of changing it (Goodman 2003).

Teaching continuous inquiry is the first of three key principles of EVC's critical literacy methodology. It is the notion that students' learning is driven by their own questions about their lived experiences; the social, cultural, and historical conditions that shape those experiences; and the media's representations of those conditions and experiences. The learner-centeredness of this approach develops the students' agency as social, political, and cultural actors in their community (Goodman 2006).

Looking for people to interview on the streets of Soweto, it didn't take long to find willing participants. So the youth were encouraged. They did, however, discover that in order to elicit the kinds of responses they wanted, they had to make a critical adjustment. All of the groups' questions had been written in English. And while the first interview was successful, the Heritage Sites group's second interviewee stumbled. He had problems understanding the questions. His responses were stilted. His answers didn't exactly speak to the question. Without skipping a beat, Thando, the interviewer, began again. This time in isiZulu, the most common African language in Johannesburg, and the interview flowed effortlessly from there. The other groups shared similar experiences. Clearly, the interviewees and often the interviewers, were more comfortable and better able to express themselves in their own language. The groups made an unannounced decision to conduct all of the remaining interviews in their own languages, whether it be isiZulu, Xhosa, Tswana, or in their own urban blend of English, Afrikaans, and native South African languages.

It is impossible to overstate the importance of this seemingly minor decision. In a country that experienced such a long-standing oppressive regime, where

Black South Africans' indigenous languages and cultures were systematically subjugated and the Black voice was intentionally demeaned and ignored in the media, using those languages represents a shift in the power dynamic. Speaking and learning in their own languages validates the richness, knowledge and power of their own cultures, communities, and family histories. After all, the Soweto uprising that took place literally on the very ground that the young people were conducting their interviews began as a protest against the imposition of the dominant culture's Afrikaans as the language of instruction in the schools' core curriculum. Speaking their own languages allowed both the young people and the community members to reinsert themselves into the national dialogue, where for so long they had been silenced. As the groups finished their interviews they headed back into the museum to debrief. *Teaching reflection* is the second key practice of EVC's critical literacy methodology. Simply engaging in an experience is sometimes not enough to get participants to think about the significance of the experience. Oftentimes during the process of reflection people make new discoveries and can make sense of what they just experienced. These new understandings might go unrealized if time isn't taken to reflect. Therefore it is important to provide multiple opportunities for students to reflect through discussion, journal writing and sometimes on poster paper as is described in the following "wall talk" activity.

We taped poster paper to the meeting room walls, and as the young people cycled back into the space, we asked them to respond to the prompts written on the paper. "Going out with the camera to interview people in the streets made me feel..." "I was most surprised by..." We all walked around the room reading each other's responses and sharing our reactions. Some of the written feedback was difficult to understand, probably as a result of the language divide and their discomfort in using English as their main language of communication. But even still, there was a lot of response. A few spoke of their desire to stay out and do more interviews with people. "I felt enlightened to hear other people's views and ideas." Some spoke of things they hadn't known could exist. One young man, Lawrence, was shocked to see a White man playing drums with a Black man on the street. They were surprised by how little it seemed some people knew about their own country and history. But mostly they talked about how proud they felt. "I felt like a journalist", one said. "I feel happy".

Now that the primary footage had been gathered, it was time to move into shaping it into a coherent piece. The teams watched their footage back to select the sound bites that they wanted to use, laughing and reliving the experience on the streets. We pulled out the laptop computers and gave small group lessons on editing. For more than half of them, it was their first time ever using a computer. Either on a PC with Adobe Premiere or a Mac with iMovie editing software, they learned to open a new project folder and "capture" footage. As one person learned, she taught the next person, until everyone in the groups had had a chance. Some were tentative, but others boldly took control of the keyboard and a mouse. A few young people in each group took the helm of

the editing task, while others concentrated on trying to figure out how the piece should flow. As with most people who have never created their own media but who have seen professionally-produced television, the groups spent a lot of time on the "bells and whistles". They debated which effects they would use, and they talked "cuts and fades". They wanted to include footage that they hadn't shot, and conjured up images that would take a full-service studio to create – things far outside of the scope of what the consumer software and limited timeframe were capable of. But they eventually came away with good ideas about how they could draw on the talents and artistry of their team mates to use text, music, and other creative elements in their documentaries.

While the incorporation of poetry in their documentaries was not discussed much in the video workshop, two of the three groups created, performed and recorded their own poems. Their poems became the most moving elements of their final documentaries. It is interesting to note that the performance of poetry also played a role historically in the underground meetings of the student Black Consciousness movement (BCM) where the cryptic language of poetry had a better chance of by-passing the government censors (Ede 2002).

Teaching multiple literacies is the third key principle of the critical literacy method. That is, in order for youth to become thoughtful, creative, and engaged citizens, they need to express themselves and be able to learn about the world through the use of visual, spoken, and printed languages. In the case of this workshop, the youth learned to use multiple literacies to tell their stories using digital editing to weave together interviews (in English and indigenous African languages), poetry, music, photographs, printed text and video images.

The groups put the final touches on their documentaries in preparation for the final screening that was to take place the next day. The US Consulate and the Museum had invited the public to view the youth producers' work in the same auditorium that we had conducted the workshop. The audience mostly consisted of the youth participants and their friends, though there were quite a few members from the US Consulate, a small contingent of media educators visiting from the World Summit, and a few museum patrons (which seemed to include an even mix of South African and international visitors) who flowed in and out as the audio caught their attention. Team by team the youth producers introduced their tapes and explained why they had chosen to explore their particular topic. Their videos were screened, and each group answered questions from the audience concerning both the creative process and the subject matter of their tapes.

The energy in the room was palpable. Many of the audience comments were congratulatory, but viewers looked to the youth as experts in the subjects they had chosen and asked them what they planned to do with both the skills they had learned in the two-and-a-half days, and with the videos themselves. The young people made grand statements that they were going to take their work to churches, schools, and community centers. People *needed* to see their videos, they said. The youth had an undeniable sense of urgency to share their work. This urgency spoke to their pride, their sense of empowerment, and their frustration at not knowing quite how to get their work to the public and not knowing when they might get the opportunity to do something like this again. When would they be able to make more videos and develop their skills as journalists, storytellers, camera operators, and computer editors, when not even the state-funded museum had technical equipment comparable to what we had packed in our carry-ons and brought to them? When would they have another platform to express their opinions – opinions not only about the topics that ended up making the final cut, but about all of the other issues they didn't have time to explore or they didn't feel comfortable suggesting?

Moving forward: youth media teams building democracy

After the workshop concluded, the Hector Pieterson Museum organized screenings for the youth producers to present their work in schools, churches, youth organizations, and clubs. The youth also presented screenings at the Museum for 15 schools that participated in International Museums Day and at a Museum Open Day Schools screening commemorating the anniversary of Martin Luther King's "I Have a Dream" speech. As Museum Education Officer Kumresh Chetty confirmed in an e-mail correspondence with us on September 5, 2007, "The responses were awesome and all inspiring as the documentaries became a vehicle and catalyst for youth empowerment .... (they raised) awareness of community and societal problems and how they can become community activists and ultimately part of the solution."

In the end, the youth participants from Soweto taught us, their teachers, as much as we taught them. We were moved by their overwhelming passion to preserve and honor their heritage, to put into practice the ideals and human rights laws of their new constitution, to make a difference and make a lasting contribution to the building of a new nation. They used video to report on public opinion and show diverse and sometimes opposing perspectives and promote discussion. They used video to critique their peers' behavior, whether in their sexual relationships, or as consumers of museum culture. And they used video as a teaching tool to raise consciousness, "conscientize" their audiences, and to move them to action. They integrated poetry, music, and imagery to create an art form that informed, engaged and moved their audiences to see and reflect on the world from a new vantage point.

The rich experience the youth participants had and the range of skills they developed in producing and screening their documentaries in such a brief period of time provoke one to imagine what could be possible if only more time and resources were invested. How many more youth could be involved? How much more in-depth might they be able to report on these issues? How many other issues might they be able to explore? Across how many different regions and communities might they screen their work? In what languages might it be translated? And what sorts of discussions and action might result?

Youth produced media can have both an important educational and activist role to play in South Africa today. In fact, access to video cameras and editing technology can enable youth producers to communicate with the non-literate, non-university audiences in ways that the apartheid era student newspapers never could.

While the legal system restricting freedom of the press has been abolished and youth enjoy the freedom to speak, write, report, photograph, and film without fear of censorship or imprisonment, the free exchange of information and ideas today still remains largely out of reach for the poorest sectors of the population. The history and ideology of apartheid has distorted and stunted the development of media and communication as a means for the free dissemination of ideas and information. Apartheid era government planning and investment still leaves the majority of township and rural area residents impoverished with little or no access to the Internet; telephone land lines are rare, and even electricity is unavailable to those living in makeshift shanties. A woefully inadequate education system has left up to 30 percent of adults functionally non-literate. Over 50 percent of students drop out of school with many finding no point in continuing (Yeh 2004). While these are formidable challenges, we argue in this paper that they need not prevent the most marginalized populations from gaining access to information and having their voices heard as part of a national dialogue. In the absence of internet connections and television, community-based youth video production can in fact be used to overcome these obstacles and promote a more informed and participatory democracy. Observing how quickly the Soweto youth teams learned to operate video equipment and create their documentaries, it is easy to image an entire network of trained community youth reporting teams who can shoot and screen short videos documenting the conditions, events, ideas, and opinions from and for the community. Mobile video screenings, followed by discussions in school and community gatherings that are in turn videotaped, could offer a voice to those "voiceless" residents and promote a direct people-to-people dialogue that would otherwise not be possible. As community journalists and activist/educators, youth media producers can play a dynamic and vital role in this democracy building project.

This approach can be successful because:

- Video is a primarily visual and spoken form of communication that can be understood by non-literate members of the community where newspapers can not.
- Video allows an entry-point for those who are not able to read English or who communicate more powerfully in their indigenous African languages. It allows people to identify with those on the screen and to feel like they have an equal place at the discussion table.
- South Africa has a rich history of youth activism and a broad array of youth organizations today engaged in community education and development that can produce and serve as sources of information and audiences for youth media.
- South Africa has 11 official languages, and many people speak several of them, but to ensure that a language barrier doesn't prevent the flow of information, dialogue in the videos can be translated and dubbed over to reach language specific audiences.
- Face-to-face neighborhood and school screenings and conversations run on social networks. While they would require a video camera, television, electric generator, and a van to drive to different communities, they don't require a vast infrastructure of telecommunications and electric wiring.

It makes sense to provide low-tech communication alternatives in a context where such taken-for-granted staples of daily life in the west as the Internet, cable television, telephone land lines, and electric power lines are limited or non-existent. Community radio has already shown the potential of non-networked communication where audiences without electricity can listen on their battery operated radios. Massive infrastructure investments are certainly needed and should move forward when the capital to do so is available. But the democratic inclusion of young and marginalized voices does not have to wait until then.

Today's generation of young South Africans stand on the shoulders of the generation that preceded them. They are now free to share their perspectives, bear witness to the conditions of life around them, and offer up solutions to the problems they encounter. Inspired by the critical and creative accomplishments and the social justice purposes of their historic counterparts, access to video technology will enable South African youth producers today to build on that legacy and promote active dialogue with young and non-literate, non-university audiences in ways that the anti-apartheid era student press never could.

It's now a matter of providing the youth with the resources, education and guidance. Then we need to stand back and watch as they "drop it to the youth" – and to the rest of us too, if we listen to what they have to say.

References

Aluka, Struggles for Freedom in Southern Africa. Retrieved 15 jan 2008 http://www.aluka.org/action/doBrowse?sa=3&sa=3&br=tax-periodicals%7Cnamed-as%7Cperiodical-title

Dewey, J. (1938/1997) *Experience and Education*. New York: Macmillan.

Ede, A. (2002) *The Black Consciousness Movement in South African Literature,* Retrieved 26 September 2007. http://www.nigeriansinamerica.com/articles/26/2/The-Black-Consciousness-Movement-in-South-African-Literature/Page2.html

Educational Video Center (Producer) (2005) *Patriarchy is Malarkey*. Educational Video Center: New York, NY.

Freire, P. (1970) *Pedagogy of the Oppressed*. New York: The Continuum Publishing Company.

Goodman, S. (2006) 'The Practice and Principles of Teaching Critical Literacy at the Educational Video Center', *Media Literacy: Transforming Curriculum and Teaching*. Boston: Blackwell Publishing, pp. 206-227.

Goodman, S. (2003) *Teaching Youth Media: A Critical Guide to Literacy, video Production and Social Change*. New York: Teachers College Press.

Hector Pieterson Museum & US Consulate Johannesburg (Producer) (2007) *Youth and Heritage*.

Hector Pieterson Museum & US Consulate Johannesburg (Producer) (2007) *Human Rights in South Africa*.

Hector Pieterson Museum & US Consulate Johannesburg (Producer) (2007) *Teen Pregnancy*.

Hertzog A. (May 4, 1967) 'Television in South Africa', *Cape Times*: quoted in *Contact,* 10(1): 4.

Horton, M. (1997) *The Long Haul: An Autobiography*. New York: Teachers College Press.

Pissarra M. (1991) *Criticism And Censorship In The South African "Alternative" Press With Particular Reference To The Cartoons Of Bauer And Zapiro (1985-1990)* B.A. Honours Dissertation, Dept. Art History, UCT, Retrieved 15 October 2007, from http://www.sahistory.org.za/pages/library-resources/thesis/mario-dissertation/index.htm

South African History online, Retrieved 15 October 2007. http://www.sahistory.org.za/pages/governence-projects/june16/organisation-list.htm

Yeh, Y. (2004) 'Programmes to Increase Literacy in South Africa', *Global Perspectives on Human Language: The South African Context*. Retrieved October 15, 2007, from http://www.stanford.edu/~jbaugh/saw/Yoo-Yoo_Literacy.html

Acknowledgement

EVC's documentary workshop in Soweto was made possible by grants from the U.S. Consulate General Public Affairs Section in Johannesburg, the 5th World Summit on Media for Children, courtesy of Chairperson Firdoze Bulbulia, and the Chen and Cox Family Fund, courtesy of Milton Chen. Thanks to Jo Ellen Fisherkeller for her support and to Kumresh Chetty and the US Consulate for the assistance and information they provided for this chapter.

Playing at Cyber Space

Perspectives on Egyptian Children's Digital Socialization

Lamees El Baghdady

In the twenty-first century, with the existence of new media environments, practicing childhood can be a totally new experience with implications for both children and their social circles. In fact, digitization has led to the birth of virtual communities that emerged from an amazing intersection of humanity and technology. This has helped in constructing new forms of social ties that goes beyond geographical locations, a concept that was first raised by Marshall McLuhan (1989) when he voiced the development of communication technologies that will bridge time and space and usher in the creation of a global village.

Generally speaking, a virtual community is defined as "social relationships forged in cyberspace through repeated contact with a specified boundary or place [a conference or a chat line] that is symbolically delineated by topic of interest" (qtd. in Jankowski 2002: 39). In fact, with the increasing population of the online communities, virtuality is no longer perceived as a characteristic of new media (Slater 2002), but rather it is a social practice that is creating new communication potentials, constructing new social ties, and raising challenging questions that need to be investigated.

One of the current virtual communities is Facebook, which is a social utility that connects people worldwide. Facebook is a free-access website that allows users to join networks, such as a school, place of employment, or geographic region, to connect and interact with other people. Users can post messages for their friends to see and update their personal profile to notify friends of happenings in their life. It is reported that the Facebook community has a population that exceeds 60 million users representing a range of ages including children, teenagers, youth, and adults from both genders and from many nationalities.

The focus of this project is to explore children's experience with their cyber space and to link this experience with the socialization process of their childhood. It satisfies two basic interrelated objectives: (1) to explore the impact of virtual socialization on children; (2) to examine Egyptian children's digital experience with Facebook. It is a multi disciplinary approach integrating the study of virtual communities, specifically Facebook, with a broader social context represented in the socialization process of children. In addition, the project integrates two levels of research. The first attempts to understand Egyptian children's experiences with Facebook, while the second examines the implications on the socialization process. Perhaps most importantly, this study is among the first academic investigation in the Arab World that deals with this scope of research.

As noted earlier, Facebook is a social networking website that exists at cyberspace. It was launched in February 4, 2004 and is ranked in seventh place among all websites in terms of traffic from September 2006 to September 2007. It is also the most popular website for uploading photos, with 14 million uploaded daily (Wikipedia 2008).

Definitions of 'New Media'

It has been argued that the term 'new media' is not only associated with the digital revolution, as it depends on the historical context of its usage (Marvin 1988) for elaboration. According to Nicholas Jankowski, newness is a relative characteristic as it is affected by both time and place; in other words, "what is new today is old tomorrow, and what is new in one culture context may be unknown or outmoded in another" (2002: 35). Although new media was once defined as "applications of microelectronics, computers and telecommunications that offer new services or enhancement of old ones" (Williams, Rice and Rogers qtd. in McMillan 2002: 164), the term is still controversial as many scholars have addressed the term with skepticism. Other researchers have argued that "the terms used to define new media are too dependent on old media forms" (qtd. in McMillan: 164). Scholars such as Janet Murray have tackled the term 'multimedia' and argued that it is a "word with little descriptor power as such additive catchall phrases are evidence that a medium is in an early stage of development is still depending on formats derived from earlier technologies instead of exploiting its own expressive power." (Murray qtd. in McMillan 2002: 164). Although the previous points illustrates that newness, as a feature of media, is to a large degree not an absolute characteristic as it depends on both the previously introduced technologies and the historical context, it is important to draw attention to the new media characteristics as a step in the right direction. According to McQuail, there are four main features that characterize new media:

- decentralization of encoded content;
- a higher capacity regarding transmission, which "overcome the former restrictions of cost, distance and capacity";
- interactivity as "the receiver can select, answer back, exchange and be linked to other receivers directly";

- flexibility in deciding on content and usage patterns (McQuail 1994: 21).

Williams, Rice, and Rogers (1998) stressed two other features of the new media: de-massification and asynchroneity. De-massifying is defined as "a certain degree of the control of mass communication systems moves from the message producer to the media consumer" (p. 13). Besides, new media are asynchronous as they "allow for the sending and receiving of messages at a time convenient for the individual user rather than requiring all participants to use the system at the same time" (p. 13).

Moreover, according to a series of essays published in *New Media and Society* (1999) ten leading communication scholars addressed the issue of the characteristics of the new media and no common definition was reached. However, it is significant to highlight that "much of the newness addressed had to do with transformation in the ways individuals are able to relate to media and to determine the place and functions of these media in their everyday lives. New media are, to a large degree, socially-constructed phenomena and often deviate substantially from the designer's original intent" (qtd. in Jankowski 2002, p. 36).

It is clear from these definitions that the newness of media is crystallized around the idea of people's usage. The existence of new media has created new horizons for the ways people communicate with others. People adopt these new media and embed them into their everyday activities; consequently, these new media become part of their social context, social practices; and more importantly, part of their social space, which played a role in creating new communication potentials and constructing new social ties.

Developments in New Media research: Four lines of research

Generally speaking, there are four lines of research that have dealt with new media development: the first line was the historical. The second is psychological. The third was 'micro-sociological/ ethnographic', and the fourth is 'macro-sociological/economic (Lievrouw 2002a).

The first line of research that has focused on new media development, historical, is concerned with the new technological innovations at that time and their introducers; for instance, scholarship about the development of the telegraph and telephone, the phonograph, wireless radio and the television (Lievrouw 2002a). More recently, research on the history of technology has integrated a blend of cultural, economic and political contexts regarding the use of these media and the economic aspects related to them (Flichy 1995). The second line of research that dealt with new media developments using research in the United States as a model, is cognitive and behavioral; it concentrates on "how people understand and use media including studies of media effects, persuasion and propaganda, and voter behavior (Lievrouw 2002a). The third research stream regarding new media development is concerned with the 'micro-sociological studies of technology'; this approach is called the *social shaping of technology* (Lievrouw 2002a). According to Lievrouw (2002a), this approach is concerned with "the everyday uses of technologies, including media, with a particular focus on the ways that people modify, avoid, reinvent or otherwise adopt technologies to their particular purpose and circumstances" (p.132). Thus, this research stream is related to the uses of technologies that were incorporated into the social environment. The forth research approach is the 'macro-sociological and economic' as it attempts to understand "how new technologies or other new ideas are introduced and spread in society" and is illustrated by the diffusion of innovation theory (Lievrouw 2002a: 132). Generally speaking, diffusion research investigates the "social process of how innovations (new idea, practice, objects, etc) become known and are spread throughout a social system" (Severin and Tankard 2001: 207).

It is important to mention that this paper offers only a brief discussion on the resource arch that deals with new media developments, giving a comprehensive mapping of the developments of new media research will be inevitably out of the scope of this paper. However, it is important to mention that by the 1990s, "new media research has progressed from its early efforts to its recent proliferation" as it has become more specialized (Livingstone and Lievrouw 2002b: 5). As Pool highlighted twenty two years ago, specialized needs will be met by the convergence of media which will create as a consequence new devices and new media use; according to him "convergence does not mean ultimate stability, or unity… and there will always be specialization, innovation, and attempts to do differently" (1983: 53). Surely the latter point cam be significantly applied to children because they represent a particular segment of new media users.

The convergence of media during the late twentieth and early twenty-first century have blurred the distinction between various media systems and the content encoded through them; nevertheless, as Lievrouw (2002a) has highlighted this issue shedding a sense of novelty that characterizes new media systems at this point of history. In this respect, and since the research stream on new media has become more specialized, the scope of this project will focus on the children's social virtual life that exist in cyberspace; specifically through Facebook.

Virtual community

Howard Rheingold one of the leading scholars on the subject of virtual community, and among the very first scholars to call attention to the study of virtual communities, defined virtual communities as "social aggregations that emerge from the Net when enough people carry on public discussions long enough, with sufficient human feelings, to form webs of personal relationships in cyberspace" (Rheingold 2000: 5). However, Rheingold's definition has faced some criticism regarding the meaning of sufficient human feeling as it does not give a criterion for judging the extent of sufficiency. Other scholars have introduced other definitions. For example, Jan Fernback and Brad Thompson (1995) argued that a virtual communities are "social relationships forged in cyberspace through repeated contact with a specified boundary or place (a conference or a chat line) that is symbolically delineated by topic of interest" (p. 10). A definition introduced by Stone emphasized that virtual communities are "incontrovertibly social spaces in which people still meet face-to face, but under new definitions of both 'meet' and 'face'" (qtd. in Jankowski 2002: 39).

To gain insight into the question of children's use of cyberspace as a social space, both surveys of children and interviews with mothers were conducted.

The participants

The participants in this project included Egyptian children, between the ages of 11 and 13, who were members of Facebook. It is important to note that the minimum age of Facebook participants is 13 years old; however, some surveyed children were able to manipulate their age in order to be members at Facebook. It was a non-probability sample based on three main qualities: the child needed to be a member at Facebook and Egyptian between the ages of 11 and 13. One hundred children participated.

In addition to the surveys, intensive interviews were conducted to provide the researcher with detailed information about the impact of virtual socialization on children's lives as observed by their mothers. Ten mothers participated in the interviews and supported their children's responses. It is important to highlight that information collected from mothers were specific to the children and no information about mothers' themselves was required for the study.

Indeed, we found, the more time children invested on their Facebook, the more socially active they appear to become. Of the 100 children surveyed, most spent an average of at least two hours every two days and many spent more in their virtual communities. While 19% spent an average of 1 hour every two days; 33% spent around two hours every two; and, 48% of the children spent approximately 3 hours every two days. We also examined the assumption that virtual socialization enhances the participant's social interactions and 79% of the children agreed, 11% were neutral, while only 10% disagreed.

In the survey, the majority of the children stated that their purpose for using Facebook was socialization: chatting with current or old friends; using virtual applications such as giving presents, playing quizzes and games, joining clubs and social gatherings; exchanging photos; and, interacting with group of people of their common interests. In addition, a majority of the children indicated that they are able to connect with old friends through the "search for friends option" that Facebook offers. Many of the surveyed children highlighted that they were able to easily find friends that they had lost contacts with. Others said that Facebook offered a highly segmented group of interests, which can give them the chance to practice the activities that they like; and more importantly enjoy.

For example, there are groups that are interested in specific types of music or singers; specific sports, books, games, and literature.

It was clear that the children established cohort relationships with other members of Facebook. Most of the research sample strongly agreed that cyber space socialization is considered to be an important factor for their late childhood interactions; further, they have highlighted that digital practices through Facebook positively affect their offline socialization process as well as helping them becoming more knowledgeable, social, and able to deal with people from different nationalities, especially because Facebook has the option of exchanging photos, and using voice and cameras through conference calls, which all increase children's socialization options.

Reflections on Facebook

The responses from the children supported the position that computer-mediated communication has furnished the opportunity to build new forms of social ties and another type of community among children, which can be perceived as a valuable resource for childhood socialization. According to the children, virtual socialization doesn't isolate the children from their physical world. In fact, it provided them with different socialization option and revitalized their physical world. Additionally, the effect of virtual socialization extended well beyond the boundaries of Facebook as it has positive effects on children's off-line world as well.

Perceptions of Egyptian children's digital socialization

The majority of the Egyptian children were able to establish coherent virtual relationships – 'coherent', is the ability to establish virtual social ties with other online members of Facebook and to be able to develop a sense of commitment to the other members of virtual communities, with whom the child is virtually communicating. The majority of the children were also able to develop strong virtual social ties with other Facebook members. Sharing a common interest with other members was a basic reinforcement to virtual relationships. The majority of respondents were able to build up a sense of commitment. Moreover, it was found that not only the use of technology shapes its essence, but also this newly emerged pattern of usage has further implications on the surrounding social context.

The Egyptian children's responses to the surveys appear to demonstrate that these children become more socially active in their physical world through cyberspace socialization. More importantly, virtual communities eradicate inequalities among various members as people focus on the content of discourse;

consequently, eliminating inequalities created by other diminutions for virtual public discourse as the participant can communicate with people who are not available at the person's social sphere at the offline world. Besides, the concept of disembedding, or the irrelevance of geographic positions to participants have further extended members' social options at virtual communities illustrates the latter point (Giddens 1990). Actually, the researcher regards all the previous points as positive effects on children's civic inclusion either at their virtual communities or on their civic life at their civic world.

In line with inequalities, the researcher believes that virtual communities are established by designers who control the civic atmosphere of the virtual community, its cultures, "social norms" and "ethos" (Bartle 2004). This has strong implications for virtual civic liberty, which consequently positively affects the civic inclusion of participants. For elaboration, it has been noted by Richard Bartle in his book *Designing Virtual Worlds*, that online communities are "20% nature and 80% nurture" (2004). In other words, designers "set up the nature- the conditions that allow a community to develop" and "the members of the community perform the nurture- how the community develops"; he further highlighted that "identical incarnations of virtual worlds will usually end up having recognizably different communities" (Bartle 2004: 213).

Having argued that virtual communities, through Facebook, encourage children's socialization and increases their options at both the physical and virtual communities, the researcher voices the importance to further elaborate on this point. Generally speaking, the Internet can be defined as a "global pool of information and services, accessible locally through individual computer stations that are each part of a global system of interconnected computer networks" (Haplin, Hick, and Hoskins 2000, p. 10). It is of paramount importance that since those children who practice cyberspace socialization have are positively affected by it, there will be a gap between children who have access to cyber socialization, and other children who do not. Since Internet sustains the existence of the virtual communities. The researcher argues that the deepening of the gap touches the civic rights of the children.

In *Communicating at the Information Society*, issued by the United Nations Research Institute for Social Development (UNRISD), Antonio Pasquali stated that "communication rights have to cover an area of praxis far greater than that covered by article 19 of the 1966 International Covenant on Civil and Political Rights" (Pasquali 2003). Pasquali pointed to six "ingredients" of communication rights among the four relevant here are:

1. communication is "an inalienable birthright of human beings, gifted like no other being for the coding/transmission and decoding/receiving of messages, for one to know the other through intercommunication in codes and channels selected them";
2. "individual and social rights to communication have the same dignity and must be harmoniously reconciled";

3. "any obstacle put in the way of the free exercise of communication rights, in regard to codes, channels, content, moment, place, or choice of receivers, is an attack on relational nature of human beings and should be considered a crime."
4. "human societies, ideally considered as a hierarchical continuum from open to closed, reflect the communicative relations prevailing in them and how their citizens exercise communication rights. Any change in the communicative model leads to social change" (Pasquali 2003, p. 209).

These stress the impact of communication media on social change, and that communication rights should be granted to every citizen and every child. The research results here demonstrate that the Internet, in the form of Facebook, has furnished the birth of another form of community for Egyptian children. A community that enjoys a high sense of democracy, harmony, homogeneity, and respected civic rights and disregards physical characteristics and focuses on the content and the core of discourse.

Conclusions and recommendations

Unlike some who have stated their concern that Internet usage may lead people to withdrawal from social engagement and abandon contact with their offline communities, the researcher have found the opposite. The 100 Egyptian children here demonstrated that virtual communities constitute part of children's socialization process. Facebook has played a role in expanding children's public sphere, and acted as a catalyst for participant's civic inclusion. Thus, it can be perceived as another form of social capital. Consequently, three recommendations are suggested and should be put into consideration. The first one is utilizing the significance of virtual civic inclusion at the social marketing campaigns as to encourage more Egyptian children to explore the virtual socialization. Second, building an African virtual community is of great importance as it can be considered as a significant mean for unifying the citizens, and children in particular of the African region away from the current political situation. Third, produce developmental awareness campaigns as to stress the importance of cyberspace socialization, and this is unlike the wide spread notion that Internet communication leads to isolation and deprivation, which can be considered as a step in integrating information and communication technologies (ICTs) as a factor of everyday life of the Egyptian children

Finally, it is important to highlight that the current developments of technology hold new structures for the civility of human kind that should always be considered, encouraged, and more importantly, to be utilized.

References

Bartle, Richard (2003) *Designing Virtual Worlds*. Indianapolis: New Riders Publishing.

Fernback, Jan and Brad Thompson (1995) *Virtual Communities: Abort, Retry, Failure?* University of South Australia.

Flichy, Patrice (1995) *Dynamics of Modern Communication*. London: Sage Publications.

Giddens, Anthony (1990) *The Consequences of Modernity*. Stanford Calif: Stanford University Press.

Haplin, Edward; Hick, Steven and Hoskins, Eric (2000) Introduction, in Steven Hick, Edward Halpin and Eric Hoskins (eds.) *Human Rights and the Internet*. Great Britain: Antony Rowe, pp. 1-15.

Jankowski, Nicholas (2002) Creating Community with Media, in Leah A. Lievrouw and Sonia Livingstone (eds.) *The Handbook of New Media*. London: Sage Publications, pp. 34-49.

Lievrouw, Leah A. (2002a)Technology Design and Development, in Leah A. Lievrouw and Sonia Livingstone (eds.) *The Handbook of New Media*. London: Sage Publications, pp. 131-135.

Lievrouw, Leah A. (2002b) Determination and Contingency in New Media Development:Diffusion of Innovations and Social Shaping of Technology Perspectives, in Leah A. Lievrouw and Sonia Livingstone (eds.) *The Handbook of New Media* London: Sage Publications, pp. 183-199.

Livingstone, Sonia and Leah A. Lievrouw (2002a) The Contributors, in Leah A. Lievrouw and Sonia Livingstone (eds.) *The Handbook of New Media*. London: Sage Publications, pp. xi-xxii.

Livingstone, Sonia and Leah A. Lievrouw (2002b) The Social Shaping and Consequences of ICTs, in Leah A. Lievrouw and Sonia Livingstone (eds.) *The Handbook of New Media*. London: Sage Publications, pp. 1-15.

Marvin, Carolyn (1988) *When Old Technologies were New: Thinking About Electric Communication in the Late Nineteenth Century*. New York: Oxford University Press.

McQuail, Denis (1994) *Mass Communication Theory*. London: Sage.

McLuhan, Marshall and Powers, Bruce (1989) *The Global Village: Transformations in World Life and Media in the 21st Century*. New York: Oxford University Press.

McMillan, Sally, J. (2002) Exploring Models of Interactivity From MultipleResearch Traditions: Users, Documents, and Systems, in Leah A. Lievrouw and Sonia Livingstone (eds.) *The Handbook of New Media*. London: Sage Publications, pp. 163-182.

Pasquali, Antonio (2003) A Brief Descriptive Glossary of Communication and Information (Aimed at Providing Clarification and Improving Mutual Understanding), inBruce Girard and Sean O Siochru (ed.) *Communicating in the Information Society* Geneva: United Nations Research Institute for Social Development, pp. 195-223.

Pool, Ithiel de Sola (1983) *Technologies of Freedom*. London: The Belknap Press of Harvard University.

Rheingold, Howard (1993) A Slice of Life in My Virtual Community, in Linda M. Harasim (ed.) *Global Networks: Computers and International Communication*. Cambridge. Mass: MIT Press, pp. 57-80.

Rheingold, Howard (2000) *The Virtual Community: Homesteading on the Electronic Frontier*, Revised Edition. London: The MIT Press.

Severin, Werner J. and Tankard, James (2001) *Communication Theories: Origins, Methods, and Uses in the Mass Media*. United States of America: Longman.

Slater, Don (2002) Social Relationships and Identity Online and Offline. Leah A. Lievrouw and Sonia Livingstone (eds.), *The Handbook of New Media* London: Sage Publications, pp. 533-546.

Williams, Frederick, Rice, Ronald, and Rogers, Everett (1998) *Research Methods and the New Media*. London: Collier Macmillan Publishers.

Wikipedia. *Facebook*. Online. Available on: http://en.wikipedia.org/wiki/Facebook

Opportunities, Challenges, & the Way Forward*

Frederick Nnoma-Addison

My address is inspired by personal connections to the subject under consideration "African Children & African Media". Firstly I reflect over the fact that I was once an African child. Secondly I was raised in Ghana by a mother who taught Kindergarten (children) her entire life and a father who was a broadcaster for over 30 years (media). Thirdly I have been academically and professionally involved in the media industries both on the African continent and in the United States for the past 14 years and lastly currently employed by a global media corporation-Discovery Communications, Inc. Beyond my own personal connection with the subject, the relevance of this subject at a time when many African governments are stressing the importance of childhood media literacy in socio-economic development compels me to join in this important dialogue.

In confronting the subject, I deem it necessary to first challenge traditional prejudices towards the African continent and demand that individuals approach the topic in a holistic manner, contrary to the usual approach fueled by media stereotypes of a grossly dysfunctional continent. In commenting on the subject I will also highlight the following Sub themes: African children, African media, African children's access to media, their use of it, participation in it and exposure to it.

The African child, once carved out primarily by African cultures, has always held an esteemed place in African societies. This esteemed place is evidenced through history, traditions and cultural practices. Today, they are exposed to and influenced by foreign pop cultures resulting in new trends such as; uncharacteristically extrovert behavior, acquired foreign tastes, knowledge of new media technology and fired ambitious among others.

In much the same way as African children and cultures are being transformed, African Media is also changing on several levels, offering tremendous opportunities to African children. In the early '90's when I was actively involved with the Ghanaian media, there was only one television station, the Ghana Broadcasting Corporation (GBC) and two radio stations in a country with a population of over 17 million at the time. All three of them were state-owned. As a result of privatization however the Ghanaian media today boasts of at least three additional private television stations and close to one hundred FM Radio stations nation-wide, a change that has already provided new opportunities to Ghanaian children through increased media participation. Re: notable and award-winning shows as "*By the Fire Side*" and *Kyekyekule* – Ghana. This trend is equally true in several other African nations. Growth of the African media inevitably includes growth of the African media practitioner. Contrary to what prevailed 10-15 years ago, the average African media practitioner has greater chances of learning from the international media community by virtue of being more exposed to and engaged with it. Such exposure only improves the professional quality of African practitioners and consequently translates positively to the African child.

The existence of international media networks like CNN, BBC, Associated Press (AP), Reuters and Discovery, also influences growth of the African media and practitioners in no small way. Additionally the fact that most of these networks hire African natives is a potential advantage for African media as it pertains to children. CNN for example boasts of Nigerian native Femi Oke who joined the Network in 1999 as weather anchor, and South African native Tumi Makgabo of *Inside Africa* fame. Femi resigned in 2005 and returned to her native country to contribute to the development of the South African media from her rich experiences and knowledge base. Being a mother of at least two young children herself, one expects that minimally she would be able to contribute a token towards children's media development in South Africa.

Other factors that present new opportunities to the African child today include growth of multi-media especially in the industrialized world, the internet and world-wide-web, digitization and introduction of multiple viewing screens. Business growth in the industrialized world has a phenomenal impact on the lives of Africans and their children. With satellite technology, this is truer for the media industry. Through the magic of a unified global market, populations across international boundaries are able to enjoy the same benefits of a product or service originally intended for consumers in one particular country. Re: the birth in the United States of the Discovery Channel in 1985, originally intended for Americans but now in 160 countries including 43 in Africa.

Thanks to the internet, school children in some of the remotest parts of Uganda (Nalinya) now have equal access to the educational resources that their counterparts in the west have. For this same reason, Discovery Channel's new online homework assistant COSMEO is no longer limited to U.S. based students alone but to children in every corner of the world where there is broadband access. Digitization of media in Africa yet another opportunity now enables more users to better manipulate and manage audio-visual information in new, innovative ways. Digitization simply implies that media assets can reach more consumers at a faster pace and at better quality than previously. In short a digital media industry is one that offers endless possibilities to all users worldwide, including African children.

The multi-platform concept of television viewing offers significant benefits to the

African child as it typically exposes media users to different formats, offering them more choices in hardware and helping them prioritize their media needs. Indeed all the mentioned developments in both the industrialized and non-industrialized worlds enhance the African child's chances of becoming media savvy.

Having listed some of the wonderful existing opportunities, it is worth noting that there are extreme challenges confronting African children and their quest for media literacy. My failure to address these challenges will therefore leave my address incomplete. In considering these challenges, access is the principal concern. "If only all had the same opportunities, all things being equal there would be fewer disparities – Source Unknown". The reality about the economies of developing African countries is that often the media's agenda for children cannot be implemented because of the overwhelming demands on these young economies, which makes the issue of the African child and media primarily an economic one. The other factors are political climates, know-how, persistent health epidemics and natural disasters.

As an example of the economic handicap, although Ghana's economy has emerged as one of the best in sub Saharan Africa according to the World Bank, it has still not reached a level where it pays adequate attention to the media needs of her children. The question then is "if Ghana, economically and politically stable as it is, is only scratching the surface of this issue then what can one expect from less stable and privileged countries like Rwanda, Liberia, Togo, La Cote d'Ivoire or Somalia, countries either living in the shadows of a just ended civil war or worse still in the middle of it?". As you would well imagine priorities are entirely different in many of these challenged countries, rendering the issue of children and media totally irrelevant and unfit even for discussion.

On the devastating effects of health epidemics I defer to South Africa and Botswana; two countries with some of the highest GDP's on the continent. For these countries the predictable consequences of the HIV/AIDS pandemic is that over time, resources intended for other sectors of the economy like education, will eventually be diverted to the health sector, if the alarming trends are not curbed through some means. For the average African government therefore the issue of allocating resources to the media needs of children remains a constant dilemma and there is no easy resolution. One of the fundamental problems facing developing countries is that often resources continues to elude those who are in need of it; if it is not education budgets being used to acquire guns then it is guns in the hands of the wrong people or a small minority having more than is needed at the expense of the entire well being of the country or community.

Having examined some of the opportunities and challenges relating to the topic, I make the following recommendations based upon my hands – on experiences and involvement with the media and Africa.

- Big Picture Approach: There is the need to strive to further understand the Africa region in totality, not just aspects of it. Study the needs of the people by conducting exhaustive research, extensive reading and most importantly interaction with the peoples and cultures on a first hand basis.

- Publishing: Capture and publish all the possibilities that media can provide African children. These could take the form of educational publications that make the subject more relevant and practical to African people.
- Dialogue & Action: Promote more dialogue both on the continent and in the Diaspora, followed by appropriate actions
- Ownership: Help African communities take responsibility/ownership of this challenge as an important step to addressing the issue.
- Policy & Enforcement: Weigh-in on government policy & legislation either in the Diaspora or on the African continent.
- Consequences for Inaction: Trumpet the fact that those in the west could share in the consequences if we fail to pay adequate attention to the subject.
- Bridge Building: Build bridges with the African Diplomatic community in Washington and other international African organizations, plus strategic partnerships with U.S. corporations already doing business in Africa. The D.C. based Corporate Council on Africa consisting of approximately 140 U.S. member companies with business interests in Africa is a great place to start.
- Funding: Encourage charitable acts within corporate America where possible. Some American companies do need fresh ideas on how to spend huge profits.
- Review and renew individual commitments to the subject since it will not be addressed overnight.
- Stay true to the mission and not be swayed by personal interests
- Accept the fact that one's efforts may never be recognized or rewarded publicly.

To conclude, I make a conscious decision to focus on the brighter side of African media and African children; including my own journey across two worlds as well as that of several other noble ones making small but very significant contributions towards giving African children a stake in media in their own countries and in the Diaspora. Indeed I do not agree with anyone who despises the current condition or thinks there is no hope, on the contrary I agree with anyone who believes that it is possible to achieve meaningful media-child relationship in Africa, identifies that this matter needs persistent and long term commitment from dedicated individuals and organizations world wide and takes practical steps towards contributing to the solution. I look forward to the day that we shall all be able to identify some of the tangible fruits of our labor.

*This article was the Keynote address at the African Children & African Media Conference sponsored by the Institute for the African Child at Ohio University, Athens Ohio, USA; June 15-18, 2006.

Children's Television Programs in Ghana

The Challenges of Local Production

Patrick V. Osei-Hwere

Over the past decades, Ghana has made some modest gains in terms of providing children's media content. The commitment of media practitioners to providing children with access to media content and production has been demonstrated by Ghana's involvement with formulating international charters and agreements related to the mass media. For example, Ghana was instrumental in preparing the Africa Charter on Children's Broadcasting including acting as host country to the African summit where the charter was adopted in 1997. Prior to this, Ghana was the first country to ratify the UN Convention on the Rights of the Child, which protects and serves the interests of children including stipulations about children's use of and access to media.

Turning from the international arena to the national stage, the ideal of providing children with access to quality media content is incorporated in Ghana's national media policy. The National Media Commission set broad media policies concerning children for the print and electronic media. With regards to print media the policy states "It is the duty of the media to protect, the identity, privacy and reputation of children" (National Media Policy 1996: 44). Radio and TV stations are expected to "produce programs that protect children's rights and support their sound psychological and social development" (National Media Policy 1996: 45). The policies regarding children in general stipulate that the media should not just refrain from doing harm to children but must also promote programs that contribute to children's development. The guarantee of freedom of the media is given with the caveat that, "the media shall exert with care its influence in shaping the sensibilities of children and minors" (National Media Policy 1996: 27). The public media are expected to provide for the information, education and communication needs of children and other marginalized groups. Advertisers are cautioned to recognize and refrain from exploiting the vulnerability of children. This case study of Ghana's children's media examines the efforts to transform such policy documents into reality.

Ghana's electronic media market overview

The population of Ghana is estimated at 23.9 million (UNSTATS 2008). The media markets in the country are considerably smaller compared to markets in other African countries such as Nigeria and South Africa. The predominant broadcast medium is radio with an estimated national radio audience of 14 million people owning about 13.4 million radio sets. The reach of each station is somewhat limited by the use of FM transmitters. Furthermore the majority of stations operate in the national capital Accra. The other stations operate mainly from the nine regional capitals with the highest number of stations located in Kumasi, Takoradi, and Cape Coast.

Some television stations in Ghana have a wider reach than FM radio stations with two stations reaching the whole nation and another reaching about a third of the country. The estimated national TV viewing audience is 11.6 million. Ghana Television (GTV), the television channel of Ghana Broadcasting Corporation (GBC) the national broadcaster, has an estimated peak viewing audience of 6.7 million while TV3, a private free-to-air station based in Accra has an estimated peak viewing audience of 4 million viewers (audience estimates are from the websites of GTV and TV3). Television viewing is largely confined to the urban areas. Although rural populations can receive transmitted terrestrial TV signals because of the use of microwave radio links, the lack of consistent electricity and the cost of TV sets serve as disincentives for rural populations to gain access to television programming. This situation is however gradually changing with the government's national electrification projects.

The media market structure in Ghana is such that all the media organizations depend on some form of advertising revenue to run their operations. This can pose a challenge when the estimated annual advertising expenditure in Ghana is $25 million (Steadman 2005). The market may be small, and advertising expenditure modest yet efforts are being made to nurture and develop the media industry.

Historical overview of broadcasting system

Before the introduction of media liberalization in the 1990s, Ghana had one broadcasting service and that was the Ghana Broadcasting Corporation (GBC) which provided both radio and television broadcasts. The origins of GBC can be traced back to "Station ZOY" launched in 1935 by the British colonial governor. Station ZOY was set up as a radio relay network in Accra to serve the expatriate and Ghanaian elite community in the then Gold Coast with news and entertainment produced by the British Broadcasting Corporation. The British government constructed a broadcasting house and introduced local language broadcasts in the 1940s and in 1953 the Gold Coast Broadcasting System (GCBS) was created as part of the government's Public Relations department. Soon after Ghana's independence from British colonial rule, GCBS was renamed Ghana Broadcasting

System and incorporated in 1968 to become Ghana Broadcasting Corporation (GBC). The corporation continued to receive state funding after it started commercial broadcasting in 1967 and this funding helped GBC to develop programs and expand its services. However, the government still had the power to influence program content as well as the appointment of the corporation's officers.

The 1990s was really a decade of significant change. At the political level, the country returned to constitutional democratic rule in 1992. The constitution made provision for the establishment of private media and that spurred efforts to establish new TV stations in the country. In 1996 GBC entered into partnership with Media Number One to launch Metropolitan Entertainment Television (Metro TV). This was a commercial station providing entertainment programs for people living in the nation's capital and surrounding cities. The government sold the Ghana Films Corporation in 1996 to one of the largest media investment groups in Malaysia, Media Prima Berhad. The Malaysian investors then established TV3 Network Limited and launched Ghana's first privately owned free-to-air TV station in 1997.

Ghana now has a pluralistic media system consisting of private commercial stations competing with the state-owned station. As at December 2006 there were 32 licensed television stations, cable and satellite subscription service providers in Ghana. Some of those operational in Accra include GTV, TV3, Metro TV, and TV Africa all free-to-air stations; cable operators Cable Gold and TV Agoro (which supplies the Cartoon Network); and MultiChoice Ghana, which operates a satellite television service providing a bouquet of channels including the Disney Channel, Boomerang, Cartoon Network, and programming from Nickelodeon. Three other pay-per-view stations operate outside the nation's capital. These are Crystal TV and *Fontonfrom* TV providing services to subscribers in Kumasi and Skyy TV in Sekondi/Takoradi.

The state-owned corporation has the public service mission of informing, educating and entertaining its audience. Broadcasting was to be used as a tool for national development. In his address at the inauguration of television in Ghana, President Nkrumah stressed that the primary goals of television were educational and political. Television was to be used for education and the socialist transformation of Ghana (Nkrumah 1965). The ideals of education and national development were included in the articles of incorporation of GBC which stated that "the objects of the broadcasting corporation shall be to undertake sound, commercial radio and television broadcasts, to prepare in the field of culture, education, information and entertainment programs reflecting national progress" (N.L.C.D. 226 1968, quoted in Anokwa 1997: 13).

The private commercial media is expected to operate in the public interest as well. The National Media Policy set forth by the National Media Commission states that "[a]ll media and media services shall be regarded as a public trust. The public interest shall therefore, be paramount in the operation of all media – public, commercial and community" (National Media Policy 1996: 27). In serving the public interest, it is expected that both state-owned and private commercial media "shall enact the role of the media to inform, educate and entertain in pursuit of dynamic, equitable and culturally endowed national development" (National Media Policy 1996: 27).

Importance of children's television programs

The debates in the United States and Europe concerning media violence should not take away from the important role educational and informational children's media content can play in children's cognitive, emotional, psychological, and social development. Various studies show the positive influence of exposure to children's media. For instance, children who are exposed to age appropriate educational and informational programs do better in school (Huston et al 2001); exposure to educational children's television programs can help preschoolers and young children with language development (Linebarger and Walker 2005); and television programs in English can help children who are learning English as a second language to develop their language skills (Colorín Colorado 2007). Furthermore, children copy the role models they see on television and learn moral and social lessons from prosocial edutainment programs (Calvert et al. 2001; Wright et al 2001). The increased production of prosocial edutainment and educational programs can serve as an alternative to violent children's programs and perhaps an antidote to the potential negative effects of violence in children's programming.

Apart from advocating for the provision of children's programs in general, the case can also be made for the importance of locally-produced media content. The frequency with which a social group is presented in the media can serve as a symbolic representation of that group's status in society. When groups are not represented or are invisible in the media it sends the message that the group is not important. In that regards, the absence of Ghanaian children in children's television programs and the prevalence of children from other countries in a variety of roles on television can send a negative message to Ghanaian children that could be detrimental to their self-esteem and development (Palmer, Taylor Smith, and Strawser 1993).

Media also play an important role in children's, especially adolescent's, identity formation. During adolescence and the early teenage years, children develop a sense of identity separate from their parents and the family unit (Huntemann and Morgan 2001; Steinberg and Silverberg 1986). Children at this age use the media more than younger children as they pursue their interests in music, film, magazines and online activities. Their interaction with the mass media exposes them to various social definitions of acceptable behavior, identity, and roles. Adolescents see characters in the media play different roles, get rewarded or punished for certain behaviors, express and affirm various values, and engage in social interaction. These media characters, stars, and celebrities serve as role models that adolescents identify with and tend to emulate. With locally produced programs, children stand a better chance of finding media characters with similar cultural values to identify with.

Finally, locally-produced content give children the opportunity to participate in the various stages of children's media production. They can contribute content, help with technical aspects such as directing, sound control, camera work or perform as actors and talent for the program. This access to media helps children appreciate how media production works and can have a positive impact on their interaction with media.

Ghana's television industry is still developing but it still cannot afford to ignore the interests of children who make up almost 40 percent of the country's population. The local broadcasting stations have not been averse to broadcasting children's programs. They acknowledge the importance of quality programming for children's development and some of the stations consider it their public service responsibility to broadcast such programs. It is therefore not surprising that children's programs have always been on the schedules of broadcasters. The next section provides a brief overview of children's television programs that have been available to children in Ghana.

Children's television programs

Programming for children has been an integral part of the mission of GBC. The Television Service of the corporation has a children's department to oversee the production and provision of children's programs (GBC 1985). GBC began producing children's programs during the early 1970s. One of the most popular children's programs during that period was "Children's Own". This was an entertainment program that encouraged children six to twelve years to engage in art, music, and drama. Another program, popular with pre-school children was "*Koliko*" – a puppet show that dramatized adventure stories with characters children could identify with. Some of the stories incorporated popular *Ananse* folktales giving it a wide appeal. Other programs such as "Young Scientist" taught children 10 to 15 years old about basic scientific concepts and laws. Special programs such as "Builders of Today" were produced to address the specific needs of teenagers. This was a magazine program where young people discussed and provided solutions to issues relevant to them (GBC 1985).

The number of children's programs and how long they run varied over the years. By 1994 GBC was broadcasting about seven locally produced children's programs each week. Some of these programs were "Toddler's Time" for preschoolers; "Hobby Time" for 3rd to 5th graders; "2nd Generation", "By the Fireside", and "*Kyekyekule*", for 6th to 9th graders; and "Dos Computer Byte", and "Brilliant Science and Math Quiz" for senior secondary school students (Heath 1996). In 1995, GBC added "Kiddie Quiz", a program for junior secondary school students to its schedule. Another educational program for elementary schools called "*Kwasasa*" was added to the schedule at the end of the 1990s.

In the early 1990s GBC adopted the policy of independent productions and sponsorship of programs. This was to encourage diversity of programs, allow GBC to focus on public service programs, and provide financing for programs. As a result of this policy, a number of children's programs telecast on GBC were sponsored independent productions. These included "*Kyekyekule*", "Teen Beat", "Smash TV", "Brilliant Science and Math Quiz", "Kiddie Quiz", and "By the Fireside". GBC complemented its locally-produced children's programs with US imports such as "Sesame Street", "Gummi Bears", and various cartoons for children. For older children, GBC imported US sitcoms such as "Cosby Show", "Different Strokes", and "Fresh Prince".

The broadcast of imported television programs can be attributed to a number of factors. Firstly, as the television station stayed on air for longer hours during the day, there was the need for programs to fill its expanding schedule. When private commercial television stations began broadcasting in Ghana there was a quantitative increase in the number of hours dedicated to children's programs. For instance, Metro TV rebroadcast programs from GBC including children's programs. It was common for Metro TV to show reruns of the same program till it was able to fill its schedule with new programs. Similarly, when TV3 started broadcasting, it filled its schedule with reruns of cartoons and children's programs till it obtained enough regular programs for adults. Since cartoons have a wide appeal in terms of audience demographics and are relatively cheaper to import, station mangers used them to keep the new station on the air and attract an audience till it was able to secure sufficient programs and advertising.

The second reason for the increasing use of imported children's television programs in Ghana is the expanding international media market. Western producers and distributors of programs in syndication have sought new markets outside America and Europe for their products. Africa has been considered a burgeoning market for western media products leading to TV stations on the continent, including Ghana, filling their schedules with imported programs. These programs for children consist of educational and entertainment programs that are animated or live-action with formats including adventure/action, drama, magazine, quiz/game, and sitcoms imported from the US, Canada, UK, Italy, Australia and South Africa.

Importing children's program is an attractive proposition for program managers in Ghana for a number of reasons. Firstly, imported programs are sometimes cheaper than local productions when one factors in the number of times it can be used in broadcast reruns. The cost of some of the programs that have been in syndication for a long time is cheaper than the cost of locally-produced programs. Secondly, there are a variety of programs to choose from which makes it easier to fill the allotted slots for children's programs in the broadcast schedule. Thirdly, the production quality of imported children's programs is sometimes higher than locally-produced programs and children tend to discriminate between high quality and low quality programs. Another reason program managers opt for imported programs is that they can have an idea of how well a program will do in the local market by examining its ratings record in different international markets where these imported programs have been in syndication. Finally, some imported children's programs have already been produced with several season's worth of episodes available for broadcast.

Besides the imported children's programs broadcast by the free-to-air stations, cable and satellite operators also offer a bouquet of imported channels to subscribers in Ghana. These operators include Cable Gold, TV *Agoro*, Crystal TV, Skyy TV and MultiChoice Ghana. Together these cable and satellite operators provide subscribers in different parts of the country with channels that have children's programs such as Animal Planet, Cartoon Network, Etv, K-TV, M-Net, SABC Africa, TBN, ZEE TV and more recently the Disney Channel and Nickelodeon. The availability of imported programs can serve as a disincentive for the local production of children's television programs.

Broadcast schedules for children's television programs

Most of the TV stations in Ghana regularly scheduled programs for children. An audit of television program schedules for the second quarter of 2005 showed that programs generally targeted preschool, elementary, junior and senior high school children (Table 1). Although the number of unique titles of television programs for children in high school was less than the number of unique program titles for children in elementary school, television programs for children in high school were usually longer and so had more time allocated to them in the broadcast schedule than programs for younger children. A majority of the children's television programs targeted children in elementary school. The private stations had more programs for this age group than the state-owned GBC. Many of the programs for six to twelve year-olds were imported cartoons or animated programs.

Table 1. Average number of hours per week of children's television programs targeting preschool, elementary and high school children scheduled by GTV, Metro TV, and TV3 during the second quarter of 2005

Television Station	Preschool Children		Elementary School Children		High School Children	
	Hrs/Wk	%	Hrs/Wk	%	Hrs/Wk	%
GTV	0.5	4	2	13	12.5	83
Metro TV	0	0	3	35	5.5	65
TV 3	0.5	7	6.5	86	0.5	7
All Stations	1	3	11.5	37	18.5	60

The number of children's programs available on TV varied by station. GTV devoted the most time per week to children's programs followed by Metro TV and TV3. Children's programs were broadcast between 9-11a.m. and 4-7 p.m. on weekdays, and between 8:30 a.m.-12 noon on Saturdays and Sundays. Educational programs were usually broadcast during weekday mornings intended for children in school to complement classroom instruction. The reason for scheduling children's programs during the afternoon time slot is that children are available to watch these programs after returning home from school. Another reason is that fewer adults watch TV during the weekday afternoon and weekend morning time slots.

GTV allocated the most hours to children's programming. This was about sixteen hours every week. However the "Distance Learning" program took up a large majority of the time allocated to children's programs. GTV regularly broadcast this program from 9-11a.m. Monday through Thursday and repeated some of the programs twice a week from 4-6 p.m. The station broadcast about an hour of additional children's programs during the week. On Saturdays mornings, GTV broadcast an assortment of locally produced and imported children's programs called the "Children's Channel".

Metro TV broadcast about nine hours of children's programs per week. During the work week, Metro TV broadcast during the "children's belt" time slot. This was typically from 4-6 p.m. "School TV" was broadcast from 4-5 p.m. and a variety of imported cartoons were shown from 5:30-6 p.m. The station also provided programs for older children on Saturday between 6-7 p.m. and Sunday from 8:30-10:30 a.m. Some of these programs included imported sitcoms such as the "Cosby Show" and "Fresh Prince" or locally produced children's variety shows such as "Smash TV".

TV3 showed about seven hours of children's programs per week. The station regularly scheduled children's programs from 4-4:30 p.m. on weekdays. Programs such as the cartoon series "Tommy and Oscar" (from Italy) and the action/adventure series "Ocean Girl (from Australia) have been shown during this time slot. From 5-5:30 p.m. on weekdays TV3 scheduled K-time, which featured a variety of imported cartoons. Other animated series such as "Dennis and Gnasher" (from the UK) were shown about twice or three times a week. On Saturday TV3 broadcast programs such as "Barney and Friends" (from the US) and "*Kyekyekule* Kids TV" in the mornings but this was not regularly scheduled all year round.

The proportion of time assigned to imported and locally produced children's programs varied by station (Table 2). The state-owned GTV was the only station with more programming hours of locally produced children's programs (93%) than imported programs. The number of hours of scheduled children's programs by GTV was more than the combined programming hours of children's programs by Metro TV and TV3. On the other hand, the privately owned TV3 scheduled more hours of imported children's programs (93%) than locally produced programs. The combined schedules of GTV, Metro TV, and TV3 had more programming hours of locally produced programs (largely due to the broadcast output of GTV) than imported programs.

Many of the imported programs were repeated so many times that children who were regular television viewers tended to lose interest in watching the program. Most of the TV stations tried to maintain the time slots designated for children's programming however it was not uncommon to see live events such as sports competitions, or trade fairs broadcast during that time slot instead of children's programs.

Table 2. Average number of hours per week of locally produced and imported children's programs scheduled by GTV, Metro TV, and TV3 during the second quarter of 2005

Television Station	Locally Produced Programs Hrs/Week	Locally Produced Programs % across	Imported Programs Hrs/Week	Imported Programs % across	Total Hrs/Week	Total %
GTV	14	93	1	7	15	100
Metro TV	3.5	41	5	59	8.5	100
TV3	0.5	7	7	93	7.5	100
All stations	18	58	13	42	31	100

Locally produced children's television programs

Many of the locally produced children's programs broadcast by GBC, TV3, and Metro TV were educational or edutainment (entertainment with educational components) programs. These programs were either based directly on the school curriculum or encouraged children to engage in extracurricular activities. Some of the programs also concentrated on teaching social skills, cultural competence and moral values. These programs used human characters and hardly any animation or cartoon characters. Children's programs produced in Ghana can be broadly categorized based on content. These categories are the formal educational content category, the informal educational content category, the traditional performance content category, and the assorted content category.

The formal educational category consists of programs that simulate classroom instruction. For example "School TV" on Metro TV and "Distance Learning" on GTV use trained teachers to present English and Mathematics lessons based on the junior and senior high school curricula. These programs were produced in response to the Government's initiative to improve education and equip the youth for the future. One of such targeted efforts at improving education by the government of Ghana is the President's Special Initiative on Distance Learning. "Distance Learning", broadcast by GTV, started as a pilot program of this initiative. Teachers from better performing schools in Ghana wrote, reviewed, and presented topics in English and mathematics on television for the benefit of students in less academically endowed schools. The program continued to run after the success of the pilot phase. Metro TV also started broadcasting "School TV" in response to the President's Special Initiative on Distance Learning.

The second broad category of programs is the informal educational content category. This consists of programs that use the quiz or game show format to educate children in an informal and entertaining way. The subjects covered could be general knowledge or topics based on the school curriculum. The questions for programs such as "Bournvita Brain Match" on Metro TV, "Sharp Brain" on TV3, and "Kiddie Quiz" on GTV were based on general knowledge and the junior high school curriculum. On the other hand, the "National Science and Math Quiz" program on GTV was based on the senior high school curriculum. Questions for the quiz programs targeting junior secondary school children were based on subjects such as mathematics, English, social studies and cultural studies. A number of these programs tended to involve viewers across the country by inviting contesting schools to a national competition. The "National Science and Math Quiz" and "Kiddie Quiz" on GTV used participants to represent the different regions of the country. The "National Science and Math Quiz" had two contesting senior secondary schools for each program while "Kiddie Quiz" used three contesting junior secondary schools per program. Winning schools advanced to the next round till the final competition where the national champion was crowned. This category of programs attempts to educate and inform children in an informal way through entertainment.

The third category of programs is the traditional performance content category. These programs are based on traditional formats such as folk songs, stories, dance and drama. Ghana has a rich cultural heritage of folktales, games, proverbs, riddles, songs, and dance that producers tap into to develop children's programs. Some of the popular programs broadcast on GTV such as *Koliko*, and "By the Fireside" have successfully utilized these traditional formats. "*Koliko*", for example, used puppets to dramatize *Ananse* folktales.

"By the Fireside" was hosted by Grace Omaboe a popular Ghana actress and radio talk show host and used junior secondary school children as actors and participants (Heath 1996). The performance was based on a traditional storytelling session. The set usually depicted scenes from traditional rural settings. The performance involved dancing, singing and the enactment of a traditional folktale with a moral lesson relevant to the viewing audience. There was interaction between the host and the performers as the children dramatized parts of the story narrated by the host. The host also asked the children with her and at home to answer riddles or think about and learn the meaning of proverbs related to the theme or moral of the story. Students from different junior secondary schools in Accra and other parts of the country participated in each episode.

The fourth category of programs is the variety content category. This format includes programs that use some of the traditional elements mentioned above such as storytelling, poetry recital, singing and dancing as well as other elements such as discussions, "field trips" to different locations, and lessons on performing various skills and activities. "*Kyekyekule* Kids TV" on TV3, the "Children's Channel" on GTV and "Fun World" on Metro TV are examples of programs categorized as the assorted content category. The education section of the GBC developed the concept for the program "*Kyekyekule*" and sought private sponsorship and an independent producer for the program (Heath 1996). Focal Point produced the program and the makers of the nonalcoholic drink Maltina sponsored it during the 1990s.

Locally produced children's programs are very popular with Ghanaian children because they can personally relate to or identify with the characters and content of the program. The programs usually use children from the school system. Adults who serve as hosts of these programs are also very popular with children. The content of most locally produced children's programs deal with the school curriculum, extracurricular activities children are familiar with, and issues relevant to children in Ghana. Children are attracted to programs that involve school participation because they can look forward to their school or themselves participating in a program that is broadcast on television.

Many of the locally-produced programs for children, for example National Science and Math Quiz, Bournvita Brain Bash, School TV, and Distance Learning are educational programs based on school curriculum. There are economic reasons for the production of educational programs. A program based on the school curriculum can command an audience from school going children. Parents are also more likely to be motivated to influence their children to watch such programs to improve their grades. With an identified audience, producers are able to approach sponsors who may be interested in reaching the targeted demographic.

Companies are more likely to sponsor programs that are educational and entertaining. The quiz format has proved over the years to meet this requirement. It is lively, there's drama and some conflict and an affable host can connect with children in the studio and at home. Educational children's programs are also relatively cheaper to produce though the cost may still be prohibitive for smaller companies or brands with smaller advertising budgets.

Local children's television program production and financing

For many years GBC was the sole producer and broadcaster of local television programs in Ghana. It was only when GBC adopted the policy to allow commercial sponsorship and private production of programs that setting up independent television production studios in Ghana became a viable option. Even then, there are very few television production companies in Ghana with a small percentage producing children's programs. There are some similarities in the general production process of children television programs used by the television broadcast stations and the independent production studios. The broadcast station conceives and produces a program in-house with funding from budget allocation for children's programs. Once the program is produced and scheduled, the television station sells advertising slots during the broadcast of the program. The other approach which is similar to what the independent production studios use is to come up with a concept, record a few pilot episodes and then seek sponsorship to finance production and the cost of airtime for broadcast. Independent production studios produce program concepts, seek sponsorship and buy airtime from a television station to air the program. The station determines whether the program will be broadcast based on the quality of the program, programming philosophy of station, and the station's broadcast schedule.

The main sources of finance for free-to-air television stations have been government subventions, TV license fees, private investments, advertising, and sponsorships. Since the inception of broadcasting the government has been the major provider of funding for the media. The amount the government spends on the media has fluctuated over the years with a steady decline in recent years. Economic conditions and the value placed on the media by the ruling government have influenced the amount of government subvention the media receives. Many of the developments in infrastructure by the GBC were initiated during the Supreme Military Council and the People's National Defense Council regimes. These military governments considered the media to be a crucial tool for national development and the dissemination of political ideology. The adoption of the World Bank's structural adjustment program that required governments to divest or reduce subventions to state-owned corporations; the transition to multiparty democratic governance; and the establishment of private media have all contributed to the decline in government subvention for national media.

Another source of revenue for the state-owned broadcast media in the past has been mandatory TV license fees. The amount was set by GBC with the approval of parliament and levied on all TV set owners. However, it has been difficult to collect or enforce the payment of television license fees.

None of the commercial stations are publicly traded companies. However, private capital from Media Number One was used to establish Metro TV while the Malaysian investment group, Media Prima Berhad provided financing for TV3. Most of the television production studios in the country are limited liability companies. Financing is one of the greatest challenges facing the media industry in Ghana.

One major source of revenue for both state-owned and private media is advertising and program sponsorships. In 1967 GBC began commercial broadcasts on both radio and television. The corporation charged clients to broadcast commercials, social announcements and obituaries. GBC began to seek sponsorships for programs in the mid 1990s. Brands could either sponsor the production and airtime costs of locally produced entertainment programs or pay for the cost of imported programs. This enabled GBC to fill its schedule with a variety of locally produced and imported programs. Children's programs, variety entertainment programs, and imported syndicated series benefited from such sponsorship.

The private commercial stations depend heavily on advertising and sponsorships for financing. The need to build the brands of companies producing alcoholic beverages, beauty products, breakfast foods and household products has been a catalyst for increasing program sponsorship in the last ten years. These brands become sole sponsors of entertainment programs on radio and television by paying for the cost of production and airtime. The brand name may be associated with the program in addition to airing commercials of the brand during breaks within the program. Some brands are able to sponsor such programs for longer periods of time than others. The challenge has been trying to win over competition for the limited advertising money the major companies are willing to spend.

Ghana's annual ad spend is estimated at $25 million with TV stations receiving about 51 percent of this amount. TV3 has the highest share of advertising dollars among the television stations. The top ten brands in Ghana in terms of advertising expenditure did not include any children's products. Breakfast and baby foods which are usually the main sponsors of or advertise during children's programs typically accounts for about 2 percent of ad expenditure in Ghana (Steadman 2005). Soft drink manufacturers tend to sponsor children's programs but ad expenditure is less than 3 percent of total annual ad expenditure in Ghana.

Brands that target or are safe to advertise to children do not always have big advertising budgets in Ghana. This may be because some of the products already have market saturation or are new products with greater overhead costs and thus smaller advertising budgets. Secondly, some brands such as soft drinks and some breakfast foods may not want to be identified solely as a children's brand thus the reluctance to spend its limited advertising budget on children's programs. Another challenge producers face is that even when they obtain sponsorship for their programs, sponsors are not able or willing to sustain sponsorship for consecutive seasons. Programs that have the brand name associated with it are left at a greater disadvantage when the brand discontinues sponsorship. New brands are unwilling to sponsor the program because of the difficulty in breaking the strong association of the former brand with the program in the minds of the audience. Finally, one drawback of program sponsorship is that brands that sponsor programs may try to influence the content of programs to reflect the image of the brand.

Conclusion

Compared to other African countries and some Western countries, the percentage of time allotted to children's programs in Ghana is commendable. However, economic factors present challenges for improving or sustaining current output of children's television programs in Ghana. Public service broadcasting all around the world is being assailed by commercialization and globalization and it questionable whether public service broadcasting can continue to provide children's programs in the long term. One alternative may be based on the Dutch model suggested by Nikken (2003) that involves establishing a fund from advertising revenues to pay for children's television productions. Another approach is for producers to explore new technology that can reduce the cost of production to assure the future of locally produced children's programs in Ghana.

References

Anokwa, K. (1997) 'Press Performance under Civilian and Military Regimes in Ghana: A Reassessment of Past and Present Knowledge', in F. Eribo and W. Jong-Ebot (eds.) *Press Freedom and Communication in Africa.* Trenton, NJ: Africa World Press, Inc., pp. 3-28.

Calvert, S.L., Kotler, J.A., Murray, W.F., Gonzales, E. et al. (2001) 'Children's Online Reports about Educational and Informational Television Programs', *Applied Developmental Psycholgy*, 22: 103-117.

Colorín Colorado. (2007) 'Using Children's Television to Learn Literacy and Language'. Retrieved August 15, 2008. http://www.colorincolorado.org/educators/teaching/television.

Forge, K.L.S., and Phemister, S. (1987) 'The Effect of Prosocial Cartoons on Preschool Children', *Child Study Journal,* 17: 83-88.

Freedman, J.L. (1988) 'Television Violence and Aggression: What the Evidence Shows', in S. Oskamp (ed.) *Television as a Social Issue.* Applied Social Psychology Annual, 8, ed., Newbury Park, CA: Sage Publications, pp. 144-162.

Heath, C.W. (1996) 'Children's Television in Ghana: A Discourse about Modernity', *African Affairs,* 96: 261-275.

Huntemann, N., and Morgan, M. (2001) 'Mass Media and Identity Development', in D.G. Singer and J.L. Singer (eds.) *Handbook of Children and the Media*, Thousand Oaks CA: Sage Publications, pp. 309-322.

Huston, A.C., Anderson, D.R., Wright, J.C., and Schmitt, K.L. (2001) 'Sesame Street Viewers as Adolescents: The Recontact Study', in S. Fisch and R. Truglio (eds.) *G is for Growing: Thirty Years of Sesame Street.* Mahwah, NJ: Lawrence Erlbaum Associates, pp. 131-14.

Linebarger, D.L. and Walker, D. (2005) 'Infants' and Toddlers' Television Viewing and Language Outcomes', *American Behavioral Scientist,* 48: 624-645.

National Liberation Council. (1968) *National Liberation Council Decree 226.* Accra: State Publishing Corporation.

Paik, H., and Comstock, G. (1994) 'The Effects of Television Violence on Antisocial Behavior: A Meta-analysis', *Communication Research,* 21: 516-546.

Palmer, E.L., Taylor Smith, K. and Strawser, K.S. (1993) 'Rubik's Tube: Developing a Child's Television Worldview', in G.L. Berry and J.K. Asamen (eds) *Children and Television: Images in a Changing Sociocultural World.* Newbury Park, CA: Sage Publications, pp. 143-154.

Steadman Group (2005) *Advertising Expenditure Data.* Retrieved March 1. http://www.steadman-group.com/monitoring_ad_expenditure.php

Steinberg, L. and Silverberg, S.B. (1986) 'The Vicissitudes of Autonomy in Early Adolescence', *Child Development,* 57: 841-851.

United Nations Statistics Division. (2008) *Social Indicators.* Retrieved August 15, 2008. http://unstats.un.org/unsd/demographic/products/socind/population.htm.

Wright, J.C., Huston, A.C., Murphy, K.C., Peters, M., Pinon, M., Scantlin, R., and Kotler, J. (2001) 'The Relations of Early Television Viewing to School Readiness and Vocabulary of Children from Low-income Families: The Early Window Project', *Child Development,* 72(5): 1347-1366.

Television Broadcasting in South Africa

Mandates to Serving the Children

Beatrice A. Boateng

It has been 30 years since the first broadcast of television in South Africa. South Africa has since come a long way from having a single channel state-owned South African Broadcasting Corporation (SABC) to having three public channels (SABC 1-3), an independent subscription service, Electronic Media Network (MNET) and an independent free-to-air channel (E-TV) ("Free-to-air" service means a service which is broadcast without encryption and capable of being received on universal receivers without payment by the end user to the broadcaster and without the use of decoders (South Africa Broadcasting Bill B94-98, p. 8). Prior to the 1990s, there were no attempts to develop children's programming that reflected the multicultural nature of the South African population (Bulbulia 1998). Most of the programs that aired, especially on the state controlled SABC were imported. The Independent Broadcasting (IBA) Act No. 153 of 1993 was the first attempt at encouraging and promoting the development of local entertainment and educational content. Although the IBA Act of 1993 was not directed at children's programming, it mandated that broadcasters provide programs that are in the public interest. The *Introduction of the First Free-to-Air Private Television Service in SA Position Paper* of 1997 published in 1997 by the Independent Communications Authority of South Africa (ICASA) is the first known policy attempt in South Africa that explicitly states the need for children's programming. ICASA is the regulator for the South African communications sector, responsible for the regulation of broadcasting and telecommunications services. It was established by the Independent Communications Authority of South Africa Act No 13 of 2000. It was originally called the Independent Broadcasting Authority (IBA).

The position paper specified the minimum amount of hours that should be dedicated to children's programming. Section 6.2.3 of the paper states that:

It is recognized internationally that special provision needs to be made to ensure that children are provided with programming that entertains, informs and educates them; programming which is made specifically for them which enhances their understanding and experience of the world and which reflects their culture, language and life experiences and which affirms their sense of self, community and place. Children's programmes should address the particular needs of specific age groups.

The Authority will require that:

- the private licensee provides programmes which are specifically made for children;
- the private licensee provides at least 12 hours per week of children's programming at times when children in large numbers are available to watch; the children's programming includes programmes for children below the age of 9 years and children between the ages of 10 to 15 years;
- early childhood programming, in particular, addresses the language needs of that audience; and,
- the children's programming includes entertaining, informative and educative programming in a range of formats (p. 13-14).

The *Introduction of the First Free-to-Air Private Television Service in SA Position Paper* was published in May of 1997 after the declaration of the Children's Television Charter in May 1995, and the adoption of the SADC Children's Broadcasting Charter in June 1996 (Southern African Developing Countries (SADC) are Angola, Kenya, Lesotho, Malawi, Mauritius, Mozambique, Namibia, South Africa, Swaziland and Zambia). Later that year (October 1997), the SADC Children's Broadcasting Charter was amended and titled the African Charter on Children's Broadcasting Charter. Changes in the South African mediascape, the local content policy and the children's programming policy have an important bearing on children's television broadcasting in South Africa. This chapter is an attempt to examine what the impacts of these factors have been on the television broadcasting for children in South Africa.

Brief history of television in South Africa

Ten years after the end of apartheid in South Africa, the media has undergone transformation from being a symbol and medium through which the National Party (NP) ruling party perpetuated propaganda to an instrument for expanding diversity and promoting unity. The state-owned SABC was established in 1936 (van Zyl 1994) and had monopoly over radio broadcasting and the print media.

Historically, the state controlled media in South Africa was plagued with censorship in all aspects. South Africa was one of the last countries to introduce television to its population because television was believed to be potentially damaging to the ruling NP government. According to van Zyl, the main arguments against the introduction of television in South Africa were that

(a) it would dilute Afrikaner culture,

(b) it would introduce communist ideology into South Africa, and

(c) it would give Blacks revolutionary ideas.

Realizing that television could be controlled, and in addition to pressure from within and the international community, the NP government permitted the SABC to introduce broadcast television in 1971. Following various discussions and trials, television services in South Africa began to air on January 6, 1976.

The first television channel to transmit signals aired by the state-owned SABC was the National Network TV (NNTV) which broadcast primarily in English and Afrikaans. The SABC added three more channels; TV2/3 in 1982 and TV4 in 1985. In 1986, a subscription based broadcaster, Electronic Media Network (MNET) was launched. This ended the television broadcast monopoly of SABC. MNET's digital broadcasting satellite service DSTV was launched in 1995. In October 1991, SABC introduced the *Topsport Surplus* (TSS) channel to carry sports programming that could not be accommodated on TV 1. The following year, TV2, 3, and 4 were consolidated into one multicultural channel, *Contemporary Community Values Television* (CCV-TV). In 1996, the SABC restructured its television channels. Three news channels were created; SABC 1, SABC 2 and SABC 3. CCV-TV was re-launched as SABC 1 and was targeted at younger audiences, SABC 2 became the family oriented channel carrying a lot of programming in Afrikaans and SABC 3 runs most of its content in English became the public commercial channel, and the majority of the programs on this channel were imported.

In 1998 E-TV, South Africa's first private free-to-air television channel was launched. E-TV is owned by the Black empowerment group Hosken Consolidated Investments Limited and Venfin Limited. Warner Bros, which owned 25% of the company, sold their shares after three years of operation in South Africa (E-TV website: http://www.etv.co.za).

In 2006, 30 years after the introduction of television South Africa, there are three main players of the television industry SABC 1, 2, and 3. The SABC is the public broadcaster which receives most of its funding through public/government funding, advertisement or television license fees. MNET is the only pay TV service and E-TV, the only private free-to-air broadcaster.

Shaping what children see on South African television

Thirty years of television broadcasting have also been shaped by numerous legislative and public debates on the media environment in South Africa. Earlier discussions on the media environment focused primarily on transforming the SABC into a politically independent public broadcaster. Following the release of Nelson Mandela in 1990, the government established the *Task Group on Broadcasting in South and Southern Africa* headed by Professor Christo Viljoen to depoliticize the public broadcasting system (Barnett 1991; Oder 1991). The resulting *Viljoen Report* was one of the first attempts at re-defining the role of public broadcasting and changing the media policy environment in South Africa.

The issue of who controlled broadcasting in South Africa in the early nineties was viewed as crucial to the outcome of the 1994 elections. During the Convention for a Democratic South Africa (CODESA) in 1991, the African National Congress (ANC) and the NP reached a compromise for the establishment of an impartial broadcaster that was to be overseen by an independent regulatory authority (Louw 1993).

In 1992, the free, fair and open media conference developed a set of proposals which were forwarded to CODESA. The result was the agreement to an independent broadcast authority. In 1993, the Independent Broadcasting Authority Act, 1993 (Act No. 153 of 1993) was enacted and this led to the establishment of the Independent Broadcasting Authority (IBA) in 1994 that was later re-named the Independent Communication Authority of South Africa (ICASA) in 2000. The IBA was to provide "regulation of broadcasting activities in the public interest" (Parliament of South Africa 1993). With regards to children and education, the IBA was mandated to:

1) promote the provision of a diverse range of sound and television broadcasting services on a national, regional and local level which, when viewed collectively, cater for all language and cultural groups and provide entertainment, education and information;

2) ensure that, in the provision of public broadcasting services . . .the need for educational programmes. . .are duly taken into account.

The IBA also pressed for local content quotas on South African radio and television broadcasters. The resulting *IBA Triple Inquiry Report* published in August 1995 included the following recommendations with regards to children and education broadcasting:

1. Educational Broadcasting should value the roles played by formal and informal learning in South Africa.

2. Educational Broadcasting should be regulated and managed in such a manner that it supports the efforts of the public in its endeavors to promote lifelong learning.

3. Educational Broadcasting should not neglect the focus on children's programmes.

4. Educational Broadcasting should forge partnerships in order to meet the educational needs of the public.

5. Appropriate equipment should be made available to learning sites and centres so that Educational Broadcasting can be accessible.

6. The capacity to produce and deliver high-quality educational programmes should be developed as a matter of urgency, and players involved in this field should start aligning their systems to cater for the development of educators' skills.

7. The establishment of an educational channel/station should be explored to play a crucial role in the provision of learning resources and distance education.

In 1994, a new broadcasting Bill was enacted by government to repeal the Broadcasting Act of 1976 (Act No. 73), amend the Independent Broadcasting Authority Act of 1993 (Act No. 153) and establish a new inclusive broadcasting policy for the South Africa. The 1994 bill set the tone for elaborate changes in the way broadcasters operate in South Africa and for streamlining the regulatory system in the industry. ICASA was given the task of regulating the South African media environment and ensuring an increase in the use of local content on television.

In December 2000, ICASA produced the *Discussion Paper on the Review of Local Content Quotas* to establish whether broadcasters were complying with the South African Music and Television Local Content Regulations that came into effect in November 1997. According to the report, Regulation 3.3 of the IBA Act of 1993 stipulated that public broadcasters must ensure that:

- 60% of its educational programming must consist of South African educational programming;
- 50% of its children' programming consists of South African education programming. (p. 46).

All five television channels were examined to determine if they complied with the local content regulation; that is, to have a minimum of 25 percent local programming. The SABC channels were monitored in August and September 2000 during their broadcast time from 05H00 to 23H00. The findings indicated that all three public broadcasters fulfilled and exceeded the local content requirement. According to the report, SABC 1 had 32% local content, 13.4% of their total programming was for children's programming; SABC 2 had 57.6% and local children's content was 66% of the total programming and although SABC 3 did not have any children's content, local programming made up 49.8%.

MNET and E-TV were also evaluated. Data was collected during this period between November 1999 and April 2000. E-TV achieved a total of 27.9% local content and 22% local children content. MNET was found to be the least compliant with the local content regulations and this was attributed to the misinterpretation of local content quotas by MNET. (ICASA 2000)

Children's programming in South Africa

Programs in South Africa are divided into 14 categories.

Comedy	Magazine	News	Sports
Documentary	Miniseries	Religious	Youth/Children
Drama	Movie	Series	
Education	Music	Shows	

For purposes of this paper, I focused primarily on the Youth / Children category within the context of educational programming. Children's programming is defined as: programming in any format, which is specifically produced for persons under the age of 15 years, which contributes to the well-being and social, emotional and intellectual development of persons in this age group, which are made from their point of view, and which are broadcast at times of the day when persons in this age group are available in substantial numbers to watch (Discussion Paper on the Review of Local Content Quotas, December 2000, p. 36).

Additional analysis was completed by this author in 2006 when it was found that all five channels, SABC 1, 2, 3, E-TV and MNET offer youth/children programming. Data was collected from the electronic program listings of www.sabc.co.za, www.e-tv.co.za and www.mnet.co.za for the last week in May and early June 2006 (May 31 2006 – June 6, 2006). The data collected is a reflection of everyday programming targeted at children aired over both public and commercial channels and is different from the one used by ICASA in 2000.

The programs were coded using information on (1) children's programmes on the channels, (2) time and day programmes are available, and whether programs are (3) local or imported.

Which channels show children programming?

The SABC has three public channels, only two of those channels (SABC 1 and 2) air children's programs. Also, there were children's programs on E-TV. MNet's KTV channel (Kids TV) had the most children's programs in a week (table 1). A total of 285 children's programs were identified.

Table 1. Percentage of children's programming per channel (May 31-June 6, 2006)

Channel	Percent of children's programming
SABC1	60 (21.1%)
SABC2	37 (13%)
SABC3	5 (1.8%)
ETV	22 (7.7%)
MNET's KTV	161 (56.5%)

Days and time where programming can be found

On the channels considered here, youth/children's programs were aired everyday, Monday through Sunday, with a greater percentage shown on weekdays (Table 2).

Table 2. Percentages of youth/children's programming aired during the sample week (May 31-June 6, 2006)

Day of Week	Percentage of Programming
Sunday	7.0%
Saturday	14.0%
Monday-Friday	78.9%

Each channel had time allocated for children's programming. MNET's KTV was the only channel that had dedicated 9 hours to children's programming per day (table 3).

Table 3. Youth/children's programming and scheduled time (May 31-June 6, 2006)

	SABC 1	SABC 2	SABC 3	MNET's KTV	E-TV±
Morning (5am – 12 noon)	5am-7am 10am*	9am*	8-11am*	6am-12pm	
Afternoon (12noon – 6pm)	2:30pm- 5pm ‡)	3-5:30pm	3-4pm*	12-5pm	2:30pm -4pm (variety)
Evening/Prime time (6-10pm)	6-7pm*				
Late Night (10pm onwards)					

*Occasional programming

As we can see in Table 3, the mornings and afternoons are popular times for the airing of children's programs (figure 3). About 61 percent of the programs were aired in the morning (between 5 am-12 noon), and 39 percent was aired in the afternoon (between 2pm and 5pm) and primetime viewing (7-10 pm) occupied only 0.4 percent of the programs.

Local vs. imported programs

Overall, there was a higher percentage of imported programming (67%) vs. local content (33%) for children. No doubt, the high percentage of imported programming is perhaps due to the longer period of programming and institutional structure of MNET's KTV. In contrast, South African public broadcaster, SABC 1 and 2, have a higher percentage of local content (figure 1).

Figure 1. Distribution of local vs. imported content across channels

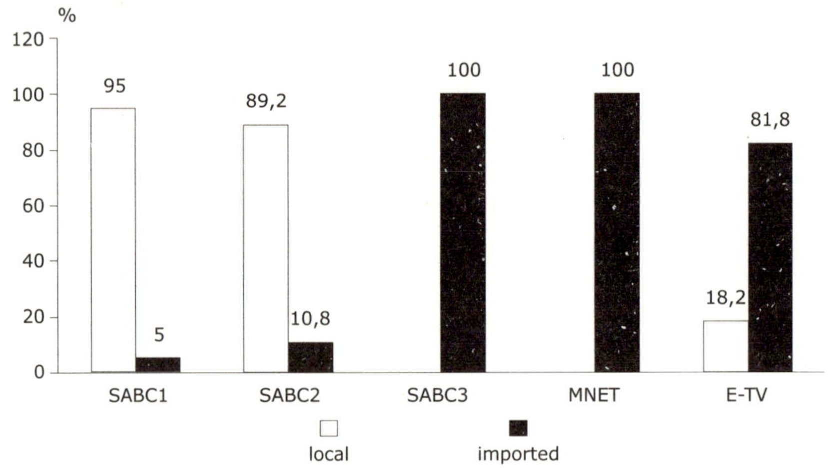

A current listing of the programs for these channels is available in Appendix A. From this list we can see that much of children's programming in South Africa, both in 2006 and more recently, is imported.

Discussion

It appears that the South African media environment have transformed over the past 30 years with an emerging local content market. Changes in the regulatory environment and the acceptance of Children's Charters on Television seem to have played a significant role in the localization of children's programming in South Africa. Also, public interest groups such as the National Association of Broadcasters and community television have played a significant role in promoting children voices in the media.

ICASA and the South African media environment are to be commended on creating environments that promote the use of local languages and local content for children's programming. However, although policies have been put in place to promote the use of locally produced children's programming, a cursory investigation South African content production revealed the lack of support in promoting local content producers. Areas that need to be considered are how to increase the production and availability of locally produced children's programming that reflect the multicultural nature of the population.

Suggestions for children's programming providers would be:

1) The exploration of funding opportunities for content producers. Presently, SABC receives its funding primarily through advertisement and television licensing fees. The government could setup grants with monies collected

from the television licenses. The SABC could then establish guidelines for programs that could be produced. Therefore, any content producer that is able to work into the guidelines set could tap into the grant monies. The monies could also be used to establish public owned privately managed local content producing companies.

2) The South African regulatory environment should be commended for setting content quotas for locally produced materials. However, more needs to be done for children's programming. I suggest that the SABC should setup a separate SABC-KIDS channel that is solely for children. The channel will provide content, preferably local content, for children during the set air time, i.e. from 5am to 10pm.

3) The production of local content is an area of concern. SABC already has a partnership with the Ministry of Education to air educational programs on television. Perhaps, one area both parties could explore is the development of a media curriculum for schools, whereby children could be taught how to produce their own content, from the script writing to acting to producing the materials. Such a subject in schools could lead to the production of new content for television. For example, the SABC together with the Ministry of Education could set aside monies for regular competitions that would encourage children to produce local content.

4) There should be incentives for the production of local content. Such incentives may include the subsidization of production costs, tax breaks for purchases of production equipment and the strengthening of distribution avenues for local content. Equally important would be the migration and transformation of materials into digital formats which would enable content to be shared across different media platforms. This could increase the flow of ideas and increase accessibility of local content to a wider audience.

Way forward

There is still a significant amount of work that needs to be done. When broadcast television started in South Africa, only English and Afrikaans were used. As of 2006, most of the children's programming is produced in all 11 official languages and sign language. The use of sign language is unique and shows the inclusiveness of children. The times that children's programs are aired on television appear to coincide with times that most children and youth are at home. Schools hours usually begin at 8am and end between 2 and 3 pm. There is a higher percentage of children's programming before school begins (5:00 am and 8:00 am) and after school (2:00 pm to 5:00 pm).

An area of concern was the lack of children's programming on SABC during primetime. The programs that were shown during that time on SABC were *That's* so *Raven*, which is an imported program and Jam Alley, a local program. Neither MNET's KTV nor E-TV aired children's programs during prime time.

In order to understand more about children's programming in South Africa, there needs to be further research in the following areas

1) A more comprehensive study needs to be done to determine trends in children's television programming from the time television started in South Africa in 1976 to date. An expansion of this study and a thirty year review would be interesting to determine the changes in television programming over the years. Although children's programming may vary from month to month, having a general idea of programming trends over the years would be interesting. The 1990s was a period of transformation in South Africa and it is possible that the children's programming will reflect that transformation.

2) It would also be interesting to examine the content of local and imported programs. What are the differences? What determines which children's programming should be imported? For example, Hamtaro and Cyborg 009 are programs being aired on SABC 2 and it would be interesting to know the processes that led to the selection of these programs.

3) Children often make decisions about which programs they should watch. A study into children decision making on programs would be interesting. Also, their preference, in terms of local versus imported content would be another feature worth exploring.

References

Permissions: The documents that were extensively quoted are the *Independent Broadcasting Authority Act 153 of 1993* and *the South Africa Broadcasting Bill B94-98*. Both of these documents are public documents in the South African public domain.

Barnett, C. (1991) 'Broadcasting the Rainbow Nation: Media, Democracy and Nation-building in South Africa', *Antipode*, 31: 274-303.

Bulbulia, N. (1998) 'An Overview of Children's Broadcasting in South Africa', in U. Carlsson and C.v. Feilitzen (eds.) *Children and Media Violence*. Nordicom: The UNESCO International Clearinghouse on Children and Violence on the Screen, pp. 231-237.

ICASA (2000) *Discussion Paper on the Review of Local Content Quotas*.

Louw, E. (1993) *South African Media Policy: Debates of the 1990s*. Bellville: Anthropos.

Oder, N. (1991) Coloring TV: South Africa. *Columbia Journalism Review*. Retrieved June 2, 2006, from http://archives.cjr.org/year/91/6/southafrica.asp.

Parliament of South Africa. (1993) *Independent Broadcasting Authority Act 153 of 1993*, Retrieved June 2, 2006, from http://www.wn.apc.org/iba/legis.htm.

van Zyl, J. (1994) Civil Society and Broadcasting in South Africa: Protecting the Right to Communicate. *Communicatio*, 20 , Retrieved June 2, 2006 from http://www.unisa.ac.za/default.asp?Cmd=ViewContent&ContentID=7156

Appendix A. Origin of children's programming in South Africa Sunday, June 29 to Saturday, July 5, 2008 (Duplicate Programmes Not Listed)

CHANNEL	LOCAL	IMPORTED
SABC1	YO.TVs Finest	George of the Jungle
	YO.TV The Breakfast Bowl	Batman
	Takalani Sesame	Ben Ten
	Kids news and current affairs	The Justice Gang
	YO.TV Paws & Claws	Boy Meets Girl
	YO.TV Land	Friends Forever (Maya & Miguel)
	Jam Alley	Cedric
	Campus Connection	
	YO.TV Blue Couch	
	YO.TV Vuvuzella	
	YO.TV Groova	
	YO.TV Blast	
	YO.TV Hlanya-Bioscope	
	YO.TV Close Up	
	YO.TV How to Win with ITU	
	YO.TV Land	
	Making Movies	
	YO.TV Wild Space	
	YO.TV Team Wild	
	YO.TV Mvubu and Friends	
	YO.TV Z'yakhipa	
	Off Camera	
	Zola 7	
	YO.TV Sports Buzz	
	YO.TV Wildroom Mega	
	Slyakholwa-We Believe	
SABC2	Thabong Thabong	Sagwa The Chinese Siamese Cat
	Jakkals Jol	In the Night Garden
	Hectic 9	Magi Nation
	Hip2BA	
	Takalani Sesame	
	Iketsetse	
	Hack Shack	
	Pfunzo	
SABC3	Snazzy Stories	The Emporer's New Groove
	Agent Fab	Harry and his Bucket Full of Dinosaurs
	Which Way!	Out of the Box
	I Crew	Code Lyoka
	URBO	The Mummy
	Vibe'z	Fun Factory
	Cooking Magic	Pinky and the Brain
	Tom and Sheenah	Little Red Tractor
		Superman
		Dragon Tales

CHANNEL	LOCAL	IMPORTED
ETV	Shiz Niz	The Untalkative Bunny
	Sistahood	Cool Catz
	Crazed Out	Tutenstein
	Frenzy	Double Dragon
	Jozi's Zoo	Jumanji
		The Get Along Gang
		Transformers
		Men in Black
		Are You Afraid of the Dark
		The Eggs
		100 Deeds of Eddie McDowd
		Real Ghostbusters
		The Frog Prince
		Care Bears
		A.T.O.M.
		The Doodlebops
		Gerald McBoing Boing
M-NET		Barney & Friends
		The Secret World of Benjamin Bear
		Pocoyo
		Postman Pat
		Little Princess
		Jakers
		Just Fun Toy Shop
		Oban Star Racer
		Serious Desert
		Barbie Mariposa
		My Life as Teenage Robot
		Romeo!
		Fairly Odd Parents
		Kappa Mikey
		Cart Squared
		El Tigre
		SpongeBob SquarePants
		Power Rangers
		Chaotic
		i Carly
		Pucca
		Grossology
		Erky Perky
		KTV Power Edition

Appendix B. Chronology of events that have shaped children's programming

- 1993
  - IBA ACT of 1993
  - Encouraged development of local content
  - 60% of educational programming = local
  - 50 % of children's programming – educational
- 1997
  - ICASA Free-to-Air Position Paper
  - 12 hours per week of children's programming
  - Target group 0 – 15 years.
- 2000
  - Review of local content quotas by ICASA (min = 25% local).
  - SABC 1: 32 % local; 13.4% children
  - SABC 2: 57.6% local; 66% children
  - SABC 3: 49.8% local, no children
  - E-TV: 27.9% local; 22% children
  - MNET: Not compliant with regulations
- 2006
  - Review of local content quotas by Boateng.
  - SABC 1: 21.1 % children
  - SABC 2: 13% children
  - SABC 3: 1.8% children
  - E-TV: 7.7 % children
  - MNET's KTV: 56.5% children

Children's Television in Kenya

The Need for a Comprehensive Media Policy Regulating Children's Content

Juliet Evusa

Kenya's media policy, like much of its constitution, is a relic inherited from the colonial government and has not kept up with the rapidly changing communication industry. Analyses of internal documents as well as newspaper reports reveal that Kenya lacks a system that prohibits the screening of adult-rated programs as well as viewer warnings about material that may be offensive during times when children are likely to be watching television. Even though there have been previous attempts to introduce media draft policies, this essay reports overwhelming evidence of the lack of a comprehensive policy regulating the broadcasting and telecommunication industry. Despite strides made as a result of the globalization of the media industry, permits issued to new entrants fail to stipulate license obligations and conditions that restrict broadcasting content. Critics charge that the recent release of a draft policy by the Ministry of Information and Communication (2006) fails to provide powers on regulation over content on advertisement, especially on television, and the Internet.

Many players in the media industry have expressed their lack of confidence in the state of the media policy in Kenya. The clergy, religious faith representatives, special interest groups as well as media scholars are frustrated by the lack of clear policy laws and ramifications on indecent material that is available to all citizens ("Faith Back Government Ban", July 30 2005; "Kenya is Ripe for Cracking the Whip on Advertising", October 13 2005; Kenya Cabinet Approves Draft Media Policy", July 25 2005; & "Z-Bottom of Form", October 13 2006). Top of the list is cultural and moral issues as they pertain to the screening of adult programs during times of the day that children may be watching. A major concern asserted by these players addresses the influx of foreign programs and new media that has led to children's increased access to indecent material. Some of the outlets for this material are changing very fast yet the laws have stagnated. The recent liberalization of the broadcasting media coupled with increased transnational concentration of media ownership and direct broadcast satellites on program exchanges calls for a comprehensive law regulating media in Kenya.

Broadcasting background

The prevailing media philosophy was rooted in the authoritarian/development tradition which advocated for state control of the press, especially broadcasting, justified on the grounds that the country was at war against illiteracy, poverty, and disease. A historical analysis of the media industry in Kenya reveals evidence of state control since the country gained its independence in 1963 to the late 1990's (Hachten 1983; Heath 1997; Mylton 1983; Nwosu 1987; and Wilcox 1975). In 1983, with independence and worries about the threat of national sovereignty posed by foreign ownership of broadcasting apparatus, the government nationalized the corporation by converting it to a department under the Ministry of Information Broadcasting and Tourism (Hatchen 1983). By drawing its revenue from advertisements, annual license fees on receiver sets and government subsidies, the corporation drew a striking resemblance with British Broadcasting Corporation (BBC). An analysis of the structural changes in Kenya's broadcasting system reveals that the Kenya Broadcasting Corporation (KBC) carried national news and ceremonies; reports of events in parliament; Kenyan popular music; development programs in which the ideology of the national elite is embedded, and advertisements of inexpensive consumer goods produced in Kenyan subsidiaries of Transnational Corporations (Heath 1997). KBC remained a monopoly over the one and only radio and TV network until 1990, when the private TV station, Kenya Television Network, KTN was launched.

The proliferation of media outlets

The emergence of the democratization, liberalization, and the globalization of the media led to the need for a change. The very first element, democratization, led to the proliferation of new media outlets. During the first decade of plural democracy – 1992 to 2002 – the media made giant strides despite frequent attempts to stunt its growth. The 1992 constitutional change that ushered multiparty politics and the subsequent 2002 defeat of the government was in no small means backed by the independent media. The late 1990's saw the liberalization of the media industry brought about by internal and external pressures. This process was accompanied by the multiplicity of media houses.

Globalization ushered in foreign influences in the advertising and communication industry. These players introduced different cultural norms namely, competition and commercialization; hence, changing the way local broadcast companies approached businesses. Also, there was an influx of new companies;

this led to more job openings and opportunities. Compared to people in other developing countries, Kenyans are now enjoying a vibrant media industry, offering opportunities for foreign as well as local entrepreneurs. As far as broadcasting is concerned, Kenyans now have access to over six television channels (some which incorporate international satellite channels), keeping them in touch with world developments as they happen. However, these channels do not offer the same opportunities to the younger audience. Although foreign programs tend to dominate as far as adult and children programming is concerned, there is less of a diversity of programs geared towards children.

A comprehensive statistical analysis of various television and radio stations reach reveals that television viewership of the six television network is dominated by two privately owned commercial networks, Kenya Television Network (KTN) and Nation Television (NTV) (African Media Development Initiative 2005). According to a study primarily based on data gathered through a representative national sample on respondents' previous seven days of listening and viewing, 91 percent of the respondents watched KTN while 89 percent watch NTV. The report adds that the other four networks – Kenya Broadcasting Corporation (KBC), Citizen TV, Stellavision TV, Family TV, East African TV (EATV) and Metro TV followed in order of viewership. In the largest urban area, Nairobi, KTN leads with a viewership of 91.2 percent, followed by NTV at 89.2 percent. KTN also leads in the second city, Mombasa, but NTV takes the lead in two cities namely, Kisumu and Nyeri. The state broadcaster, KBC, leads in two other smaller towns – Nakuru and Bungoma. A major shortcoming of the report was its failure to provide viewing preferences according to age, gender as well as socio-economic status. Although television remains a preserve of the middle class urban dwellers, others are able to watch videos and television programs (especially sports and news) in 'video-show rooms.'

The reason attributed to KTN's leadership in viewership is the fact that it offers entertainment content mainly geared towards the 18 to 39 demography. These programs comprise of drama series, reality shows, children entertainment, news magazine shows, investigative reporting, movies, talk shows, and comedy shows. Most of the older generations, on the other hand, are attracted to NTV and Citizen TV niche mainly because they offer up-to-date national and regional news reports as well as parliamentary reports.

Dependency on imported programming

The issue of foreign content has been most controversial. To cut down on production costs, most stations are dependent upon imported programs (soap operas, series, documentaries, and films) and some complement local newscasts with international news relayed from *CNN*, *Deutsche Welle, Sky News*, *BBC* and others. As a result, there has been no attempt to encourage any local programming hence, the lack of utilization of local talent. Analysis of the *Daily Nation* newspaper articles disclosed that the permits issued to new entrants fail to stipulate any licenses obligations and conditions that restrict broadcast content material (Kisero 2003 August 19; Gitahu 2003 September 1; Bindra 2003 July 13; Tengo 2003 July 20).

In response to this controversy, local newspapers have been featuring new developments in the broadcasting sector. According to these reports, the Broadcasting Content Advisory Council has proposed that Kenyans own at least 30 percent of any broadcasting firm as a way of limiting foreign ownership (Irungu 2004 December 6). This will help limit the amount of foreign programming that is believed to contain violent and sexually explicit content that might be accessible to children. The report goes on to mention that one of the function of the council would include advising the government on monitoring and regulating broadcasting content and standards relating to scenes of violence, sexually explicit conduct, offensive language as well as audience advisory (Irungu 2004, December 12). The CCK has already drawn up recommendations for the broadcast policy, which will introduce a quota system in the content mix to address the dominance of foreign programs on Kenyan television, especially children programming, with the aim of increasing local content.

An analysis of the type of programming offered by the most viewed private network, (KTN), during the week of July 27, 2008, reveals that 71 percent of broadcast material is imported: the majority being drama series (22 percent), children programs (21 percent) and reality shows (12 percent). Apart from local news, the leading locally- produced shows are magazine style programs.

Table 1. Programming offered by KTN, June 27, 2008 (%)

	Type of Productions			
Programming Type	Foreign	Local	Co-prod	Total
Drama	22	0	0	22
Comedies	7	0	0	7
Reality	12	2	0	14
Game Shows	4	0	0	4
Talk	2	0	0	2
Magazine	0	11	1	12
News	1	9	0	10
Gospel	0	5	0	5
Sports	2	0	0	2
Children	21	1	0	22
Total	71	17	1	100

Source: KTN TV Schedule http://www.ktnkenya.tv/

Of the six available channels, KTN offers the most programs geared towards children. While KBC and Metro TV offer only two programs per network that target children (*Kids Unlimited*, *Cartoon Hour*, *Toons* and *Sesame Street* respectively). An examination of the network's schedule also reveals that all but one children's programming, during the week of July 27, 2008 is imported (http://

www.ktnkenya.tv/). What is also most appalling is the fact that, out of the total percentage of children programs offered by these networks, only one, *Child Kiboko*, is locally produced. Therefore, majority of the younger audiences will naturally be attracted to this network due to the quantity of children shows it offers. Table two attests to this phenomenon.

Table 2. List of childrens' programming on Kenya television network (KTN), June 27, 2008

Program Title	Country of Origin	Program Title	Country of Origin
ART Attack	UK	Justice League	USA
Brace Face	USA	Lilo and Stitch	USA
Club Kiboko	Kenya	My Dad the Rock Star	USA
Disney Recess	USA	Phil of the Future	USA
Fairly Odd Parents	USA	Superman	USA
Fatherhood	USA	Hi-5	Australia
Jackie Chun Adventures	Hong Kong	Hoobs	USA
Jacob Two Two	Canada	Fun Factory	UK
Jonny Bravo	USA	X-Men Revolution	USA

Source: KTN TV Schedule, http://www.ktnkenya.tv/

An attempt by the Minister of Information and Tourism to stop issuing licenses to those who broadcast 100 percent foreign content sparked criticism amongst private advertisers (Kisero 2003 August, 19). This attempt was triggered by public outcry on the amount of inappropriate advertisement featured in both television and as well as print media that is likely to be consumed by minors. Although both the UK and Kenya hold the same broadcasting regulation standard that discourages foreign media from engaging in local broadcasting, such an attempt raises questions on the lack of clarity in broadcasting content regulation. For instance British Broadcasting Corporation (BBC) that broadcasts foreign programs is not allowed to engage in advertising (that is left to the local media) while the country's leading newspaper, *The Daily Nation*, does advertise yet it is foreign owned. There is therefore, need for licensees to be given an obligation to air within a certain time frame with a target population in mind. This way, the government introduces measures that ensure that the public interest is taken on board.

Lack of a rating system

Another issue of major concern is failure by the Kenya Broadcasting Act of 1990 to institute a rating system that will prohibit the screening of adult-rated programs during times when children are likely to be watching television as well as warning viewers about material that may be offensive. This act is increasingly becoming obsolete in a market with several players because KBC cannot be both a competitor and a regulator.

At present, television stations use their own discretion to determine what programs to screen and when to screen them. Station owners are increasingly airing material – particularly – films meant for adults at inappropriate peak viewership times. This phenomenon is common with KTN, the most watched television network in Kenya. An examination of the type of programming aired by KTN's during the week of July 27, 2008 reveals that most drama series containing violent and indecent material are broadcasted between 2:00 to 9:50 pm. Majority of the 18 foreign drama shows broadcasted between 2:00 to 9:50 pm contain violent and indecent content despite the risk that children will be in the audience at that time.

Table 3. KTN's Summary of TV Schedule, July 27, 2008

	Time Slot	PTC Rating
Drama Shows		
24	8:05 pm	Red
Cold Case	10:10 pm	Red
Desperate Housewives	9:50 pm	Red
Gilmore Girls	8:05 pm	Yellow
Justice	11:15 pm	N/A
Lois and Clark	3:10 pm	N/A
CSI NY	2:00 pm	Red
NAVY NCIS	2:00 pm	N/A
Law & Order: Criminal	10:10 pm	Red
One Tree Hill	2:00 pm	Red
The Practice	10:10 pm	N/A
ER	2:00 pm	Red
The Pretender	4:45 pm	N/A
Monk	5:35 pm	N/A
How I Met Your Mother	7:35 pm	Red
Fashion House	10:35 pm	N/A
8 Simple Rules	7:35 pm	N/A
Eve	9:50 pm	N/A
Reality Shows		
America's Next top Model	9:50 pm	Red
Dance 360	7:35 pm	N/A
Wrestling TNA Impact	2:00 pm	N/A
So You Think You Can Dance?	6:30 pm	Yellow
American Idol	7:35 pm	Yellow
Survivor	4:50 pm	N/A
Fear Factor	6:15 pm	N/A

Source: KTN TV Schedule http://www.ktnkenya.tv/

Figure 1. PTC Rating Legend, June 27, 2008

Red	Yellow	Green	Blue
Show may include gratuitous sex, explicit dialogue, violent content, or obscene language, and is unsuitable for children	The show contains adult-oriented themes and dialogue that may be inappropriate for youngsters	Family friendly, show promoting responsible themes and traditional values	Not yet rated by the PTC

Source: http://www.parentstv.org/ptc/shows/main.asp?shwid=1538

The parental television council (PTC) ratings of the most popular shows confirms the fear that the most watched private network in Kenya is airing shows not suitable to children during peak viewership times yet Kenya continues to lack a rating system that will warn viewers of content that is inappropriate to children. Members of the Film Censorship Board of Kenya and senior Communication Commission of Kenya's (CCK) officials have proposed various measures to eradicate this problem. If approved, the bill will give CCK the legal authority to oversee all aspects of electronic media as well as content of TV programs. The policy will not only prohibit the screening of adult-rated programs during times when children are likely to be watching television, but also warn viewers about indecent material. The Film Censorship Board of Kenya, on the other hand, has proposed a bill that will require individuals who display or exhibit any video cassette or DVD to the public to acquire a Certificate of Approval. This certificate will require them to affix on the DVD or video cassette material, the following labels:

U: Green labels with letter U in a triangle for films approved for general exhibition;

PG: Yellow labels with letters PG in a triangle for films approved as unsuitable for children under the age of ten years;

15: Blue labels with the number 15 in a circle for films approved as unsuitable for children under the age of 16 years;

18: Red labels with the number 18 in a circle for films approved as unsuitable for children under the age of 18 years and for adults only

(Kenya Law Reports: Capp 222, 11 Films and Stage Plays)

Internet access exposing the youth to obscenity

The introduction of new technologies and mediums of content delivery has even heightened the confusion further because part of regulation that addresses content is not very clear. Yet, the Internet is the latest in a wave of technologies that have seized the African culture and lifestyle. An analysis of Kenyan newspaper reports on this issue revealed that, the advent of the Internet has contributed a great deal in introducing the youth to obscenity (Church Men Also Enjoy, 2004 September 13; Mulaa and Kwamboka 2004, September 13; Ndunda 2004, September 13). The reports expressed concerns that cyber cafés are becoming a hangout especially for bored teenagers. The reports added that minors are frequenting the cafes to browse pornography and yet the law seems helpless in controlling the obnoxious Internet menu. As a result, the 'Children Media Policy draft' was released in September 2004 to ensure that minors are protected against harmful and destructive information in media content in print, radio and television (Policy fails 2004, September 13). However, most critics contend, its narrow description of media content falls short of incorporating the Internet. Authored by the Kenya Children's Parliament Foundation, the draft fails to specifically examine the current trend where children are getting hooked on Internet obscenity (Ndunda 2004, September 13). The lack of an adequate policy calls for the need to integrate the broadcasting and telecommunication industry in order to catch up with the convergence of technology.

Analysis of newspaper reports indicate that some cyber café owners have voluntarily introduced self-regulation by turning away clients who try to open pornographic websites. Others are blocking the sites using filtering software designed to block selected material. However, these reports also indicate that the majority of cyber café owners in Nairobi, the capital city, are not interested in monitoring the activities of their clients so long as they pay for the services (Mulaa and Kwamboka 2004 September 13; Ndunda 2004 September 13; Mugo 2004 September 13; 'Church Men Also Enjoy', 2004 September 13; Kwamboka 2004 September 13; 'Policy Draft' 2004, September 13). There is therefore, need for the national ICT policy draft to address Internet security issues so that people do not use these tools to the detriment of society.

Lack of a comprehensive media policy

The final major issue of concern is the lack of a comprehensive media policy that regulates content in the broadcasting and telecommunication industry. The sector has previously been regulated by a variety of legislation, such as the Science and Technology Act of 1977, the Kenya Broadcasting Corporation Act of 1988 and the Kenya Communications Act of 1998. Because ICT policy is spread over various legislative acts, a comprehensive policy is needed to merge all the different policies. While the media sector is growing during the current political climate, the absence of comprehensive media policy and law is undermining the development of a strong media to play its full role within the democratic era. Meanwhile, the three bodies commissioned by the government to oversee and advise the country on ICT policy issue – namely the Communication Commission for Kenya (CCK), the National Communication Secretariat (NCS), and the

Department of IT services within the Ministry of Planning and Finance – have all come up with overlapping ICT policy drafts (*The Kenyan Gazette* 2001; National Communication Secretariat 2003; Ministry of Planning and National Development 2003).

Political wrangling and opposition by special groups triggered the release of a draft ICT Policy by the Ministry of Information and Communications in 2006. The overall objective of the policy was to assert the important role that broadcasting will continue to play in the 21st century as a communication tool. The draft provided detailed guidelines on broadcasting aimed at, among other things, converting the KBC from a state to a public broadcaster; improving the local broadcast content production industry through the development of appropriate local content; establishing a sector-wide code of conduct; encouraging diversity in ownership and control, discouraging the concentration of ownership of print and electronic media in a few hands; and finally encouraging the development of, and respect for, codes of practice by all licensees, and hence, adhering to social responsibility. The policy would also establish the development of a pluralistic broadcasting landscape through continued licensing of private commercial broadcasting services that would, in turn, be expected to provide a diversity of programming content, contribute to job creation and ensure human resource development. In addition, the policy aspires to promote local content by promoting local production of advertisements and above all, cultivate an enabling environment for production and export of local broadcast and media products, with the end result being a contribution towards job creation. The policy also proposed the formation of a broadcasting Content Advisory Council to advise the Communication Commission of Kenya on: content and broadcasting standards; monitoring and regulating such content; handling complaints from operators and consumers; as well as monitoring compliance with broadcasting ethics (Irungu 2004 December 6). The council is expected to work in conjunction of the Kenya Film Censorship Board to ensure that all broadcasters broadcast material suitable for children (National ICT Policy 2006: 18).

However, the policy has been largely criticized for its vagueness on matters of public interest, such as the proposed local content ratio, and the assumption that the government is representative of the public's view. The draft bill also seems to have forgotten to regulate the content of advertising, particularly in television, as well as keeping in touch with local situations. Critics content that these advertisement are insensitive to time schedules when airing adult material. Opposition to the bill grew quickly. The lack of a line-item-veto meant that the draft had to be either passed as whole bill or rejected in its entity. This 'all-or-nothing' approach led to the defeat of the bill, even though there were good parts of the bill, the opposition to contentions parts was overwhelming. The straw that broke the camel's back was the provision that stated journalists had to disclose all their sources. Although the Bill reasserts that the government is committed to self and co-regulatory approaches and that the converged regulator will work alongside industry in developing regulations and systems that continue to safeguard children, citizens and business and respect of the privacy of all persons, the policy fails to provide powers on regulation over content on the Internet (African Media Development Initiative 2006).

Summary

This essay has demonstrated that Kenya's telecommunication industry is still developing its commercial telecommunication orientation after decades of state control. With the liberalization of the mobile cellular market, supply and installation of VSAT terminals coupled with the issuance of licenses to 73 Internet Service Providers, it is clear that the telecommunication environment is different from that of its predecessors. The competition has increased the penetration of communication services in Kenya. There are however, concerns about the lack of culturally relevant content. One critical area that needs more careful consideration is the need to formulate a national ICT policy that is internal and specific to the country. A common national ICT policy will go a long way in harmonizing the telecommunication, broadcasting and communication sectors. A national ICT policy therefore needs to take culture into account for purposes of an extensive and widespread use of ICT.

However, it appears that despite the presence of a draft in the making, the government lacks a standard policy that addresses pertinent issues that have arisen in the telecommunication sector as well as one that harmonizes the telecommunication, broadcasting and communication sectors. On the negative side, the introduction of new technologies brought about confusion because part of the regulation that addresses Internet content is not very clear. Questions emerged about the cultural significance of foreign programming at the expense of local program development and absence of laws enacted to regulate the current trend where minors have accesses to immoral material, specifically pornographic material in electronic and print media. Results from the analysis revealed two important issues: one, there has been no attempt to encourage any local programming because of the influx of foreign programs, hence, the lack of utilization of local talent; and secondly, the children's media policy draft that ensures the protection of minors against harmful and destructive media content falls short of incorporating the Internet as an instrument of communication. The conclusions arrived at supporting those who argue that print and electronic broadcasting content is at conflict with rural African set-up because most content emanates from the western world. This calls for the need to emphasize and encourage local content developers to develop content that is culturally relevant. In view of this, clearer national polices and guidelines that also harmonize the various ICT initiatives found across ministries are recommended to avoid the duplication of organizations. In order to effectively deal with a converging communication environment, it was evident from the study that the convergence of traditionally regulatory structures was inevitable. At the time of this study, the cabinet had approved a draft media policy and was in the process of negotiating with broadcast media to ensure programs were suitable, mainly to children. From the trends and patterns that reappeared across the different document analysis, case studies and newspaper analysis, it is obvious that despite advancements made as a result of globalization of the media industries, Kenya still has a long way to go.

References

African Media Development Initiative. (2005) Kenya Country Report Case Study.

Bindra, S. (2003, July 13) 'In Africa, Big Brother is Always Watching us', *The Daily Nation,* p.16, Opinion & Analysis section.

Bourgault L. (1995) *Mass Media in Sub-Saharan Africa.* Bloomington & Indianapolis.

Church Men also Enjoy. (2004, September 13) *East African Standard.* Retrieved November 1, 2004. http://www.eastandard.net. Indiana University Press. *Cambridge*: Cambridge UP, 1960. Press, Inc.

Draft Information and Communication Bill Released. (February 09 2006) *The Daily Nation.* Retrieved October 2, 2007. http:lexisnexus.com/us/Inacademic/delivery/PrintDOc.do?

Faith Back Government Ban on Tobacco and Beer Adverts. (July 30, 2005) *The East African Standard.* Retrieved October 2, 2007. http:lexisnexus.com/us/Inacademic/delivery/PrintDOc.do?

Gathu, F.W. (n.d.a) *Freedom of Expression in Kenya and USA: A Comparison.*

Gitahu, M. (2003, September 1) Points to Ponder Over Censorship. *The Daily Nation,* p.11 (Spot-Light).

Hachten, W. (1993) *The Growth of Media in the Third World.* Iowa: Iowa State University Press.

Heath, C.M. (1997) 'Communication and Press Freedom in Kenya', in W. Jong-Ebot, F.F. Eribo (eds.) *Press Freedom and Communication in Africa.* New Jersey: Africa World Press, pp.29-50.

Irungu, G., (2004, December 6) Government set broadcasting standards for media. *Daily Nation.* Retrieved December 6, 2004. http://www.natioaudio.com.

Kenya Cabinet Approves Draft Media Policy. (July 25, 2005) *The East African Standard.* Retrieved October 2, 2007. http:lexisnexus.com/us/Inacademic/delivery/PrintDOc.do?

Kenya is Ripe for Cracking the Whip on Advertising. (October 13, 2005) *The East African Standard.* Retrieved October 2, 2007. http:lexisnexus.com/us/Inacademic/delivery/PrintDOc.do?

Kenya Law Reports. (n.d.) Capp 222, 11 Films and Stage Plays. Retrieved September 30, 2007. http://www.kenyalaw.org

Kisero, J. (2003, August 19) 'Confusion Dogs Broadcast Industry Regulation', *Daily Nation,* p. 27.

Kwanboka, E. (2004, September 13) Law Disregard. *East African Standard.* Retrieved November 1, 2004. http://www.eastandard.net.

Ministry of Information and Communications. (January, 2006) National Information and Communications Technologies (ICT) Draft Policy.

Moggi, P. & Tiesser, R. (2001) *Media Status Report: Kenya.* Nairobi, Kenya: Communications Department, Tangaza College, GRET (Groupe de recherche et d'echanges technologiques Research and Technological Exchange Group)

Mulaa, A., & Kwamboka, E. (2004, September 13) Caught in a Web of Ruin. *East African Standard.* Retrieved November 11, 2004. http://www.eastandard.net.

Murunga, A. (2003, August 27) 'Kenya a Safe Haven for Cyber Gangsters', *Daily Nation,* p.9, Opinion.

Mytton, G. (1983) *Mass Communication in Africa.* London: Edward Arnold.

National Communication Secretariat (NCS) (2003) Government Information and Communication (ICT) Policy Draft. Nairobi, Kenya: Government Printing Office.

Ndunda, E. (2004, September 13) Mombasa Gives Porno a Wide Berth, *East African Standard.* Retrieved November 11, 2004. http://www.eastandard.net.

Nwosu, I. (1987) 'An Overview of the Mass Media and the African Society', in J. Domatob, J. Abubakar, & I. Nwosu (eds.) *Africa Media Monograph Series: Mass Media and the African Society.* Nairobi: The African Council on Communication Education.

Policy Fails to Address Internet Issues. (2004, September 13) *The East African Standard.* Retrieved November 1, 2004. http://www.eastandard.net.

Rule, S. (1987, June 14) To Cut Births Kenya Turns to TV Show. *New York Times.* Retrieved October 16, 2007. http://query.nytimes.com/gst/fullpage.html

Tengo, D. (2003, July 20) 'Big Brother Evictions: Who Will go Next?', *The Sunday Nation,* pp. 4-5 (Young Nation)

The Kenya Gazette (2001) The Kenya Communication Act: Telecommunication and Postal Sector Policy Guidelines. (Vol. CIII_Publication No. 77) Nairobi, Kenya: Government Printing Office.

Urges Regulation of Local TV Advertisements. *BBC Monitoring International Reports.* Retrieved October 13, 2006. http:lexisnexus.com/us/Inacademic/delivery/PrintDOc.do?

Wilcox, D. (1975) *Mass Media in Africa: Philosophy and Control.* New Jersey: Africa World.

Z-Bottom of Form; Z-Top of the Form; Sample; Strong; Typewriter; Variable; Kenyan Writer

Children's Television in Zambia

Local vs. Imported

Musonda Kapatamoyo

Television broadcasting was an urban phenomenon where according to Scott (2002) nearly half of all Zambians lived. Initially, Zambia used television as a tool for development that was managed by and for the benefit of government programs. However, like most African countries, the industry has evolved to accommodate private ownership and content management. This trajectory, as Bourgault (1995) observed is within the context of Africa's transition into democratization and the global free market economy in the 1990s that emerged alongside the transformation of national broadcasting systems connected to hitherto authoritarian regimes, the promotion of independent and plural media, and the proliferation of new media channels. This led to the character and role of the broadcasters to be transformed from a state monopoly to a largely open, independent, and plural media. Elsewhere, others observed this trend across the whole African continent that led to the emergence and growth of independent media; particularly radio (Fardon and Furniss 2000; Panos Institute 1993).

This essay discusses the evolving nature of television in Zambia, its role in national development, and the various attempts at creating and supporting programs directed at children. It highlights the deregulation and liberalization policies of the 1990s, which had a collective impact on the transformations that led to competition, expansion in scope and reach in the broadcasting industry. It ends with a discussion of the opportunities and challenges facing television as a medium for development when Zambian broadcast organizations struggle to balance between the need for profit and accommodation of children's programs.

Media nationalization and national development

The evolution of television broadcasting in Zambia can be traced to the first station that was built in 1961 by the London Rhodesia Company (LONRHO) based in on the Copperbelt province. LONRHO was owned by the industrialist 'Tiny" Rowland, whose interests included mining and manufacturing in several African countries and Europe. Setting up the station in the Copperbelt province was strategic because it was home to the largest copper mines in Africa and was inhabited by large numbers of white immigrant mine workers. The station primarily accommodated that demographic.

The television station was nationalized after Zambia's independence from Britain in October 1964, and following the passage of the Broadcasting Act of 1966, which created the government-controlled Zambia Broadcasting Services (ZBS). Eventually, all television operations where relocated to Zambia's capital city, Lusaka, in 1967. Twenty years later, ZBS was transformed into a body corporate called the Zambia National Broadcasting Corporation (ZNBC) that would generate its own operational funds and rely less on state funding (Banda 2003). ZBS and later ZNBC where tightly controlled by the United National Independence Party (UNIP) government until 1991 when a change in government led to a shift in ownership policies. According to Banda (2006), the new government, led by the Movement for Multiparty Democracy (MMD) passed the Zambia National Broadcasting Corporation (Licensing) Regulations to liberalize the broadcasting sector for private investment. Liberalization allowed private operators to own radio stations and television stations.

Several factors brought about sweeping changes in media ownership. The first was the broader historical circumstances surrounding the nationalization era and the desire by the Zambian government to secure its borders from foreign interference in the region. Foreign-owned institutions were nationalized as part of sweeping away the institutions of colonial influence (Noll 2000). In Zambia, like in most post-independence African countries, the media were perceived as a critical machinery of nation building and heavy emphasis was placed on the social and development role of the media (Blankson 2007).

The second factor as Noll (2000) observed was a view of development that emphasized escape from colonial influence through strong domestic control over key institutions and comprehensive central planning to guide the path of economic growth. A great deal of emphasis was placed on self-reliance and self-control (Mwanakatwe 1994). The Zambian government used the media to mobilize citizens around the common interests of infrastructure development.

The third factor that justified nationalization and consolidation of media under government control pertained to regional uncertainties. During the post-independence era, Zambia's geo-political situation was volatile because most countries in the southern African region were still colonized. As a result, large numbers of freedom fighters moved their military bases into Zambia, with support from the Zambian government. Media were once again used for propaganda and mobilization towards the liberation of neighboring countries. The fourth factor, socialism, reached its crescendo as an ideology and economic model in the 1950s and 1960s. Socialism, characterized by centralized government, appeared to offer a viable alternative to Western market capitalism as a means to achieve long-term economic development. In Zambia, the new independent government in 1964 adopted "Humanism", a derivative of socialism, which permitted the government to exert a lot of control on the media as a vital instrument of government power (Kaunda 1967).

As a result of the circumstances described above, the Zambian government co-opted all media into its arsenal of instruments to achieve rapid economic development, pursue ideological transformation, and facilitate social cohesion. The media institutions were expected to help disseminate information relevant to national development (Banda 2003).

According to Moore (1992), the Zambia government used these laudable goals of economic development to abuse the power with which the people vested them. Consequently, the media were inefficiently utilized to combat illiteracy, health problems, poverty, and building political consciousness. According to Blankson (2007), the media evolved in a culture in which the government concentrated their political power and influence over civil society institutions and the citizenry through the enactment of parliamentary bills, legislations, and Acts aimed at controlling information flow.

Zambia, like most African governments during the 1990s, moved away from complete monopoly management of the broadcasting sector and implemented reforms that included liberalization and deregulation. Banda (2006) called this policy shift as "cautious deregulation" because the policy did not advocate for privatization of the government owned and operated broadcasting services. It only allowed for new competitive entrants. The pressures for sector reform were usually subtle and emanated from domestic and external factors (Afeikhena 2002). For a long time, one television broadcaster (ZNBC), operating from its two stations in Lusaka and Kitwe, was the sole medium and operated without any competition. This arrangement necessitated creation of fewer programs that mostly exhibited low production quality as well. Following regulatory changes in the 1990s that allowed competition in the industry, programming improved. The regulatory changes have had a positive impact on the diversity and scope of programs directed at children. For instance, the privately owned MuviTV in Lusaka produces children-centric programs like "Z Kids News @ 5"; a news program anchored by young people with a presentation style that appeals to young people.

Broadcasting system in Zambia: the role of political influences

According to Mytton (1983) the media in Zambia were a legacy of the country's colonial past. The Zambia government initially used the British Broadcasting Corporation (BBC) model to create an organization in which government appointees oversaw the management of operations. Operationalization of this sector, however, revealed stack dissimilarities. Whereas the BBC worked independently of direct government interference, the supervision of mass communications was the responsibility of the Ministry of Information and Broadcasting whose top three government officials, including the minister; deputy minister and a permanent secretary were all appointed by the Zambian President and served at his pleasure. Within this framework, the Zambia National Broadcasting Corporation (ZNBC), headed by a government appointed Director General, was designated as the state broadcaster and saw as its primary goals to inform, to educate, and to entertain on behalf and within the mandates set by the government (Kasoma 1986). To ensure that government programs received priority in television programming, the President of Zambia had decreed that, "Zambia television would, apart from disseminating information and entertainment, express in depth the various cultural aspects of this nation" (Kaunda 1975).

Despite the dedicated government support, the decree suffered set backs in implementation: Presenting "in depth the various cultural aspects" did not happen because the economic decline in Africa between 1970s and the 1980s had a huge impact on the state of media systems. As noted by Ocitti (1999), the number of African countries unable to meet there basic needs increased profoundly by the end of the 1980s. Average incomes fell by as much as 30 to 40 percent annually in the more affected countries. Revenue for the media tumbled drastically as the purchasing power of the public and business community declined. Broadcasting became a very expensive profession because of the decline in commercial advertisements that supported the media (Blankson 2007). This situation could be credited for the large number of imported programs on ZNBC television.

Policy prescriptions and media turnaround

President Kaunda's United National Independence Party (UNIP) lost elections in 1991 after 27 years in-charge of government to the Movement for Multiparty Democracy (MMD). The MMD government swiftly moved away from the policy positions of Dr. Kaunda's government. They liberalized and deregulated the media industries. The entry of private television and digital broadcasting operators following the deregulation of the industry had a remarkable impact on the broadcasting landscape in Zambia. As it was to be expected, private players, though fairly new in the market, immediately introduced diversity and keen competition to a sector until that time dominated by the ZNBC.

In the early years of television in Zambia, programming on weekdays was primarily in the evening and began promptly at 5:00 pm and ended at midnight. On weekends it started at noon and ended at midnight. Therefore, during the morning and afternoon, the television set was just a piece of furniture to decorate the living room. In the 1990's, the digital satellite broadcaster – MultiChoice – introduced 24 hours programming of which a large segment catered for a children audience. Even the smaller MuviTV programmed for 24 hours a day. In what could be termed an improvement, ZNBC commenced their broadcasts earlier; at 10:00 am on weekdays and 7:00 am on weekends. Despite the limited hours, ZNBC maintained the majority of the audience share, largely due to a near national coverage of its free-to-air transmission.

Table 1. Broadcasting television in Zambia

Station/Channel	Established	Transmission Format	Ownership
ZBS (became ZNBC in 1987)	1966	Free-to-air[a]	Government
DStv	1995	Subscription[a]	MultiChoice Africa*
TBN	1998	Free-to-air[a]	US-Christian Trinity Broadcasting
MuviTV	2002	Free-to-air**	Private
CASAT	2002-2006	Satellitea	Private

* Also 30% ownership by ZNBC. ** Concentrated in Lusaka only: most of the content is for the urban audience.
[a] = National coverage

Source: African Media Development Initiative: Zambia Content (n.d.).

Table 2. Television audience share in Zambia[1]

Station/Channel	Audience Share in Percentage
ZNBC	81%
TBN (Trinity Broadcasting Network)	8%
MultiChoice (DStv)	7%
Others	4%

Note: Adapted from Banda 2003.

Table 2 illustrates the rapid diffusion of private television in Zambia. The Audience share for private television in Zambia grew steadily from 1995 to capture 25 percent of the viewership within eight years. The first foray into this market began when ZNBC entered into joint-venture partnership with South Africa's Electronic Media Network (M-Net) to create MultiChoice (Zambia) Limited. ZNBC maintained a 30 percent shareholding while M-Net controlled the other 70 percent of shares (Banda 2006). In 1990, M-Net launched the popular K-Net children's channel that is dominated by imported programming primarily from the U.S. (History of SA Media, n.d.). MultiChoice operated high-end satellite based television programming, also dominated by popular foreign (mostly American) movies (Banda 2003).

In quick succession the government awarded new private operator's licenses the Trinity Broadcasting Network (TBN), an evangelical-Christian television station from the United States to provide free-to-air programming (in 1998); and to Zambian owned and operated CASAT (2002-2006) and MuviTV studios (2002) (African Media Development, n.d.). Despite the tremendous popularity of private television operators, ZNBC continued to maintain a dominating lead in terms of audience share because its services were free-to-air and its revenues were subsidized by government and supplemented by commercial advertising.

The private operators, on the other hand, were subscription based and relied entirely on commercial advertisements, which presented a challenge to capture the market in tough economic times.

Children's media policy

Zambian broadcasters rely on several international charters as benchmarks to ensure that children's programming is prioritized. The two most important benchmarks are the International Children's Television Charter and the Africa Charter on Children's Broadcasting.

Government officials, including representatives from Zambia National Broadcasting Corporation signed on to the internationally accepted International Children's Television Charter that was adopted in Munich, Germany, on the 29th of May 1995, and ratified it in 2000 (Commonwealth Broadcasting Association, n.d.). ZNBC collaborates with such organizations as the Commonwealth Broadcasting Association (CBA) and United Nations Children Education Fund (UNICEF) to comply with this charter. The charter obligates public service broadcasters like ZNBC to provide programming for children that will inform, entertain and educate, even though the quality and quantity of some such programming varies enormously. UNICEF for its part champions initiatives that create quality broadcasting for children, and involve children in the broadcasting process. As a result, UNICEF and the International Council of the Academy of Television Arts and Sciences established the International Children's Day of Broadcasting that takes place on the second Sunday of every December, and has engaged 2,500 TV and radio station in 170 countries over the past decade (Jempson 2003).

CBA's mission is to help publicly owned national public service broadcasting organizations, or groups of such organizations, with planning, production and presentation of broadcast program in Commonwealth countries. As a result, Zambia participates in regular CBA conventions where standards are discussed. In addition, CBA provides Zambian Journalists with scholarships for undergraduate and graduate studies in other commonwealth countries. This in turn helps with quality management of children programming as well as ensuring that it is prioritized (Commonwealth Broadcasting Association, n.d.). '

In 1996, Zambia National Broadcasting Corporation and civil society representatives signed the Africa Charter on Children's Broadcasting which affirmed that:

- children should have programs of high quality;
- children should be protected from commercial exploitation;
- children should be ensured access to programs and, where possible, be actively involved in production;
- children should hear, see and express themselves and their culture;

- children's programs should create opportunities for learning and empowerment;
- children's programs should offer a range of genre and content;
- children's programs should be aired at regular times when children are available;
- sufficient resources must be made available.
  (Africa Broadcast Charter, n.d.)

This Charter was established by the Children and Broadcasting Forum (CBF) formed at the first World Summit on Children and Television which took place in 1995; Zambia formally joined CBF in 1999 with representatives from ZNBC and the Children's Education and Social Fund. CBF is registered locally to promote the Africa Charter on Children's Broadcasting (adopted by all CBF Charters in Africa and the Commonwealth Broadcasting Association) and to aid ZNBC and other broadcasters in abiding to all treaties and agreements that further the cause of children through such organizations as the United Nations, the African Union, and the Commonwealth (Children and Broadcasting Forum, n.d.).

Evolution of children's television programming

Children's programming has routinely been part of ZNBC's offerings since the introduction of television in Zambia. According to Soremekun (1973) television was instrumental in early outreach to children through schools. Urban schools would watch instructional videos broadcast by Zambia Broadcasting Services (the forerunner to ZNBC). However, there was never an official definition of what constituted children's programs nor was there a guarantee that the "children's" programs listed in the television guides would be broadcast, a practice that continues today. According to the corporation's Website, ZNBC could switch any program at short notice. The change would be necessitated by any number of causes such as unavailability of the listed program and censorship by government or management. Similarly, MuviTV offers no guarantee that the listed programs will be aired and placed a disclaimer on their Website to that effect (MuviTV 2008).

According to Jabes Mvula (a senior ZNBC news anchor; personal interview May 1, 2006), censorship was never an official government policy. However, given the strength of government in appointing the management of the national broadcaster, very little was done that was outside what was permitted by senior government officials. On occasion, government ministers would publicly call for certain programs to be removed, and got their wishes oftentimes.

Program ratings

Children's Programming Zambia has never had a formal rating system for television programs even though care is taken to ensure that the edicts of the International Children's Television Charter and Africa Charter on Children's Broadcasting are implemented. The rationale used in this discussion to define children-specific programming is based on the time of day that programs appeared on the schedule and the title used to identify children's programming in the television guide. For example, a cursory look through the Websites of ZNBC and MuviTV indicates that most programs aired before the 7:00 pm newscast had light content and could easily accommodate a child-friendly audience (ZNBC 2008; MuviTV 2008).

In general, these programs include imported cartoons and local dramas interspaced with telenovelas and soap operas. MuviTV does better than ZNBC at children's programming by providing at least 2 hours of children's programs compared to average 1 hour provided by ZNBC. Programs shown after 9:00 pm are evidently geared towards an adult audience. They include actions movies and talk show programs like Eyeball 2 Eyeball (MuviTV, n.d).

The government's heavy-handed approach of censuring the public broadcaster for "extreme" programs does not have any basis on directly observed effects on Zambian children. However, many scientific theories and studies exist in literature dealing with the issue of media effects. The studies, of which none was done in Zambia yet, cover a broad range of different paradigms such as cultural studies, content analyses of media programs and behavioral research (Groebel 2002). The most influential theory on this matter is probably the Social Learning Approach by Albert Bandura (1977), which suggests that people learn through observation in their immediate environment and media.

The power of television on children's behavior presents both an opportunity as much as it can be a problem. Negative effects may not always be the outcome of television viewing, based on the findings by Seymour Feshbach (1985) (Inhibition Theory) who posits that inhibition would occur when the stimulation of one's aggressive tendencies would lead to learned fear of punishment and thus contribute to its reduction.

Diversity of Programs

In spite of the few programs on offer by both ZNBC and MuviTV, they had a variety of programs aimed at different audiences, but mostly irrelevant to children. Upwards of 50 percent of broadcast minutes went to imported programs and less than 7 percent devoted to children's programs. In general ZNBC had large portions of time dedicated to such global satellite feeds as the BBC World Service, the Oprah Winfrey Show and German and British football (soccer). Its regional imports included the popular South African soap opera 'Isidingo' (Cowling 2005).

For children, ZNBC offered the following schedule as illustrated in Table 3.

Table 3. Children's television programs on ZNBC, downloaded July 20, 2008

	Mon	Tues	Wed	Thurs	Fri	Sat
9:30	n/a	n/a	n/a	n/a	n/a	Fun Time
10:15	n/a	n/a	Skyland	n/a	One Cubed	n/a
5:00	Team Galaxy	Eckhart	Kids TV	Lighthouse Tales	n/a	n/a
5:30	n/a	Fun Time	Opening the Book	n/a	Nilas the Sandman	n/a

Legend: n/a = time slots allocated to something else during a period when most children's programs are broadcast.

From ZNBC's website (www.znbc.co.zm)

According to Moore (1992), ZNBC opted to give a significant portion of its programming to pre-packaged, pre-recorded syndicated satellite international news feeds (most often with little relevance to the Zambian audience and frequently in the language of the originating country). A snapshot of programs in July 2008 showed that children's programs where a mere 7 percent of total scheduled programs. There appeared to be no children's programs on Sunday. The private television stations and the satellite television providers offered a wider range of programs though many still imported. MuviTV, a privately owned Zambian company, programs 24 hours a day. They also provide few programs for children and then only in a generic block every Monday through Saturday from 9:30 to 10:00 am every morning. However, MuviTV has one of the few children's news divisions – Z-Kids News (www.zkidsnews.com). This innovative division is staffed by journalists with a wide range of background and experiences. In addition, the Z-Kids News site links to the websites for many of the U.S. public broadcasting's children's programs such as "Arthur", "Maya and Miguel", and "Postcards from Buster".

Finally, some children in Zambia have access to K-Net available by subscription through South Africa's MultiChoice satellite system. Using DStv, the satellite system, children can have access to several U.S. children's channels including: Boomerang, Cartoon Network, Disney, and Nickelodeon. K all Day and K-Net DStv's children's block include programming from the U.S., Australia, and U.K. such as "Sponge Bob Square Pants", "Barney and Friends", "Hi-5", and "Raggs".

Local content

ZNBC has missed a great opportunity to design and present locally produced children's programs no doubt due to the poor economic situation and perhaps limited skills that confined local content to news broadcasts in English and local languages at ZNBC. Very few adult programs tend to be locally produced except for budget-low soccer and other sports and local soap operas such as

Chintobetobe. Chintobetobe is a contemporary on topical issues ranging from politics to health matters.

Clearly MuviTV demonstrates with "Z Kids News @ 5" that quality children's program can be produced. This particular program is supported by UNESCO's Media and Democracy and relies heavily on the MuviTV staff and resources. The synergy is, nevertheless, essential and is an obvious must-have if future programs of this kind will be produced. Apart from "Z Kids News @ 5", MuviTV shows the generic cartoon shows (one can safely assume these cartoons are imported). Finally, the digital satellite television network M-Net whose service covers nearly all countries in Africa provides a lot of children's content, although none is about and by Zambian children per se, those with subscription will benefit for the large selection of programs (M-Net, n.d). M-Net has cleverly used other programs to create a local identification in Zambia (and other African countries as a matter of fact). In order to gain credibility in those geo-cultural markets, the company participates in making 'locally' produced and other 'African' programs (Conradie 2000). "Local content", which is applicable to all Africa, is mostly local versions of international competition-themed formats. Some popular imported formats include British quiz shows like "Who Wants to be a Millionaire?"; talent shows like "Pop Stars" and "Project Fame" and reality shows like "Big Brother Africa" (Cowling 2005). These shows feature participants/actors from several African countries. Zambia was proud that two Zambians won the best performances on the reality show 'Big Brother Africa" in 2004 and talent show "Project Fame" in 2005, respectively. The participation of nationals increases M-Net's popularity and adds to their profits. Even with these expanded schedules, locally produced children's programs where far between as indicated on "K-Net/K All Day"[2].

Summary

Children's television in Zambia is still undeveloped. The national broadcaster ZNBC, has operated television as an instrument of state propaganda for nearly three decades following independence from Britain. Over reliance on government funding has constrained creativity at ZNBC. As the Zambian economy weakened, so did revenue coming to ZNBC. As a result ZNBC was forced to show out dated foreign programs.

According to Scott (2002), nearly half of Zambians live in rural areas. This results in limited access to television by children in rural areas. In addition, it is estimated that less than 36 percent of the population has access to television, further limiting access. Most children's programming represents a Western culture. The one bright spot is MuviTV's "Z Kid's News @ 5; even though its primarily addresses an older teen audience. Clearly there is a need for more local programming but in a country identified as one of the poorest in the world and with a high incidence of HIV/AIDS, children's television is no doubt of minor concern (United Nations 2008). As a result, the advocacy by the International

Children's Television Charter and the Africa Charter on Children's Broadcasting for broadcasters to prioritize quality children's programming is undermined.

Notes

1. Table 2 does not include MuviTV, which was established in 2002. MuviTV now boasts a sizable following in Lusaka even though hard figures are yet to be assessed. These stations are not mutually exclusive, therefore, MultiChoice subscribers, for example, also receive ZNBC transmission. A more accurate determinant of audience share would be advertising revenue. That too is yet to be assessed. The percentages are rounded off.
2. K-Net is M-Net's children's block and K All Day is listed under MultiChoice as their children's block of programs yet when one clicks on programming for K All Day the link is K-Net's web page and program schedule.

References

Afeikhena, J. (2002) *Public Enterprise Reform in Nigeria: Evidence from the Telecommunications Industry*. AERC Research Paper 129. Nairobi: Africa Economic Research Consortium.

Banda, F. (1995) *The Media and the Challenge of Human Rights: The Case of Zambia*. Leicester: University of Leicester (MA Diss.)

Banda, F. (2003) Community Radio Broadcasting in Zambia: A Policy Perspective. Pretoria: University of South Africa (Unpublished Dr. Diss.).

Banda, F. (2006) 'Commentary: Negotiating Distant Influences: Globalization and Broadcasting Policy reforms in Zambia and South Africa', *Canadian Journal of Communication*, vol. 31(2006): 459-467.

Bandura, A. (1977) *Social Learning Theory*. Englewood Cliffs: Prentice-Hall.

Blankson, I. (2007) 'Media Independence and Pluralism in Africa', in Isaac Blankson, and Patrick Murphy (eds) *Negotiating Democracy; Media Transformations in Emerging Democracies*. New York: SUNY Press.

Bourgault, L.M. (1995) *Mass Media in Sub-Saharan Africa*. Bloomington, Indiana University Press.

Calvert, S.L (2008) 'Children as Consumers: Advertising and Marketing'. *The Future of Children*, vol. 18(2008)1, Spring.

Children and Broadcasting Forum (2008) Retrieved August 6, 2008 on http://www.thezambian.biz/clients/cbf/default.htm.

Commonwealth Broadcasting Association (2008) Retrieved August 06, 2008 on http://www.cba.org.uk/index.php.

Conradie, P.D. (2000) 'Reactions to Globalization by the Television Industry in Post-apartheid South Africa', *Electronic Journal of Communication*, 10(1, 2).

Cowling, L. (2005) 'South Africa', in Anne Cooper-Chen (ed.) *Global Entertainment Media; Content, Audiences, Issues*. Mahwah, NJ: Lawrence Erlbaum Associates.

Fardon, R. and Furniss, G. (2000) *African Broadcast Cultures*. Westport, CT: Praeger.

Feshbach, S. (1985) 'Media and delinquency', in Groebel, J. (Chair) *Scientific Aspects of Crime Prevention*. Milan: Symposium 7th United Nations Congress on the Prevention of Crime.

Groebel, J. (Sept. 1998) 'Media Violence and Children', *Educational Media International*, vol. 35(3): 216-227.

Groebel, J. (2002) 'Media Violence in Cross-Cultural Perspective: A Global Study on Children's Media Behavior and Some Educational Implications', in Singer, D. and Singer, G. (Eds.) *Handbook of Children and the Media*. Beverly Hills: Sage Publishers.

Hachten, W.A. (1996) *The World News Prism*. Ames, IA: Iowa State University Press.

History of SA Media (n.d.) http://www.mediamanager.co.za/MediaLibrary/ML_History/chapters/historySector_Broadcast.htm. Retrieved on August 10, 2008

Kasoma, F.P. (1986) *The Press in Zambia: The Development, Role, and Control of National Newspapers in Zambia, 1906-1983*. Lusaka: Multimedia Publications.

Kasoma, F.P. (1997) 'The Independent Press and Politics in Africa', *International Communication Gazette*, vol. 59(4): 295-310.

Kaunda, K.D. (1967) 'Humanism in Zambia and its Implementation', Part 1. Lusaka: Government Printers.

KTV (2006) http://www.ktv.co.za/shows/

Lerner, D. (1958) *The Passing of Traditional Society*. New York: Free Press.

M-Net. (2007) Retrieved January 10, 2007 on http://www.M-Net.co.za/

Moore, R. (1992) *The Political Reality of the Press in Zambia*. Lanham, MD: University Press of America.

MuviTV (2008) Retrieved August 06, 2008 on http://www.muvitv.com.

Mwanakatwe, J.M. (1994) *End of Kaunda Era, A Multimedia Publication*. Lusaka, Zambia.

Mytton, G. (1983) *Mass Communication in Africa*. London: Edward Arnold.

Noll, R.G. (2000) 'Telecommunications Reform in Developing Countries', in Anne Krueger: *Economic Policy Reform, the Second Stage*. Chicago: The University of Chicago Press.

Ocitti, M. (1999) *Media and Democracy in Africa: Mutual Political Bedfellows or Implacable Arch-Foes*. Harvard University: Weatherhead Center for International Affairs.

Olorunnisola, A.A. and T.M. Akanni. (2005) 'Nigeria', in Anne Cooper-Chen (ed.) *Global Entertainment Media; Content, Audiences, Issues*. Mahwah, NJ: Lawrence Erlbaum Associates.

Panos Institute. (1993) *Radio Pluralism in West Africa: A Survey Conducted by the Panos Institute Paris and L'Union de Journalistes d'Afrique de l'Quest, Vol. 3*. Paris: Institut Panos and L'Harmattan.

Scott, G. (2002) 'Zambia: Structural Adjustment, Rural Livelihoods and Sustainable Development', *Journal Development Southern Africa*, vol. 19(3): 405-418.

Soremekun, E. (1973) 'Educational Television in Zambia', *Innovations in Education and Teaching International*, vol. 10(3): 196-207.

United Nations Human Development Index Report (2007) Retrieved August 2, 2008 on http://hdr.undp.org/en/countries/.

Villani, S. (2001) 'Impact of Media on Children and Adolescents: A 10-Year Review of the Research', *Journal of the American Academy of Child and Adolescent Psychiatry*, vol. 40(4): 392-401.

Zambia National Broadcasting Corporation (2007) Retrieved January 10, 2007 on http://www.znbc.co.zm/.

Television Programming for the Youth in Zimbabwe

Studio 263 and Handspeak

Wenceslous Kaswoswe

In Zimbabwe locally produced television programs are being used to inform, instruct and empower the youth to desist from risk behavior. *Studio 263* and CHIPAWO Media's *Handspeak* are examples of local television programs whose themes focus on challenges faced by the Zimbabwean youth. Dominant themes in these programs include HIV/AIDS, unwanted pregnancy, relationships, and challenges faced by deaf people. This paper addresses how television programming for the youth is an effective vehicle for disseminating information relating to challenges facing the youth in Zimbabwe. The success of these programs implies that policy makers in Zimbabwe need to open up the airwaves to community and private players to allow the production of quality, locally produced television programs with relevance to the socio-economic and political context of the Zimbabwean youth. The paper provides a thumbnail history of television broadcasting in Zimbabwe; discusses the current broadcasting system; and the broadcasting policy reforms of 2001. Lastly, the paper discusses television programming for the youth and the problems confronting producers of these programs.

Broadcasting in Zimbabwe, 1980-2008

Television was introduced in Southern Rhodesia, now Zimbabwe, in 1961 during the colonial European settler era. It was the first such service in Southern Africa as South Africa, the first African country to provide radio broadcasting in 1924, later introduced television broadcasting in 1976. Television became part of the state controlled Rhodesian Broadcasting Corporation (RBC) that was in charged of radio broadcasting (Akers and Yates, 1973). Television was confined mainly to urban centers and programming targeted the dominant European minority.

Color television was introduced in 1984, four years after the collapse of colonial rule. A second channel was introduced in 1986 and was only accessed in Harare, the capital city of Zimbabwe. This channel was taken off the air in 1997 and was immediately replaced by Joy TV. In 2002, Joy TV was taken off the air in a controversial move; many believed that Joy TV was killed off because it posed a threat to the monopoly enjoyed by ZBC (Soros 2002).

At independence, the RBC was renamed Zimbabwe Broadcasting Corporation (ZBC) and key positions within the corporation were filled by members of the ruling party, Zimbabwe African National Union-Patriotic Front (ZANU-PF). Since its inception, ZBC has remained state-controlled and has been accused of being a mouthpiece of the ZANU-PF regime, with no editorial independence. Today, ZBC operates four radio stations and a national television channel, providing a mix of news, current affairs, educational programming and music in English, Shona and Ndebele.

The transition from the colonial broadcasting system to broadcasting in independent Zimbabwe saw the retention of colonial broadcasting policies, structures, and organization. Broadcasting remained state-owned and it was controlled and operated like other government units that received their budgets from the central government. All broadcasting operations were centralized in the capital city, taking orders directly from the ministry of information. This centralization was not only unique in Zimbabwe, but characterizes the organization of broadcasting in post-colonial Africa. The philosophical justification for this centralization of broadcasting in most African countries hinders on effective management, national integration and cohesion (Ziegler and Asante 1992). In Zimbabwe, the new political leadership argued that broadcasting had a central role to play in nation-building that included unity among the ethnic groups, propelling uniformity of values and reinforcement of nationalism and African heritage.

The government in Zimbabwe in fact accentuated the colonial authoritarian media system they had fought against. Even though the Supreme Court ruled in 2000 that state monopoly over the airwaves was unconstitutional, ZBC remains as the only broadcaster in the country. Zaffiro (2002) notes of striking continuity with usage and management of radio and television by the ZANU-PF led government. These continuities include "retained structures and process of broadcast organization; regime-selected; politically-screened executives; inter-locking management arrangements; closely monitored training programs' dependent finance; formal and informal content controls; day-to-day regime guidance and restricted access to opposition groups" (2002: 76). Throughout the twenty-six years of independence government's democratic rhetoric has not been matched with proper media reforms to enhance democratic practices.

In 1981 over 250,000 radio and 70,000 television receivers were in use and by 1994, radio and television receivers had increased to 801 000 and 137 100 respectively. To facilitate centralization of both radio and television, broadcasting studios outside Harare were closed and those in Harare were guarded 24 hours by members of the Zimbabwe National Army (Zaffiro 2002). The broadcasting content was directly influenced by the Ministry of Information which produced documentary films whose themes were based on glorifying ZANU (PF) and its leader Mugabe (Zaffiro 2002). The documentaries presented ZANU (PF) as though it was the only vanguard in the fight against colonial rule, trivializing, if not negating, the contribution made by other political parties. The Media Monitoring Project of Zimbabwe (MMPZ), an organization, established in 1998, dedicated to monitoring of the media, has well documented the apparent bias by ZBC towards the ruling party. A report by MMPZ in 1999 noted that there was a serious problem regarding the government's attitude towards ZBC, which structured the corporation to behave as a government mouthpiece rather than a vehicle for general matters of public interest. This attitude is reflected in the intermittent sacking or suspension of broadcasters who display a degree of independence (MMPZ 1999).

The 1990s witnessed a renaissance in media reforms throughout Southern Africa. Debates on the role of the media in democracy and freedom of expression and the media took center stage in government, academic and policy arenas (Ronning 1994). As a topic of debate among media scholars, the concern over freedom of the press and its fundamental role in democratization superseded the issues that had previously dominated communication studies in developing countries, namely the flow of information and news between the first world and the third world.

Zimbabwe's television marketplace

Most governments in Southern Africa reformed their media policies, transforming the once state monopolies into competitive, plural and diverse media systems. Zimbabwe embarked on broadcasting policy reform that resulted in the enactment of the Broadcasting Services Act (BSA) in 2001. It is important to highlight that both colonial and post-colonial Zimbabwe have never had an independent, plural and diverse broadcasting system and the enactment of the BSA was an attempt to establish such a system. Research on media reforms in Zimbabwe reveals that the promulgation of the BSA has failed to transform the broadcasting terrain into a competitive, plural and diverse sector. Kaswoswe (2005: 10) There is a huge gap between the stated objectives of the Act and the actual administration of the Act. This explains why, despite the promulgation of the Act in 2001, no single radio or television station has been licensed. This broadcasting monopoly system has had a negative impact on television programming in particular and development of cultural industry in general.

The state-owned Zimbabwe Broadcasting Corporation (ZBC), now operating as Zimbabwe Broadcasting Holdings (ZBH) operates the only television station in the country. In the 1990s, the ZBC had two channels and rented one of them (TV2) to private broadcasters who would air their content at different times and pay the ZBC (Mukundu 2006). These private broadcasters were Munhumutapa

African Broadcasting Corporation and Joy TV who were thrown off the air in 2001 when the Broadcasting Service Act was enacted. Apart from the one state-owned ZTV channel, the South African-based MultiChoice Africa DStv, a subscription pay-TV is also available in Zimbabwe. DStv's channels are all foreign-produced and are accessed by the few Zimbabweans who can afford to pay monthly subscription in foreign currency.

Programming for the youth: An entertainment-education approach

It has been argued and proven that television and radio play a vital role in raising awareness of community, national and global issues among children thereby playing a fundamental role in shaping their lives. International bodies such as UNICEF have been at the forefront in urging "broadcasters to advance overall child development in their countries by producing documentaries that detail the plight of children, dramas that help break down gender stereotypes and reduce discrimination and animation that both teaches and entertains" (www.unicef.org/videoaudio/video_children.html). The International Children's Day of Broadcasting depicts the efforts of broadcasters worldwide in promoting children's rights, children's participation in broadcasting and promoting quality children's programming (www.unicef.org/videoaudio/video_children.html). Thus, when television and radio are constructively designed, they can become meaningful and positive media experiences for young people.

Broadcast programming targeting children have been a major component of both radio and television in colonial and post-colonial Zimbabwe. The first program focusing on children was a radio show called the Children's Hour and was established in April 1935 (Akers and Yates 1973). At independence, ZBC continued with the tradition of children programming. These programs are of both local and foreign origins, with the majority of the programs imported from the United States and Britain. Cartoons and soap operas dominate the imported television programs, whose contents do not always reflect the reality of life situations that confront the youth on a daily basis.

A few locally produced television programs, written and produced by Zimbabweans, such as *Studio 263* and *Handspeak* address issues that affect the young people and these programs adopt the entertainment education theoretical framework. These programs differ from most of the imported children television programs in that the local productions focus on real life situations that confront the Zimbabwean youth on a daily basis. Studio 263, for example, empowers the youth by providing information about the importance of education and dramatizes health issues such as sex, HIV/AIDS, and effects of unwanted pregnant amongst the teens.

These popular locally produced children television programs utilize the entertainment education approach to engage children. Entertainment education entails embedding of educational content in entertainment programs presented through such mediums as television, radio, and video. Singhal and Rogers (1999) argue that entertainment-education directly or indirectly facilitate social change. As noted by Melkote (2003), the entertainment education framework influences, at the individual level, awareness, attention, and behavior toward a socially desirable objective. This approach has been used in other parts of Africa such as South Africa's Soul City that began in 1994.

STUDIO 263

Studio 263 is a serial television drama, an entertainment-education program that is designed to educate viewers, particularly the youth, about HIV/AIDS, unwanted teenage pregnancy, abstinence and the importance of education in one's life. The aim of this television soap opera, whose name refers to the international calling code for Zimbabwe, is to provide an entertaining, educational format and an arena for reflection and discussion of health issues and risk behavior. It was created by Population Services International Zimbabwe in partnership with United Kingdom Department for International Development, Embassy of Japan, and USAID (www.usaid.gov/stories/zimbabwe/cs_zimbabwe_aidstv.html).

The soap opera, written and directed by Zimbabweans, tackle issues that confront the Zimbabwean youth and seeks to provide choices, solutions and ideas to help the country's youth move toward a better future. The medium of television is used to engage young viewers by disseminating information about HIV/AIDS, abstinence, risky behavior and education. The program airs thirty-minute episodes five nights per week and its characters and plots reflect situations that Zimbabwean youth face. The storyline in the drama centers on Vimbayi, a young woman who took control of her life after experiencing the horrors of unwanted pregnancy. The man who fathered Vimbayi's child refuses responsibility and Vimbayi goes back to school and completes her education and becomes economically independent. The producers of the show present Vimbayi as a role model for the majority of the youth to emulate. The importance of this soap opera is that it helps the Zimbabwean youth to understand the risks and responsibilities associated with sexual activity especially HIV/AIDS and unwanted pregnancy.

HANDSPEAK

Another locally produced television series targeting young people is *Handspeak*, a television program featuring deaf children. Handspeak is a product of the Children's Performing Arts Workshop (CHIPAWO), founded in 1989. The main objective of CHIPAWO is to enrich "the cultural experience of Zimbabwean children by introducing them to the culture and performing arts of Zimbabwe, the region and the continent" (www.chipawo.co.zw/aboutus.html). CHIPAWO is for and by the children where children are encouraged to freely express their creativity and originality and the development of all-round versatility. In 1995 CHIPAWO Media introduced a television series Welcome to CHIPAWO, a 13-part series that target young people to express themselves freely through arts programs. Some of the CHIPAWO television productions include the CHIPAWO Christmas shows, Welcome to the World and the CHIPAWO Showcase.

In 2005 CHIPAWO made history when it aired on television the first episode of the television series, *Handspeak*, for and by the deaf. The 13-part magazine program, initiated by CHIPAWO media in 2005, was designed mainly for deaf audiences, but utilised sub-titles so that hearing audiences could also watch the show and learn about the deaf community (Chimbodza 2005). The program is produced as a weekly magazine show, and each episode features a Sign Language lesson, news about and for the deaf, a drama on the topic of the week followed by a discussion with studio guests. The program also profiles deaf people who are having success in their lives. According to Nyasha Nyamwanza, as quoted by Chimbodza (2005) the objective of this television program is to challenge and change people's attitude towards the deaf. Thus, the program is designed to provide information to deaf people, change the way deaf people are perceived by society, and highlight some of the problems and challenges deaf Zimbabweans face and in the process fostering positive change.

CHIPAWO Media has launched two sequels to *Handspeak*. The first sequel, *Deaf Dialogues*, was a 4-episode mini-series that presented performances filmed on stage for television (www.comminit.com/en/node/272759/38). This mini-series included "Give Us a Chance", a documentary based on a Handicap Advocacy Arts Festival featuring performance and discussion on issues relating to the handicapped, and involving handicapped and other children. It also included the small dramas that had been featured in Handspeak, which were gathered into two episodes of drama in Sign Language entitled "Dialogues of the Deaf". The second sequel, *Action Power*, launched in April 2008, is a magazine program similar to Handspeak which focuses on: (a) profiling deaf artists and craftspeople, (b) a continuation of Sign Language lessons for the hearing, but also includes more advanced words for the deaf, and (c) featuring discussion by children, youth, parents, teachers, and government on education and careers for the deaf in Zimbabwe (www.comminit.com/en/node/272759/38).

Conclusion

Studio 263 and *Handspeak* reveal that locally- produced television programs for children play an integral part in raising their awareness about social, economic, and political issues in their communities. The locally produced programs have more relevance to the realities of their target audience as compared to foreign produced television programs and it is in this regard that policy makers in Zimbabwe need to open up the airwaves to other players to promote the production of local programs to serve the interests of the youth in Zimbabwe. Maintaining state monopoly over television stifle the empowering ability of locally produced television programs because the state controlled ZTV has demonstrated historically that it does not have the capacity to produce quality programming hence its reliance on foreign produced programs. In Zimbabwe 10% of the content of the national television broadcaster, ZTV, is expected to be for the hearing impaired (McLaren 2003). However, state monopoly over the airwaves means that there is no competition among service providers to fill the gap with programming for all segments of the nation including the hearing impaired.

Themes dominant in these two programs, Studio 263 and Handspeak, reveals that locally produced programs are deeply rooted in socio-economic and political conditions confronting Zimbabwe and they empower the youth to make informed decision based on sound judgment regarding their behavior. In a country where an estimated 3,290 deaths due to AIDS are recorded each week, policy makers in Zimbabwe have an obligation to promote entertainment-education television programming by opening up the airwaves so that more players, both community and private broadcasters, can join the state controlled broadcaster in creating quality television programming that address problems and challenges facing the youth in Zimbabwe. Audience tracking surveys show that Studio 263 is rated the best television program in Zimbabwe and, with over 2.8 million viewers, it is also the country's most watched program (Hales, D., et al (2004: 5). As noted by the Zimbabwe All Media Products Survey (ZAMPS) report, Studio 263, using the entertainment education theoretical framework has been very successful in influencing behavior change amongst the young people (www.usaid.gov/stories/zimbabwe/cs_zimbabwe_aidstv.html), The survey report reveals that 88% of 11-29 year-olds watches Studio 263 and that its messages influenced 48% of 15-19 year-olds to delay the onset of sexual activity). Thus, television programming for children, when properly designed, plays a fundamental role in national development.

References

Akers, M. and D. Yates (1973) *Encyclopedia Rhodesia*. Salisbury: The College Press.

Children's Broadcasting and Partnership. www.unicef.org/videoaudio/video_children.html

Chimbodza, B. (2005) *Handspeak– TV Program*. MS Zimbabwe (Danish Association for International Development). www.ms-dk/sw2575.asp

CHIPAWO. www.chipawo.co.zw/aboutus.html

Hales, D., Attawell, K., Hayman, J., and Khan, N. (2004) *PSI Zimbabwe Assessment Report*. USAID Zimbabwe.

Handspeak. www.comminit.com/en/node/272759/38

Kaswoswe, W. (2005) *The Politics of Broadcasting Policy Reform in Zimbabwe, 2000-2005: Breaking away from the Past?* Dr.Diss. Ohio University, Athens: Ohio.

McLaren, R. (2005) *Deaf Children Make Zimbabwean Television History*. Deaf Today, Vol. 3. At www.deaftoday.com/v3/archives/2005/06/deaf_children_m_1.html

Media Monitoring Project-Zimbabwe (1999) *A Duty to Inform: A Report on Zimbabwe's Publicly-owned Media*. Harare: Zimbabwe.

Melkote, S. (2003) 'Theories of Development Communication', in Bella Mody (ed.) *International and Development Communication: A 21st-Century Perspective*. London: Sage Publications.
Mukundu, R. (2006) *African Media Development Initiative: Zimbabwe*. BBC World Service Trust
Ronning, H. (1994) *Media and Democracy: Theoretical Principles with Reference to African Context*. Harare: SAPES.
Singhal, A. and E.M. Rogers (1999) *Entertainment-education: A Communication Strategy for Social Change*. Mahwah, NJ: Lawrence Erlbaum.
Soros, E. (2002) *The Death of Independent Zimbabwean TV?* At www.worldpress.org/print_article.cfm?article_id=675&don't=yes
Studio 263 TV – HIV/AIDS Programming A Hit, At www.usaid.gov/stories/zimbabwe/cs_zimbabwe_aidstv.html
Zaffiro, J. (2002) *Media and Democracy in Zimbabwe*. Colorado Springs: International Academic Publishers.
Ziegler, D. and M.K. Asante (1992) *Thunder and Silence: Mass Media in Africa*. Trenton, NJ: African World Press.

The Authors

Dr. Norma Pecora

Professor
School of Media Arts and Studies
Scripps College of Communication
Ohio University
Athens, OH 45701
USA
pecora@ohio.edu

Dr. Enyonam Osei-Hwere

Assistant Professor
Department of Communication
Sybil Harrington College of Art and Humanities
West Texas A & M University (WTAMU)
PO Box 60754
Canyon, TS 79016-0001
USA
eosei-hwere@wtamu.edu

Dr. Ulla Carlsson

Professor and Director
International Clearinghouse on Children, Youth and Media
Nordicom
University of Gothenburg
PO Box 713
SE-405 30 Göteborg
Sweden
ulla.carlsson@nordicom.gu.se

Sarah Akrofi-Quarcoo

President
Women in Broadcasting
PO Box 4707
Cantonments
Accra
Ghana
saroaq2000@yahoo.com

Dr. Beatrice A. Boateng

Assistant Professor
Office of Educational Development
University of Arkansas for Medical Sciences
4301 W. Markham St., Slot #595
Little Rock, AR 72205
USA
BBoateng@uams.edu

Priscilla Boshoff	Lecturer Journalism and Media Studies Rhodes University PO Box 94 Grahamstown 6140 South Africa p.a.boshoff@ru.ac.za
Mimi Brazeau	Senior Partnership Program Advisor Plan West Africa Regional Office 136 Sotrac Mermoz BP 21121 Dakar Ponty Senegal mimi.brazeau@plan-international.org
Firdoze Bulbulia	Chairperson, 5th World Summit on Media and Children/ Children and Broadcasting Foundation for Africa (CBFA), and Secretary General, International Centre of Films for Children and Youth (CIFEJ) 72 Keurboom Street Atholl 2196 Johannesburg South Africa moments@icon.co.za
Lamees El Baghdady	Lecturer/Doctoral Candidate Faculty of Mass Communication Modern Sciences and Arts University 14 Amer St. Messaha Sq. Dokki, Giza Egypt lamegdy@aucegypt.edu
Dr. Juliet Evusa	Assistant Professor Department of Communications Roger State University Claremore, OK 74017 USA jevusa@rsu.edu
Steven Goodman	Executive Director Educational Video Center 120 West 30th Street, 7th Floor New York, NY 10001 USA sgoodman@evc.org

Dr. Steve Howard	Director African Studies Program Professor School of Media Arts and Studies Scripps College of Communication Ohio University Athens, OH 45701 USA howard@ohio.edu
Dr. Musonda Kapatamoyo	Assistant Professor Department of Mass Communication Southern Illinois University PO Box 1775 Edwardsville, IL 62026 USA mkapata@siue.edu
Dr. Wenceslous Kaswoswe	MFA Candidate Film and Electronic Media American University 4400 Massachusetts Avenue NW Washington, DC 20016 USA wence.kaswoswe@gmail.com
Christine Mendoza	Specialist North American Language & Culture 6711 Fort Hamilton Parkway, apt. B3 Brooklyn, NY 11219 USA cmendoza@gmail.com
Frederick Nnoma-Addison	President, CEO African Media-Image Project, Inc. PO Box 1090 Washington, DC 20013 USA Frederick_N_Addison@afroimagetv.org
Dr. Francis B. Nyamnjoh	Head of Publications CODESRIA Avenue Cheikh Anta Diop X Canal IV BP3304 Dakar CP 18524 Senegal francis.nyamnjoh@codesria.sn nyamnjoh@gmail.com

Patrick V. Osei-Hwere	Doctoral Candidate Department of Telecommunications Indiana University 1229 East 7th Street Bloomington, IN 47405 USA poseihwe@indiana.edu
Charles Owen	Director Children SABC Content Hub Private Bag X 41 Auckland Park 2006 Johannesburg South Africa owencg@sabc.co.za
Dr. Jeanne Prinsloo	Professor Journalism and Media Studies Rhodes University PO Box 94 Grahamstown 61410 South Africa j.prinsloo@ru.ac.za
Dr. Mastin Prinsloo	Associate Professor School of Education University of Cape Town Private Bag X3 Rondebosch 7701 Cape Town South Africa mastin.prinsloo@uct.ac.za
Rebecca Renard	Director and Educator Minds Consulting 2812 Erie Street, SE #34 Washington, DC 20020 USA rrenard@InquiringMindsConsulting.com
Dr. Marion Walton	Lecturer Film and Media Studies University of Cape Town Private Bag X3 Rondebosch 7701 Cape Town South Africa marion.walton@uct.ac.za

Tewodros Workalemahu
Lecturer
Department of English Language & Literature
Arba Minch University
Arba Minch
Ethiopia
teddywork@ethionet.et